. . . .

Family Matters

FAMILY MATTERS

SECRECY AND DISCLOSURE IN THE HISTORY OF ADOPTION

E. WAYNE CARP

HARVARD UNIVERSITY PRESS

Cambridge, Massachusetts, and London, England · 1998

. . . .

Library of Congress Cataloging-in-Publication Data

Carp, E. Wayne, 1946–
Family matters : secrecy and disclosure in the
history of adoption / E. Wayne Carp.
    p.   cm.
Includes bibliographical references and index.
ISBN 0-674-79668-3 (cloth : alk. paper)
1. Adoption—United States—History.
2. Open adoption—United States—History.
3. Adoptees—United States—Identification.
4. Birthparents—United States—Identification.
5. Family social work—United States.
6. Confidential communications—United States.
I. Title.
HV875.55.C38   1998
362.73'4'0973—dc21   97-40023

Designed by Gwen Frankfeldt

. . . . FOR PAULA

Contents

Preface

I had originally planned to write a more general book on the history of adoption in America, not a history of secrecy and disclosure in adoption. I was initially drawn to the subject of adoption by stories my father told me of his temporary placement as a small boy at the Jewish Children's Society in Bridgeport, Connecticut. While some of the children there were adopted, he was not, and after two years he returned home. Being a professional historian, I was curious about the historical circumstances that led to some "orphans" being adopted and others returning to their parents. I went to the library and was surprised to discover that there were no histories of adoption. It was the combination of curiosity about my father's experience and the challenge presented by the absence of an adequate historical study of adoption that impelled me to undertake this study.

One can speculate about the reasons why there existed no comprehensive history of adoption. First, most child welfare professionals are underpaid and overworked, too busy dealing with everyday crises to research and write history. The dictates of their profession place a priority on research that is useful to their everyday work. Thus, most history written by child welfare experts covers only the recent past. Second, I suspect that professional social workers are wary about revisiting a past that is replete with failed policies, a trip that could prove both unhelpful and embarrassing. But most important, a reliable, long-term history of adoption has not been written because the primary sources necessary for writing such a history—adoption case records—have been sealed from researchers by tradition and state law. For historians this has been an almost insurmountable barrier: no sources, no history. The few articles and dissertations written about adoption have gotten around this problem by writing legal histories of adoption based primarily on state statutes and case law. Although valuable, they are methodologically narrow and chronologically limited and have little to say about how adoption practices actually worked or how they affected members of the adoption triad—birth parents, adopted persons, and adoptive parents.

Although there were no general histories of adoption, I quickly learned that there were literally thousands of books and articles on the subject by anthropologists, lawyers, pediatricians, psychiatrists, psychoanalysts, and especially social workers and adoption professionals. As I read these works, I realized that it was important to have practical, experiential knowledge of adoption as well as information derived from historical research. Since I was neither an adopted person nor an adoptive parent, I did the next best thing. In the fall of 1987, with the aid of a John M. Olin Foundation Faculty Fellowship, I took a one-year leave of absence from Pacific Lutheran University, where I teach American history, and volunteered to work part-time at the Children's Home Society of Washington (CHSW).

The CHSW is a private, statewide, voluntary nonprofit organization founded in 1895 by a Methodist minister, the Reverend Harrison D. Brown, and his wife, Libbie Beach Brown, the former superintendent of a Nebraska orphanage, the Home for the Friendless. Its mission was to seek out homeless, neglected, and destitute children in order to place them in families for adoption. Throughout the twentieth century, as the demand for child welfare services increased, the Society slowly added staff members, expanded geographically, and began to develop all the services related to adoption. By 1970, just before it ended the practice of placing children in adoptive homes, the Society operated six branches throughout the state and administered programs that included homes for unmarried mothers, foster care for children prior to adoption, and institutional or group care for older children as well as adoption. In the 1960s, the CHSW averaged 421 adoptions a year, approximately 25 percent of Washington's adoptions. During the first ninety-four years of its existence the Society oversaw some 19,500 adoptions.[1]

I was assigned to the CHSW's Adoption Resource Center, where I organized an adoption library and wrote reviews of new books for the institution's clientele. Within a month of my arrival, the Center's director, Randy Perin, asked me if I would be interested in looking at the CHSW's 21,500-odd adoption case records. Perin is sympathetic to the adoption rights movement and also is one of those rare adoption professionals who believe in the importance of historical research, whether it reflects well or ill on the profession in general or the CHSW in particular. Needless to say, I immediately recognized the value of his offer and gratefully accepted. For the next eight months, I read the CHSW adoption records, which ran continually from 1896 to 1973, when, due to the shortage of Caucasian infants, the CHSW all but ceased placing children for adoption.

My initial impulse was to read them *all.* I was the first professional historian to have access to confidential adoption case records, and I felt a responsibility to bring to light as much information about adoption agency policy and practice as I could. Of course, time constraints made that ambitious goal impossible. As a roughly random sample, I read one out of every ten of the Society's 21,500 adoption case records. (The CHSW continues to add information to the case records on postadoption contact, so I was able to examine data through 1988.) The 2,500 cases I read provided me with both a representative sample and a larger body of cases than an ordinarily constituted random sample would have to use for descriptive purposes. I supplemented the adoption case records with the disorganized and incomplete minutes of CHSW supervisors' meetings, personnel files, and annual reports, which I found buried and forgotten in the CHSW's garage.

But if my sample of the CHSW's adoption case files was representative of that institution's policies and practices, how could I be sure that it was typical of the nation's other child-placing institutions? To test the CHSW's representativeness, I attempted to gain access to other agencies' records. I was granted permission to view the case records of the Children's Home Society of Minnesota, but officials there restricted my use to quantifying the data I extracted from the files. My efforts to gain access to East Coast adoption agencies, which I sought for geographical diversity, were repeatedly rebuffed. Nevertheless, I am fairly confident that my findings are representative because of corroborative evidence I found from a host of other sources. In particular I have used the vast manuscript sources of the U.S. Children's Bureau and the Child Welfare League of America—a privately supported national organization of four hundred affiliate adoption agencies—and the annual reports and correspondence of geographically diverse child-placing agencies, such as the Illinois Children's Home and Aid Society, New York's Spence Alumnae Society, the Cleveland Protestant Orphan Asylum, Washington, D.C.'s Hillcrest Children's Center, and the Children's Home of Florida. I also studied professional social work journals, such as *Child Welfare, Social Service Review, The Family, Social Work,* and *The Child.* What I found supports the contention that the CHSW's policies were not unique, but were representative of mainstream adoption agencies' attitudes and practices. In evaluating the CHSW's representativeness, it must be kept in mind that most adoption agencies' records are sealed by law, and most agency officials refuse to give researchers access to them. I invite scholars to test the representativeness of my findings by attempting to conduct research at other adoption agencies. Until adoption agency officials permit researchers access to the case records, however, the data presented here may be the best available.

. . . .

A Note on Language

A few words about the language used in this book are in order here. Language describing issues involved in adoption, like all language, is historically constructed and emotionally charged. For example, children of unmarried women have been variously said to be "bastard," "illegitimate," or "born out of wedlock." Reformers viewed each succeeding descriptor as reducing the social stigma surrounding the circumstances of the unmarried birth, even though all three sound stigmatizing to us. To complicate matters even further, a group of adoptees on the Internet have created a Web page that they defiantly call Bastard Nation, thus reappropriating the original term of opprobrium and turning it into a term of pride and commitment in their quest to secure access to their adoption records. After much thought, I have decided to use the terms that were commonly used in the periods I describe rather than sanitizing the history of secrecy and disclosure in adoption by using language less harsh to modern sensibilities. Although using such language may offend some people, I am not making a value judgment. Rather, I believe that the historian's highest duty is to attempt to reconstruct the past as closely as possible to the way it was, given the inherent limitations of evidence and the historian's own bias. Using terms like "bastard," "illegitimate child," and "natural parents" conveys the authentic flavor of how, before the 1970s, everyday language stigmatized those involved in adoption; it also underscores my contention that throughout American history, biological kinship has occupied a privileged position in American culture.

. . . .

Family Matters

CHAPTER ONE

The Rise of Adoption

Because of the decision by the federal government in 1975 to stop collecting statistics on adoption, Americans today can only guess at how many children are adopted each year. The ostensible reason was economy, but the decision also reflects America's pervasive cultural bias against adoption. When it comes to family matters, most Americans view blood ties as naturally superior to artificially constructed ones.

Yet despite the stigma surrounding it, an enormous number of people have a direct, intimate connection to adoption. Some experts put the number as high as one out of every five Americans. Others estimate the number of adoptees at 2 to 4 percent of the population, or some 5 to 10 million individuals. According to incomplete and partial estimates by the National Committee for Adoption, in 1986 there were a total of 104,088 domestic adoptions, of which half were biologically related to family members and half were nonrelated, or "stranger," adoptions. A more comprehensive study completed in 1990 calculated the number of domestic adoptions at 118,779.[1] In short, adoption is a ubiquitous institution in American society, creating invisible relationships with biological and adoptive kin that touch far more people than we imagine.

Any social organization that touches so many lives in such a profound way is bound to be complicated. Modern adoption is no exception. While raising any family is inherently stressful, adoption is filled with additional tensions that are unique to the adoptive parent-child relationship. From the moment they decide they wish to adopt a child, couples begin to confront a series of challenges. First comes the problem of state regulation. A host of state laws govern every aspect of legal adoptions: who may adopt, who may be adopted, the persons who must consent to the adoption, the form the adoption petition must take, the notice of investigation and formal hearing of the adoption petition, the effect of the adoption decree, the procedure for appeal, the confidential nature of the hearings and records in adoption proceedings, the issuance of new birth certificates, and the payment of adoption subsidies. Accustomed to thinking of themselves as autonomous in the sphere of family and social life, prospective adoptive parents find themselves intricately involved with administrative practices and dependent on social workers, lawyers, doctors, and in some cases surrogate mothers in order to "qualify" to receive a child. And after successfully negotiating the legal and bureaucratic maze, the new parents must come to grips with a society that views adoption as inferior to blood kinship.[2]

Further complicating the entire edifice of modern adoption is the issue of secrecy and disclosure. Records of adoption proceedings are confidential. They are closed both to the public and to all the parties involved in the adoption: birth parents, adoptees, and adoptive parents. They may be opened only upon a judicial finding of "good cause" or, increasingly, upon the mutual consent of all parties. In addition to legal proceedings and adoption case records, an adopted person's original birth certificate is also considered confidential and is sealed by the state bureau of vital statistics. In its place, a new birth certificate, containing the child's new name and the adoptive parents' name, is issued.[3]

The tensions inherent in keeping secrets affect all aspects of the adoptive process. Everyone involved in adoption must confront at one time or another questions about secrecy and disclosure. Should a child's birth certificate indicate that he or she has been adopted? How many details about a child's birth should social workers disclose to the adoptive parents? When and how should adoptive parents tell their children they were adopted? Should adoptive parents impart to their child all the information that social workers have given to them? When adult adoptees return to an adoption agency, should social workers give them all the facts in the file, including the names of their biological parents? When birth mothers return, should they learn how to contact the children they relinquished? Disclosure is also fraught with anxiety. Adoptive parents worry that they will forfeit the love of the child after telling about the adoption. They worry that they will lose their children when the children seek and find their biological family. Some adult adoptees worry that they will hurt their adopted parents if they make deeper inquiries into their past or want to meet biological family members. Unwed mothers who have married and started new families worry that the child they relinquished for adoption, now grown, will appear unexpectedly on their doorstep. Others worry the opposite: they will never again see the child they gave up for adoption.

It was not always this way. At the beginning of the seventeenth century, the institution of adoption hardly existed. There were no established legal processes, no confidential court records, birth certificates, or adoption case records, no social workers, no standards for determining the best interests of the child or, for that matter, any criteria of what constituted desirable qualities in adoptive parents. And in place of secrecy, there existed an ethos of openness, a bias toward disclosure, for most of the people directly involved in adoption. How American adoption went from its initial climate of openness and disclosure, which lasted until the end of the Second World War, to one of secrecy in the postwar era, and how it then began to return to openness in the 1970s cannot be understood unless these issues are first set into their broadest historical context.

Adoption, the method of establishing by law the social relationship of parent and child between individuals who are not each other's biological parent or child, is doubtless as old as humanity itself. It appears in the Code of Hammurabi, drafted by the Babylonians around 2285 B.C., which provided that "if a man has taken a young child 'from his waters' to sonship and has reared him up no one has any claim against the nursling." Adoption was practiced in ancient Egypt, Greece, Rome, the Middle East, Asia, and the tribal societies of Africa and Oceania. But there are many differences between modern adoption and its counterpart in the past, when the purpose of adoption was not the welfare of the child but the needs of adults, whether for the purpose of kinship, religion, or the community.[4]

Anthropologists have identified significant differences between modern Western adoption norms and practices and those of non-Western societies in the South Pacific. Whereas in Western societies modern adoption is infrequent, private, formal, and involves a complete transfer of parental rights, on some South Pacific islands adoption is common, public, casual, and characterized by partial transfer of the adopted child to the new family and dual parental rights and obligations. In contrast to Western societies, where parental ties are always broken, in Africa and Asia, adoption is a method of enriching and strengthening ties between two family groups. Similarly, in the South Pacific, it is common for adopted children to maintain a relationship with their biological parents. In contrast, modern Western societies and especially the United States define kinship by the unalterable nature of blood ties and view the biological family as "a state of almost mystical commonality and identity."[5]

By the seventeenth century, the West's emphasis on the primacy of biological kinship and the concomitant prejudice against adoption resulted in the demise of adoption in most European countries. The virtual disappearance of adoption in the West was also the result of a number of specific factors. For centuries, the Church had discouraged adoption as a strategy for inheritance. Adoption was also denounced by sixteenth-century Catholic and Protestant reformers who, in their insistence that marriage should be the sole arena for sexual activity and procreation, wanted to stop the long-standing practice of fathers bringing their illegitimate sons surreptitiously into the family. Fears of adoption were spread by stories of accidental incestuous unions between unsuspecting blood relatives. As a result, people hesitated to adopt: childless couples who adopted invited public scrutiny of their infertility; other presumptive adoptive families worried that neighbors might perceive them as challenging the natural order. In short, by the early modern period adoption had almost died out in Europe, being judged "unchristian" and "unnatural."[6]

England, whence the American colonists derived their culture and laws, emulated European attitudes and practice toward adoption. English common law did not recognize adoption. This legal opposition to adoption stemmed from a desire to protect the property rights of blood relatives in cases of inheritance, a moral repugnance of illegitimacy, and the availability of other quasi-adoptive devices such as apprenticeship and voluntary transfers. Not until 1926 did England enact its first adoption statute.[7]

The history of adoption in early America reveals a past that initially broke away from Europe's and England's prohibition against adoptive kinship. Although the United States would eventually manifest typically Western attitudes toward adoption—that biological kinship was superior to adoptive kinship and that adoption was an inferior type of kinship relation—these would wax and wane throughout American history. What is noteworthy about the history of adoption in America is that at its beginning, colonial Americans showed little preference for the primacy of biological kinship, practiced adoption on a limited scale, and frequently placed children in what we would call foster care. This was primarily due to the multifaceted functions of the colonial American family: it was the cornerstone of church and state, the center of all institutional life, and the fundamental unit of society. As Lawrence Cremin has noted, the family "provided food and clothing, succor and shelter; it conferred social standing, economic possibility, and religious affiliation; and it served from time to time as church, playground, factory, army, and court."[8]

Most important, the family served as a school and as a system of child care for dependent children through the institution of indenture or apprenticeship. Colonial America inherited from England a three-tier system of apprenticeship, by which children of all classes were placed in families to learn a trade. Merchants paid fees to apprentice their adolescent sons to lawyers or doctors or silversmiths. Middle-class parents voluntarily entered into contracts to "put out" their children to learn a craft and ease their economic burden, or as an alternative for parents "who did not trust themselves with their own children" because they were "afraid of spoiling them by too great affection." And church and town authorities involuntarily "bound out" orphans, bastards, abandoned children, and impoverished, neglected, or abused children to families to labor and be educated.[9]

Involuntary or compulsory apprenticeship stemmed from the Elizabethan poor laws that had been designed to suppress vagrancy and idleness and provide for the relief of poverty. Under the legal doctrine of *parens patriae,* derived from the belief that the king is the father and protector of his people, the role of the state included the right to intervene, on behalf of the child, in the biological family. It was not unusual for English Overseers of the Poor to remove children from impoverished families and place them with those more fortunate, saving the taxpayers from additional financial burdens. Similarly, Parliament, under Henry VIII, saw nothing wrong with passing an act ordering that all vagrant children between the ages of five and fourteen be arrested and bound out as apprentices. Compulsory apprenticeship was designed to relieve the community from the cost of supporting vagrant or impoverished children while at the same time ensuring that they received the basic necessities of life—food, clothing, and shelter.[10]

Colonial Americans copied the English poor law system when it came to caring for children born out of wedlock, orphaned, or neglected. Statutes permitted town and parish authorities to remove children from pauper families and place them with masters who, in exchange for their labor, would provide them with an adequate maintenance. Thus, for example, in 1648, at a town meeting, the inhabitants of Salem, Massachusetts, resolved that "the eldest children of Reuben Guppy be placed out, the boy till the age of 21 years and the mayd till the age of 18 years." Nearly a century later, Boston town officials authorized the overseers of the poor to bind out children whose parents were unable or neglected to support and educate them. During the 1750s, the churchwardens of Virginia's Frederick County removed 7.3 percent of the children from their families and bound them out as apprentices.[11] Primarily as a result of the indenture system, both voluntary and involuntary, colonial American family life was far from the stable, nuclear family so idealized by many twentieth-century Americans: a substantial number of colonial American children grew up in families other than their own, many with the consent of their parents.

The fluid boundaries between consanguine and nonconsanguine families in colonial America led in some cases to the adoption of children, particularly in Puritan Massachusetts and Dutch New York. Informal adoption occurred when children were adopted without a legal proceeding. In 1658 in Plymouth Colony, for example, Lawrence Lichfeild, while lying on his deathbed, adopted out his youngest son to John and Ann Allin "for ever." Colonial Americans also practiced testamentary adoption, by which childless couples used their wills to provide generously for young relatives or children who had been "put out" to service in their homes. The most famous example and "the first known case of adoption" in colonial Massachusetts, as Jamil S. Zainaldin has noted, occurred in 1693 when Governor Sir William Phips mentioned his adopted son in his will. The adopted son was Phips's nephew, who legally changed his name in 1716. The concept of adoption also appeared in the more informal device of the godparent-godchild relationship, in which godparents not only bequeathed part of their estate but also frequently their names.[12]

By the middle of the nineteenth century, the number of adoptions increased, though it is impossible to know precisely by how much. In addition to informal and testamentary adoption, many private bills providing for the adoption of children by adults were enacted by state legislatures. Parents who sought a change of name for their adopted children often had recourse to these private legislative enactments. For example, a 1848 Pennsylvania statute directed that "henceforth the name of David Richardson Blair, an adopted son of Thompson Richardson . . . shall be David Richardson . . . and he is hereby invested with all the legal rights of a legitimate son of said Thompson Richardson." In Massachusetts between 1781 and 1851, the General Court enacted 101 private name-change acts, compared to just four in the previous century.[13]

The increased incidence of private legislation legalizing informal adoptions reflected profound changes occurring in American society. By the mid-nineteenth century, under the impact of large-scale immigration, urbanization, and the advent of the factory system and wage labor, the compact, stable, agricultural communities of colonial America were giving way to crowded, sprawling, coastal cities. One of the effects of these wrenching economic and social transformations was that both urban and rural poverty became major problems. Consequently, humanitarian and religious child welfare reformers all over the United States turned to large-scale institutions such as public almshouses and private orphanages to reduce the expense of poor relief and, with utopian expectations, to reform, rehabilitate, and educate paupers.[14]

Although private orphanages had existed in six cities before 1800, urban poverty, cholera and yellow fever epidemics, and evidence of child abuse in almshouses provided the impetus for the founding of an additional 164 orphan asylums in the next half-century, 75 of them between 1831 and 1851. In the following twenty years, another 126 private institutions came into existence. Before 1850, the primary aims of these institutions were to withdraw their charges from association with harmful adult influences, tutor boys and girls separately in practical and moral instruction, and then indenture them for apprenticeship or, less typically, place them out for adoption. In the first forty-five years of its existence, for example, the Boston Female Asylum adopted out 1.9 percent of its children.[15]

In the decades that followed, neither almshouses nor orphanages lived up to reformers' expectations. In almshouses, where conditions were abysmal, orphaned, impoverished, abandoned, neglected, or delinquent children were routinely housed with adult criminals, paupers, and the insane. A select committee of the New York State Senate in 1857 reported on the state's almshouses and condemned their "filth, nakedness, licentiousness, general bad morals and disregard of religion and the most common religious observances, as well as a gross neglect of the most ordinary comforts and decencies of life." Similarly, many child welfare reformers became disillusioned by the failure of orphan asylums to reform or rehabilitate their charges. They began attacking these institutions for their high expense, rigid routines, harsh discipline, and failure to produce independent and hardworking children. In contrast to the artificial environment of the institution, these reformers extolled "God's orphanage," the family, and its natural ability to produce sociable, independent, and industrious citizens at little expense. Changing attitudes toward the nature of children reinforced reformers' renewed appreciation of the family. Supplanting older Calvinist views of innate evil, infant depravity, and original sin, more optimistic doctrines derived from John Locke and Horace Bushnell emphasized the malleability of children and the importance of the environment in shaping their character. Child reformers' disillusionment with institutions and their newfound belief in the ability of a family environment to shape and reform dependent children lay behind the full-scale home-finding movement (which included foster care, boarding out, and adoption) that gained increasing momentum with child welfare reformers throughout the second half of the nineteenth century.[16]

The most influential of these charity organizations, New York's Children's Aid Society (CAS or Aid Society) was founded in 1853 by the Reverend Charles Loring Brace, a transplanted New Englander and graduate of Yale Divinity School, who began his celebrated career as an evangelical missionary working with "street arabs" at New York City's Five Points Mission. In the four decades following the CAS's founding, Brace enjoyed such great success that most existing charity organizations switched over to the CAS's placing-out system. In addition, dozens of new children's aid societies replicating CAS methods sprang up in the 1870s and 1880s, and imitators also appeared in Great Britain and Australia.

Upon arriving in New York City, Brace was appalled at the large numbers of impoverished immigrant children. To him they seemed a threat to the city's social order. His major goal during his forty-year tenure as secretary of the CAS was to rescue poor and homeless children from New York City's crowded, dirty streets and to place them out West in good Christian families where they would be cared for, educated, and employed. For Brace, "placing out" was superior to traditional antebellum institutional care in almshouses, orphanages, or reformatories because it promised to transform these "little vagabonds and homeless creatures" into "decent, orderly, industrious children." When Brace quickly discovered that placing children individually in families was slow and expensive, he turned to group placement, thus setting in motion the movement that became known as the orphan trains. In March 1854, the CAS sent the first large "train" of 138 children to western Pennsylvania. In the following twenty years, the CAS placed out 20,000 Eastern children in the "western" states of Michigan, Ohio, Indiana, Iowa, Missouri and Kansas; by 1890 the number had climbed to 84,000.[17]

The boys and girls whom Brace placed out came under the authority of the CAS by a variety of routes. A small number of children were removed from asylums and prisons. Some came of their own volition to CAS headquarters and volunteered for resettlement. Others were brought by their poor, immigrant, working-class parents, who hoped to give their children a better life, employing what historian Bruce Bellingham has called a "family strategy of economic calculation." Critics of the child-placing system accused the CAS of stealing children, and there was truth in these charges. Brace or a "visitor" would frequently roam lower-class neighborhoods, going "from house to house," recruiting poor, destitute, and delinquent children for the program. The net result of such recruitment was that a high percentage of Brace's clientele—some 47 percent by his own calculations—were not in fact orphans, but had one or both parents living. As Brace remarked, "the great majority were the children of poor and degraded people, who were leaving them to grow up neglected in the streets."[18]

Brace's comment reveals one of the most controversial aspects of the child-placement system: a decided preference for breaking up biological families in order to "save" children. Brace claimed it was a CAS principle to receive the parents' consent before taking the children. But misunderstandings often occurred. Communication with immigrants whose English was often deficient coupled with CAS mismanagement and highhandedness resulted in lawsuits and sometimes in tragedy. In one case, a man sued the CAS for sending his son West without his permission. The father lost the suit when it was discovered that the boy had used the CAS to run away from home, but the fact that the CAS never checked with the boy's father before placing him out suggests its casual attitude toward separating children from their parents. In another case, a father who placed his daughter with the Salvation Army Brooklyn Nursery and Infants Hospital returned to retrieve her, only to be told that she had been "put out on a farm in Kansas" by the CAS. The Salvation Army and the CAS refused to provide him with any other information; father and daughter never saw each other again.[19]

Brace broke families up to "rescue" the children from the evils of an urban environment. He assumed that a rural setting was morally superior and that the farm families desiring a child partook of this rural virtue and would treat the children well. Brace's romantic optimism was reflected in the way the CAS placing-out system differed from the traditional idea of binding out: Brace did away with the written contract of apprenticeship. The CAS relied on an oral agreement with the adult, while retaining custody of the child. Brace counted on the farmer's "sense of Christian duty and of affection" for his young charge to resist overworking or abusing the child. If farmers mistreated children, the CAS could reclaim them. If the children proved unsatisfactory to the farmers, they could be returned.[20] In addition to reducing the threat of social disorder in New York City and providing cheap labor for western farmers Brace anticipated that the children would be "treated not as servants, but as sons and daughters." This latter goal was often achieved. After several years, bonds of affection often sprang up between the family and child, which eventually led, in Brace's words, to "very many" of them being adopted.[21]

The large-scale placing-out movement inaugurated by the widely imitated CAS had enormous consequences for the history of adoption. The origins of America's first adoption laws can be traced to the increase in the number of middle-class farmers who wished to legalize the addition of a child to the family. By the mid-nineteenth century, state legislatures began enacting the first general, as opposed to private, adoption statutes. These were designed to ease the burden on legislatures caused by the many private adoption acts and to clarify inheritance rights. First enacted in Mississippi in 1846 and Texas in 1850 (states that were originally subject to the laws of France and Spain, respectively), the general adoption statutes were influenced by the civil law tradition embodied in the Napoleonic Code. They merely provided a legal procedure "to authenticate and make a public record of private adoption agreements," analogous to recording a deed for a piece of land.[22]

Alongside adoption by deed, state legislatures began to enact a second type of general adoption statute. The 1851 Massachusetts law, "An Act to Provide for the Adoption of Children," is commonly considered the first modern adoption law. It codified earlier state court decisions that had transformed the law of custody to reflect Americans' new conceptions of childhood and parenthood, which emphasized the needs of children and the contractual and egalitarian nature of spouses' rights of guardianship.[23] The Massachusetts statute differed from all earlier statutes in its emphasis on the welfare of the child—it made the adopted person the prime beneficiary of the proceeding—and the evaluation of the adopters' parental qualifications. The Massachusetts Adoption Act, as it was commonly called, was the first statute to establish the principle of judicial supervision of adoptions. It required the judge to ascertain that the adoptive parents were "of sufficient ability to bring up the child, before issuing the decree, and furnish suitable nurture and education," and that in general the magistrate was satisfied that the adoption was "fit and proper." The concern for the child's welfare drew on the "best interests of the child" doctrine, which had been evolving slowly in custody cases since the early 1800s, and which would become the cornerstone of modern adoption law. The statute also required the written consent of the natural parents, if living, or of the guardian or next of kin if the parents were deceased. The law also ended the power of natural parents over the children they relinquished by severing the legal bonds between them and freeing the child from all legal obligations to them. The enactment of the Massachusetts Adoption Act marked a watershed in the history of Anglo-American family and society. Instead of defining the parent-child relationship exclusively in terms of blood kinship, it encouraged adoptive parents to build a family by assuming the responsibility and emotional outlook of natural parents. In the next quarter-century, the Massachusetts Adoption Act came to be regarded as a model statute, and twenty-five states enacted similar laws.[24]

Not only did the CAS play a pivotal role in the origins of America's first child adoption laws, but Brace's reckless child-placing system was also indirectly responsible for initiating a fifty-year child welfare reform movement that culminated in the professionalization and bureaucratization of social workers and an expanded state role in regulating adoptions. Beginning in 1874 and continuing for the next half-century, Brace's methods ignited a heated controversy in the annual meetings of the National Conference of Charities and Correction over the relative merits of institutionalization versus family homes for homeless children. In the course of the debate, the child placement system came under attack from a variety of groups highly critical of Brace's methods. Representatives from Midwestern states accused Brace of dumping into their communities "car loads of criminal juveniles, . . . vagabonds, and guttersnipes," which resulted in a steep increase in vagrants and the state prison population. Catholic authorities viewed the CAS child placement system as an aggressive and covert form of Protestant proselytizing, equivalent to kidnapping. Eastern child welfare reformers voiced concern that their states were losing valuable human resources that were needed closer to home.[25]

Child welfare reformers also criticized the CAS for failing to investigate the families the children were placed with or supervising them afterwards. As early as 1857, Brace himself admitted the inadequacy of placement procedures, noting that letters of references even from clergymen or magistrates were given "with too little care." By 1882, at the ninth annual National Conference of Charities and Correction, the criticism reached new heights. J. H. Mills, the superintendent of an orphan asylum in North Carolina, accused the CAS of distributing large numbers of children to farmers "without asking any questions or obtaining any information regarding them or any security for their proper care or protection." The result, Mills stated, was that the farmers treated New York children like slaves. Delegates from Ohio, Michigan, Wisconsin, and Pennsylvania followed with additional charges about the lack of supervision. Brace denied the charges and conducted several investigations by his own agents, which invariably exonerated the CAS of any wrongdoing. However, in 1884, Hastings H. Hart, secretary of the State Board of Corrections and Charities and a respected child reformer, conducted an independent investigation of 340 CAS children placed out in Minnesota and confirmed Mills's criticism: there were numerous hasty placements and inadequate supervision, which resulted in many abused and exploited children. A further indictment of Brace's methods was Hart's inability to find any information on nearly one quarter of the children placed.[26]

Child welfare reformers' criticism of the CAS's unsound child placement practices led to the emergence of a second generation of reformers, who changed the procedures surrounding the placing of orphaned, abandoned, and dependent children in families. This movement was initiated by Catholic leaders, state officials, and reformers who advocated modifying or abolishing many of the CAS child-placing practices, particularly the unnecessary breakup of families, casual solicitation of parental consent, poor investigatory procedures, inadequate supervision of the children placed, and deficient record-keeping. Originating in the last quarter of the nineteenth century, the movement to reform child-placing practices faced an uphill struggle for the next seventy-five years. The implementation of its goals became the raison d'être of professional social workers.

Led by Catholic religious leaders, child welfare reformers repudiated the needless breakup of families. Catholic authorities' initial concern was Brace's placing of Catholic children in Protestant families.

To counter Brace's proselytizing, they founded in 1863 the Society for the Protection of Destitute Roman Catholic Children in the City of New York to ensure that dependent or delinquent Catholic children would be brought up within the faith. In its first annual report the Protectory, as it was known, pointedly repudiated Brace's placing-out system by denouncing the "serious evil of weakening the family tie by unnecessary separating children from their parents." To ensure that families were not needlessly broken up, it was essential that each case involving the separation of a child from parents be investigated thoroughly. Here was an important origin of "social casework," the methodology of the nascent profession of social work. Second-generation child-savers like the Reverend Martin Van Buren Van Arsdale led the way. As a college student, Van Arsdale was inspired by the shocking sight of ragged children in a county poorhouse and set himself the goal of finding individual homes for homeless children: the first child he placed was in his own home. In 1883, Van Arsdale, by then a Presbyterian minister, founded the National Children's Home Society (originally called the American Education Aid Society), a private, voluntarily supported, nonprofit organization that sought to establish branches in every state. By the 1890s, Children's Home Societies had arisen in Iowa, California, Missouri, Indiana, Michigan, Minnesota, and Washington state; twenty years later there were twenty-eight Societies placing children in adoptive homes in thirty-two states.[27]

In 1886, Van Arsdale started his own state organization, the Illinois Children's Home and Aid Society (ICHAS) and instituted standards of child placing that reformed most of Brace's unsound practices. Like Catholic authorities, Van Arsdale made it a cardinal principle to investigate each case thoroughly in order to avoid "severing the bonds of blood relationship." ICHAS officials would accept children who had parents or guardians only if a written surrender or commitment was given by the courts. To ensure a good home for the child, the ICHAS employed local advisory boards and trained agents to screen applicants requesting children. Officials began keeping exact records of all children placed out. ICHAS agents also made "visits of inspection" before and after the child's placement in a new home. The ICHAS thus was in the forefront of establishing standards for child adoption. During the Progressive Era, professional social workers would lobby state legislatures to enact these standards into law.[28]

Beginning at the end of the depression of the 1890s and extending to the conclusion of World War I, many Americans responded to the profound strains, widespread misery, and deep class divisions produced by a new industrial society by demanding reforms. Progressivism took the form of a political movement that sought by collective action and government intervention the reorganization and improvement of American life. Originating among a shifting coalition of mostly Protestant, newly professionalized, middle-class men and women, these "evangelistic modernizers," according to John Whiteclay Chambers, "wedded a quasi-religious idealism and scientism in a movement that worked for specific reforms while seeking to restore [America to] a sense of community and common purpose." Progressive reformers engaged in countless national and local campaigns to mitigate the impact of brutal factory conditions, concentrated economic power, corrupt politics, crowded and unsanitary cities, and a newly arrived, heterogeneous immigrant population. In reality members of a set of loosely connected movements, Progressives set about to regulate big business, democratize and reform the political system, aid the urban poor and exploited workers, and impose homogeneous cultural values on the entire population, especially Catholic and Jewish immigrants and blacks.[29]

Progressive reformers were particularly concerned with protecting women and children from the harsh effects of urban and industrial changes. From the 1909 White House Conference on the Care of Dependent Children that proclaimed "home life is the highest and finest product of civilization . . . Children should not be deprived of it except for urgent and compelling reasons" to the 1921 Sheppard-Towner Infancy and Maternity Protection Act that provided for federal spending to promote infant and maternal health, the Progressive Era witnessed a flurry of child welfare reforms instituted by Congress and state legislatures. Prominent among these reforms was the establishment of the U.S. Children's Bureau and legislation providing for mothers' pensions. It was also during the Progressive Era that a number of innovative institutions and practices first appeared in the field of adoption. The first private adoption agencies were created; social workers began the long process of professionalization; and social workers sought the aid of the state to regulate adoptions.[30]

Paradoxically, the number of dependent children in institutions nearly doubled during the first three decades of the twentieth century, while adoptions increased slowly. By 1900, breaking up families had become practically taboo, at least in theory, and family preservation had become a fundamental principle among all child-savers. This social work ideal would continue to be axiomatic among professional social workers until the end of World War II. As Galen A. Merrill, a child welfare reformer, noted in 1900 at the twenty-seventh annual meeting of the National Conference of Charities and Correction, "the permanent separation of a child from its natural parents is such a grave matter that it should be permitted only when parents cannot be helped or compelled to meet their obligations as parents."[31] By the early twentieth century, in the effort to prevent Brace's reckless child-placing policies, child welfare experts and social workers went to the other extreme and stressed the cultural primacy of the blood bond in family kinship. While they continued to extol the family as superior to the institution, the "family" they now meant was the child's *natural parents,* the family of origin.[32]

It is this emphasis on the preservation of the biological family that above all explains why the number of adopted children failed to increase significantly during the first third of the twentieth century. Rather than break up families, child welfare experts' new strategy was to emphasize the prevention of the causes of child dependency in the first place. To this end, they stressed that families should not be broken up merely because of poverty and that children should be separated from their natural families only as a last resort, for reasons of "inefficiency and immorality." Taking their cue from President Theodore Roosevelt's 1909 appeal to help the widowed mother "keep her own home and keep the child in it," a coalition of child welfare experts, powerful women's organizations, and influential social workers lobbied state legislatures for mothers' pensions. Their campaign met with considerable success. In 1911, Illinois passed the first statewide mothers' pension law. Other states rapidly followed. By 1920, forty state legislatures had passed similar statutes. Theda Skocpol has calculated that monthly grants for "deserving" widows "ranged from $4.33 a month in Arkansas to $69.31 a month in Massachusetts; and the median grant was $21.78." Despite the inadequacies and restrictiveness of these programs, especially toward minority mothers, the Children's Bureau in 1931 estimated that they resulted in 93,600 families with 253,00 children receiving mothers' pensions, more than twice the number of children adopted or in foster care.[33]

An aversion to adoption was the flip side of the popular and professional ideal that families should be kept together. Professional social workers made it a point of pride that they rarely recommended that children be adopted. Speaking before the prestigious National Conference of Social Work, Albert H. Stoneman, the Michigan Children's Aid Society's general secretary, noted approvingly that the twenty most respected child-placing organizations he studied all refused to receive children for adoption if it was possible for them "to be properly cared for by their own people." Similarly, Children's Bureau researchers reported that the ten child-placing agencies they examined "were unanimous in their opinion that no child, whether of legitimate or illegitimate birth, should be placed for adoption if there were decent, self-respecting parents or other family connections who might later, if not at the moment, provide a home for him." In teaching the art of child-placing, William H. Slingerland, special agent in the Russell Sage Foundation's department of child-helping, instructed social workers to conduct an intense investigation of the child's parents and especially "all near relatives, grandparents, brothers, sisters, uncles and aunts." Slingerland, noting that "Blood is thicker than water," confidently predicted they would find some near relatives "fit, able, and willing to care for children whose parents have died, failed, or broken down." Thus, social workers turned to adoption only as a last resort when other means to keep families together failed. As a result, the number of children available for adoption remained small.[34]

Americans' cultural definition of kinship also stigmatized adoption as socially unacceptable. Social workers had to overcome widespread popular prejudice in order to convince would-be adopters that taking a child into the home was not abnormal. During the late nineteenth and early twentieth century, a broad segment of the American public believed that adoption was an "unnatural" action that created ersatz or second-rate families. Most Americans would have agreed with Dr. R. L. Jenkins that "the normal biologic relationship of parent and child is more satisfactory . . . than an artificially created one." They would have nodded their heads in agreement when hearing the opinion that "though it is better to be adopted than institutionalized, no adopted relation is likely to be as good as a natural one." The very language underscored the inferior nature of adoption: in popular discourse, adoptive parents were always juxtaposed with "natural" or "normal" ones. Discriminatory laws reinforced the notion that the adoptive relationship was inherently flawed. Jurists regularly ruled in inheritance cases, for example, that adoption violated the legal principal of consanguinity or blood ties. In practice, this meant that adopted children did not have the same inheritance rights as birth children. In 1881 an Illinois court ruled against a girl's right to inherit from her recently deceased intestate adoptive parents because she was "not a brother or sister in fact." In other cases dealing with disputed custody rights of adopted children, both courts and legislatures favored natural parents' appeals to restore their children to them.[35]

Medical science contributed to popular cultural prejudices against adopting a child by coupling the stigma of illegitimacy with adoption. After 1910 the rise of the eugenics movement and psychometric testing led adopted children to be linked to inherited mental defects. Studies like Henry H. Goddard's *The Kallikak Family* (1912) claimed to demonstrate the tendency of generations of children to inherit the social pathology of their parents, particularly criminality and feeblemindedness. Using the Yerkes-Bridges modification of the Binet-Simon intelligence test, psychologists and social workers uncovered a strong connection between unmarried mothers and the purported hereditary trait of feeblemindedness. It was but a small conceptual step to include adopted children in the equation. As Ada Elliot Sheffield, director of Boston's Bureau of Illegitimacy, noted in 1920, "the children of unmarried parents, who doubtless make up a large number of adoptions, may turn out to show an undue proportion of abnormal mentality." The supposed link between feebleminded unwed mothers and their illegitimate children cast a pall over all adoptions; even popular magazines warned adoptive parents against the risk of "bad heredity." Adopted children were thus burdened with a double stigma: they were assumed to be illegitimate and thus tainted medically *and* they were lacking the all-important blood link to their adoptive parents.[36]

The general strategy that social workers employed to combat popular prejudice and negative medical opinion was to argue that environmental circumstances were more important than heredity. Prominent Progressive child welfare reformer Hastings H. Hart summed up social workers' beliefs: "a good environment will overcome a bad heredity." But while professional social workers downplayed the importance of heredity, they could not ignore it. At the height of eugenics influence, roughly from 1910 to 1925, they advocated separating the feebleminded unwed mother from her child and ruled out the possibility of adoption for what they called "defective" children. As Albert H. Stoneman remarked, "With our present knowledge of biology and heredity we seem justified in general not to offer for adoption the child of feebleminded parentage." Instead, social workers like Stoneman counseled that both mother and child should be placed in separate institutions that would care for them. Rather than fight the "science" of eugenics, social workers borrowed its methodology in order to assure prospective adoptive parents that the children they received were mentally sound. As early as 1910, leaders in the field of adoption urged upon their colleagues the use of psychometric tests, a recommendation they embraced with alacrity. But even with their best efforts, the cultural and medical stigmatizing aspects of adoption made many potential adopters extremely wary.[37]

Potential adoptive parents were also reluctant to adopt children because the chaotic, free market in child placement, which sprang up at the beginning of the twentieth century, gave adoption a distinctly disreputable aura. Although the first generation of state laws provided a mechanism for legalizing adoption, they did not compel the state to regulate the transfer of children from one family to another. Consequently, the first private adoption agencies, created at the beginning of the twentieth century, were largely unsupervised by federal or state agencies. Moreover, these amateur child-placing institutions were staffed by nonprofessional volunteers. Wealthy, socially prominent women with little social work training volunteered to care for homeless infants. They soon found themselves running adoption agencies, initially supplying their friends' requests for babies and later expanding their operations to meet childless couples' demands for infants. A number of these private adoption agencies first sprang up in New York City. One of the first was the Alice Chapin Adoption Nursery, started in 1911 by the wife of the prominent pediatrician Dr. Henry Dwight Chapin. Five years later, Mrs. Louise Wise, the wife of the famous Reform rabbi Stephen Wise, sought assistance from three wealthy members of her husband's Reform congregation, the Free Synagogue of New York, to expand and systematize her ad hoc adoption activities. Their financial assistance led to the incorporation of the Child Adoption Committee, which eventually became the largest Jewish adoption agency in New York City, the Louise Wise Services.[38] Similarly, in Chicago, several wealthy businessmen donated the money that permitted Mrs. Florence Dahl Walruth to purchase the residence that became The Cradle Society, Chicago's first adoption agency. Unlike professional social workers, these upper-class female amateurs made little effort to keep families together. They vigorously recommended adoption for children born out of wedlock and, on this issue, were sometimes supported by the influential print media.[39]

A host of other institutions seeking to place for adoption children born out of wedlock engaged in similar dubious practices. These included private maternity homes, family welfare agencies, hospital social service departments, state court probation departments, child protective agencies, and legal aid societies. Doctors and lawyers facilitated private nonagency or independent adoptions, acting as liaisons between childless couples and unmarried mothers trying to avoid social stigma. In many states only a minority of adoptions were regulated. Studies conducted in Massachusetts and New Jersey during the 1920s revealed that only one-quarter to one-third of children adopted in those states were placed by state-licensed child-placing institutions. Moreover, many parents succeeded in circumventing all institutions, whether licensed by the state or not, by advertising in newspapers that their infants were available for adoption. Adding to the disreputable aura of adoption were the commercial maternity homes and baby farms that sold infants born out of wedlock to childless couples. A 1917 study, commissioned by Chicago's Juvenile Protective Association, investigated adoptions and confirmed the worst fears of Progressive reformers. It found that there was "a regular commercialized business of child placing being carried on in the city of Chicago; that there were many maternity hospitals which made regular charges . . . for disposing of unwelcome children; and that there were also doctors and other individuals who took advantage of the unmarried mother willing to pay any amount of money to dispose of the child. No name, address, or reference was required to secure the custody of a child from these people." The combination of cultural, medical, and social stigma surrounding adoption during the first quarter of the twentieth century kept the number of potential adoptive parents relatively low and thus depressed the number of children who were adopted.[40]

Studies such as those by Chicago's Juvenile Protective Association underscored the need for state regulation of adoptions. Working in public and private child-placing institutions and in federal and state agencies, professional social workers from Massachusetts to California adamantly denounced unregulated adoptions by unwed mothers. They attacked independent adoptions because they contributed to high infant mortality, deprived the child of living with his or her own family, foisted feebleminded children on unsuspecting adoptive parents, and discredited conscientious and competent child-placing agencies. They advocated two courses of action to reduce and ultimately end unregulated adoptions. First, in their professional journals and at national conventions, social workers vigorously recommended keeping an unwed mother and child together as the most desirable course of action and proposed adoption only as a last resort or if the unwed mother insisted on it. Second, they lobbied state legislatures strenuously for changes in laws concerning illegitimacy and adoption. In the ten years following the 1909 White House Conference on Dependent Children, lawmakers in seventeen states created commissions to revise child welfare legislation.[41]

The most important product of the child welfare commission movement was the Children's Code of Minnesota, enacted in 1917, which became the model for state laws in the next two decades. The Children's Code of Minnesota was the first state law that required a social investigation to determine whether a proposed adoptive home was suitable for a child. It became the responsibility of the state's Board of Control to examine the adoption petition and advise the court in writing on every adoption case. The statute also provided for a six-month probationary period of residence by the child in the home of the adopting parents and ordered that adoption records be closed to inspection. Child welfare reformers hailed Minnesota's Children's Code as a model law, and for the next two decades the major theme in the history of adoption centered on their efforts to lobby state legislatures to provide safeguards—consent decrees, social investigations, probation periods, and confidential records—protecting everyone involved in the adoption process.[42]

State legislation received guidance from two national child welfare organizations, one public and the other private. The U.S. Children's Bureau and the Child Welfare League of America were instrumental in reforming adoption laws, instructing professional adoption workers, and educating the American public on adoption issues. Established in 1912 within the Department of Commerce and Labor, the U.S. Children's Bureau marked the first Federal recognition of a responsibility for the welfare of *all* children, not just poor and dependent ones. The Bureau's budget was small—$25,640, with a staff of fifteen—and it was not permitted to initiate legislation. Its mandate, however, was broad. It was charged by Congress to "investigate and report . . . upon all matters pertaining to the welfare of children and child life among all classes of our people."[43]

Julia Lathrop, the first chief of the Children's Bureau and the first woman to head any federal bureau, used that mandate to conduct "research aimed at the national conscience." Under her leadership, the Bureau issued reports detailing the inadequacy of American birth registration, the high incidence of infant mortality, and the evils of child labor. By 1919, the Bureau had issued 38 publications with a total circulation of 3,020,448. The Bureau also published popular pamphlets instructing mothers on how to raise their infants, recommending prenatal health care, and arguing the benefits of breast-feeding. Lathrop had a genius for publicity and organization. She soon had Children's Bureau officials writing editorials, articles, and columns of advice on infant and maternal health in such popular magazines as *Ladies' Home Journal, Woman's World,* a magazine with two million subscribers, and a host of others. In short order, the Children's Bureau was receiving 125,000 letters a year from women of every class and region in the United States and had established itself as the nation's leading expert on children.[44]

Until the late 1940s, the Children's Bureau played a similar commanding role for adoption officials, caseworkers, and those most directly involved in adoption: natural parents, adoptees, and adoptive parents. Through intensive survey research, the Bureau established itself as the repository of authoritative information on adoption at a time when not much was known about the issue. The publication of studies such as *Adoption Laws in the United States* (1925), *The Work of Child-Placing Agencies* (1927), *The ABC of Foster-Family Care for Children* (1933), and *Problems and Procedures in Adoption* (1941) broke new ground by instructing adoption workers on every aspect of the adoption process. They provided social workers with statistical data identifying who adopted children, where they were adopted, and how many children were adopted. No one could answer these simple questions before the Children's Bureau researched them. The Bureau recommended professional adoption practices, including careful child placement, investigation of adoption petitions, and the importance of the report to the court. Keeping with the Bureau's reformist ideology, publications insisted that adoptions should be carried out only by properly trained social workers in state-licensed agencies using sound casework procedures and campaigned for restricting independent adoptions. They pointed out the wide disparity in state laws and campaigned for uniformity. They described common practices in child-placing that adoption workers should avoid, such as needlessly breaking up families, pressuring unwed mothers to relinquish their children before they had recovered their physical and emotional equilibrium, and failing to investigate the physical, mental, social, and family history of the child and the adoptive parents before placement.[45] In addition, the Bureau disseminated the latest information on child welfare and adoption through its monthly journal, *The Child*. Offprints of valuable articles on adoption from various sources were made available to agencies and researchers. For example, in 1943, 2,000 reprints of "Problems in Safeguarding Adoptions" from the *Journal of Pediatrics* were distributed to a variety of child welfare agencies and state social service consultants.[46]

Because it was viewed as the nation's expert on adoption, the Bureau's staff was frequently called upon for advice. Lawyers and bar associations asked about adoption laws; child-placing agencies requested advice about psychological tests for children, the proper age of child placement, treatment of unmarried mothers, and countless other questions. Thousands of letters from prospective adoptive parents poured in, asking for children to adopt or for the location of a child-placing agency. Advice was sought on how to get a birth certificate, locate a parent, or tell a child of the adoption. Prominent adoption researchers, such as Dr. Florence Clothier of the New England Home for Little Wanderers and Sophie van Senden Theis of the New York State Charities Aid Association, requested Bureau staff to review their articles and monographs. Producers of radio soap operas like *The Guiding Light* submitted scripts for approval. Editors of and writers for popular magazines such as *Life, Collier's, The Woman, Cosmopolitan,* and *Parade* requested Bureau experts to vet their manuscripts before publication. No request for information was too trivial or too complex. The Bureau staff responded politely and professionally. By these means, the Bureau gained a remarkable influence in conveying to lawyers, social workers, researchers, and the public its reformist vision of child care, especially its views on the evils of independent adoptions and the importance of state licensed agency adoptions.[47]

The Bureau acted as a watchdog on the media, actively countering misleading or what it considered malicious information on adoptions. When some California radio stations attempted to place children for adoption, the Bureau's chief wrote to the head of the Licensing Division of the Federal Radio Commission to halt the practice. Similarly, Bureau staffers sought correction from editors and authors when their articles exaggerated the number of black-market adoptions, mistakenly blamed agencies for delaying adoptions, or advocated withholding information about the child's social history from adoptive parents.[48]

The Bureau also exercised great influence on local adoption policies and procedures by conducting inspection tours of state child welfare services. In November 1938, for example, Mary Ruth Colby, head of the Social Science Division, spent four days in Maine, during which she conferred about adoption issues with officials from the state's Division of Vital Statistics and Department of Health and Welfare and interviewed a probate judge about legal procedures in adoption. Colby concluded her visit by attending a social work conference at which she introduced a plan for studying Maine's adoption petitions to representatives from private and public child-placing institutions and persuaded them to investigate the state's probate courts and identify problems needing reform. Similarly, Children's Bureau staffers kept abreast of local initiatives and adoption practices by communicating regularly with state adoption committees.[49]

Working in conjunction with the Children's Bureau was the Child Welfare League of America (CWLA). Founded in 1921 with headquarters in New York City, with sixty-five organizations as charter members and a renowned social worker, Christian C. Carstens, as its first director, the CWLA became in the 1920s the most important private national agency for child welfare. Among its many activities, the CWLA conducted on-site investigations of child care facilities in order to suggest improvements, sponsored regional conferences for social workers, and published the Child Welfare League of America *Bulletin,* which eventually evolved into the influential social work journal *Child Welfare.* Beginning in the late 1920s it also provided advanced training institutes for experienced social workers. One of its primary contributions was to encourage a standardized national child care program by promoting recognized child welfare principles and standards. In pursuit of this goal the CWLA published *Standards for Children's Organizations Providing Foster Family Care* (1933), which stressed temporary rather than permanent institutional care for dependent children and insisted on the preservation of the family in potential foster care cases.[50]

Soon after the onset of the Great Depression in 1929, unprecedented levels of adult unemployment, homelessness, hunger, and misery provided additional impetus for legislation applying to children, as local governments and private agencies were unable to cope with massive suffering and unemployment. Forty percent of the eight million people on relief were children under sixteen. Infant mortality rates rose, and the material circumstances of many children declined dramatically. Large numbers of impoverished single mothers and their children exhausted state poor relief funds and mothers' aid appropriations. President Franklin Roosevelt's Federal Emergency Relief Act (1933) delivered a measure of support by funding states' general assistance and mothers' aid programs, but fell seriously short. The 1935 Social Security Act provided additional federal funding for child welfare services. The resulting influx of federal financial support strengthened and expanded existing adoption programs while creating new state welfare departments where none had existed previously. By the end of 1937, thirty-nine states had enacted new adoption laws or revised old ones; many provided for a social investigation by the state welfare department or a licensed children's agency before the court hearing, and a trial period in the prospective adoptive home.[51]

In the late 1930s, the CWLA began to address the issue of adoption standards. The impetus came from a number of the CWLA's member societies complaining of the practices of commercial adoption agencies and maternity homes. Notorious adoption mills like The Cradle Society of Illinois, The Willows of Kansas, and the Veil Maternity Home of West Virginia accepted payment from adoptive parents upon receipt of a child, ignored commonly accepted social work practices, and provided inadequate safeguards for everyone directly involved in the adoption. The Cradle Society, for example, shunned the primary tool of professional social workers, individualized casework. It accepted without question the decision of the unwed mother to relinquish her child and made no effort to ascertain whether her action was appropriate to her circumstances. Moreover, The Cradle Society failed to investigate prospective adoptive parents thoroughly, failed to record the child's family history or make a study of the child's mental development, refused to inform the adoptive parents of the child's family history, and made no provision for a probationary period after placement to supervise the child. By the 1930s, all of these policies that The Cradle Society ignored had become tenets of professional social work.[52]

The large number of independent adoptions made by physicians also concerned CWLA member agencies. In the 1940s, the Children's Bureau estimated that almost half of the adoptions in America were made outside the purview of licensed agencies. Adoption officials believed that the lack of a proper social investigation often led to tragedy. As one agency executive wrote, "Only last year we had an unfortunate experience when a physician in good standing insisted on placing a baby with one of his patients who was unmarried, in her 40's and psychopathic, having been committed to the State Institution some years previous."[53]

Responding to the widespread deviations from sound adoption casework principles and the increasing number of independent adoptions, the CWLA in 1938 published its first set of adoption standards, which fit on a single page. They were grouped under three separate headings providing "safeguards" for the child, adoptive parents, and the state, respectively. The first safeguard for the child could also be considered one for the natural parents: the child was not to be unnecessarily deprived of kinship ties. Maintaining the family of origin was still considered by professional social workers to be the most desirable course of action for treating children threatened by depen-

dency. The second and third safeguards for the child revolved around
the adoptive parents' motivation and suitability for the adoption. It
was necessary that the adoptive parents desire the child "for the purpose of completing an otherwise incomplete family group," have "a
good home and good family life . . . and be well adjusted to each
other," and promise to love, support, and educate the child. The safeguards that the adoptive parents should expect from a reputable
child-placing institution were that it would keep their identities from
the natural parents; physically and mentally match the child in accord
with their expectations; and complete the adoption proceedings
"without unnecessary publicity." Finally the state should require "for
its own sake and the child's protection" that there be a trial period of
residence before the adoption was finalized and the child's birth records be revised to prevent "unnecessary embarrassment in case of
illegitimacy." The standards recommended that for "good advice and
best results" both natural and adoptive families consult a "well-
established children's organization." The League's adoption standards
presented member agencies with a model of the most desirable practices to which child-placing organizations should aspire. Failure to
conform to CWLA standards would result in suspension.[54]

Both the Children's Bureau's increasing attention to adoption and
the CWLA's formulation of adoption standards in the decade before
World War II were symptomatic of the beginning of far-reaching
changes in adoption policy and practice. Over the course of the next
generation, roughly from 1940 to 1970, strong demand by childless
couples for adopted children, an increase in the number of children
available for adoption, repudiation of the standard of the "unadoptable" child, and more liberal attitudes on race transformed the field
of adoption. The initial sign that the old order was changing was the
decline during the 1920s and 1930s of the stigma of eugenics surrounding adopted children. In 1924, Sophie van Senden Theis published her pioneering study, *How Foster Children Turn Out*, which
reported that 88.1 percent of 269 children placed out for adoption
by the New York State Charities Aid Association had made a "capable"
social adjustment in adult life, thereby repudiating the eugenicists'
claims about the "menace of the feebleminded." By then, medical
authorities had distanced themselves from the "science" of eugenics
and were embracing the new theories of psychiatry and mental hy-

giene. Also by the 1930s, adoption agencies routinely administered to children the Stanford revision of the Binet-Simon intelligence test, while popular magazines assured prospective adoptive parents that "the 'danger' of adoption has been largely obviated by scientific advance."[55]

Not only were children represented as "safer" to adopt after 1940, but there were also more of them to adopt. In addition to the continued large number of homes broken by death, divorce, and desertion, there was a veritable demographic revolution in the number of children born out of wedlock. With social bonds loosened by wartime, illegitimacy rates, especially among nonwhites, began to soar and continued their upward flight for the next fifty years. In 1938, 88,000 children were born out of wedlock; a decade later, 129,700; by 1958 the figure had climbed to 201,000, reaching 245,000 by 1962, a 306 percent increase in a quarter-century. The largest increase in the number of out-of-wedlock births occurred among nonwhite mothers, climbing 2.5 times, from 46,700 in 1938 to 130,900 in 1957.[56]

The crucial ingredient in the origins of the revolution in adoption practice was not the increase of supply factors, though these were important, but on the demand side, as childless couples besieged adoption agencies pleading for a child to add to their household. Even before the war years, the nation found itself in an adoption boom. Startled Children's Bureau officials initially attributed the unexpected demand for adopted children to the low birth rate of the Depression years and subsequent wartime prosperity, as previously economically strapped couples found they could now afford to start adoptive families. But it was the baby boom, beginning in the mid-1940s and reaching its peak in the late 1950s, with its dramatic rise in marriages and births, that exacerbated the increased demand for children to adopt and resulted in adoption agencies being inundated with requests for children.

The baby boom was both the cause and the effect of a profound change in the national political culture that tied the security of the nation and personal happiness to an ideology of domesticity and the nuclear family. Parenthood during the Cold War became a patriotic necessity. The media romanticized babies, glorified motherhood, and identified fatherhood with masculinity and good citizenship. The consequences of this celebratory pronatalist mood, as the historian Elaine Tyler May has written, "marginalized the childless in unprecedented ways." Uncomfortable with being childless and the subject of public opprobrium, many of these childless couples sought adoption in record numbers as one solution to their shame of infertility. Contributing to the unprecedented numbers of childless couples applying for children to adopt were new medical treatments—semen examination, tests for tubal patency, and endrometrial biopsies—permitting physicians to diagnose physical sterility more easily and accurately early in marriage.[57]

Wartime prosperity, a postwar pronatalist climate of opinion, and medical advances in infertility diagnosis combined to produce a remarkable increase in the number of applications to adopt a child. In 1937 child welfare officials used incomplete returns to estimate that there were between 16,000 and 17,000 adoptions annually, of which one-third to one-half were adoptions by relatives. By 1945, the Children's Bureau estimated that adoptions had increased threefold, to approximately 50,000 annually; a decade later the number of adoptions had nearly doubled again, to 93,000, and by 1965 climbed to 142,000. In less than thirty years, the number of adoptions had grown nearly ninefold.[58]

In the decade after World War II, this new interest group—white, middle-class, childless couples—overwhelmed the understaffed and underfunded adoption agencies, which had failed to anticipate the increase in adoption applicants. The demand far exceeded the number of available children. By the mid-1950s one expert estimated that of the four and a half million childless couples, fully one million were seeking the approximately 75,000 children available for adoption. By 1957, depending on what region of the nation a prospective adoptive couple inhabited, CWLA executive director Joseph P. Reid estimated that the odds were between 18 to 1 and 10 to 1 against receiving a child.[59]

Frustrated couples blamed adoption agencies, not the scarce supply of infants, for their inability to find a child. Their hostility toward adoption agencies was fed in part by popular magazines. Articles reported that one million children in the United States languished in institutions while social workers dithered. Prospective adoptive couples, turned down by adoption agencies, lashed out at the apparent injustice. Rejected applicants and childless couples on waiting lists blamed "red tape," which usually meant social workers' perfectionist rules. These were rules concerning age limitations (applicants could not be over forty years old); requirements of religious uniformity (applicants had to belong to the same church); and policies concerning the length of marriage (applicants had to be married more than two years). They also complained of long delays between application and child placement (up to eighteen months in New York City, and as much as four years in Louisiana); the social workers' intrusiveness (overzealous prying into the applicant's private life); and partiality toward wealthy and famous applicants (favoring Hollywood celebrities). One young woman succinctly captured childless couples' resentment of and antagonism toward adoption agencies when she remarked, "These agency people are all trying to play God—and to beat Him at His own game . . . This business of matching babies to the parents' complexion and personality—did all your brothers and sisters look and act alike? And the idea of holding a child under observation for months, even years, to see if his IQ will improve or to make sure some hereditary disease won't crop out—did your mother get a guarantee of perfection when you were born?" Being denied a child was hard to bear for tens of thousands of childless couples who desperately wanted to start families. In droves, they circumvented professional social work standards by securing children from unregulated institutions like The Cradle Society, from third parties (doctors or lawyers), and to a lesser extent from the black market, where unscrupulous operators sold infants for a profit. By 1955, the ubiquity of black-market baby rings spurred a Senate subcommittee to hold public hearings to investigate them.[60]

The upsurge in postwar adoption applicants and the drumbeat of adoption applicants' complaints prompted professional social workers to defend themselves. The staffs of the Children's Bureau and the Child Welfare League of America spent countless hours rebutting critical or inaccurate articles in popular magazines. They emphasized that children eligible for adoption were in short supply and that the vast majority of the children receiving temporary care in institutions were not legally free for adoption. They justified this situation by maintaining the need to protect everyone involved in adoption from hasty placements. By way of example, they cited the case of a mother going to court six years after her child was placed for adoption because she did not understand the permanence of her decision when she signed the release papers. Such could be the tragic result of unsupervised adoptions. Similarly, the time-consuming testing of children and investigations of their background protected adoptive parents from assuming responsibility for a child who was physically or mentally disabled. And, of course, the thorough investigation of adoptive parents was necessary to place the child in a healthy, nurturing environment and to prevent abuse. The social workers upheld their professional standards by stating pointedly that their function was "not to supply a baby to every childless couple but to find the best possible parents for the babies in their charge."[61]

But childless couples' resentment of long delays and the inflexibility of adoption agencies' rules provoked anxiety in adoption workers. As early as 1937, CWLA officials worried that childless couples seeking children to adopt were avoiding accredited agencies and instead were pursuing independent adoptions—receiving children from doctors, lawyers, relatives, or directly from unwed mothers. After surveying its member agencies, CWLA officials concluded that "the fact that such a large amount of adoption work is going on beyond the reach of the organized social agencies seems to indicate that in some way we have failed to meet the community's need—why has the stream passed us by? This calls for a frank scanning of program and policy. Are we so inflexible that we cannot find a way to serve this group in need and yet serve them in a socially safeguarded way?"[62] Another decade would pass before the social work profession could provide a negative answer to that question.

In 1948 and again in 1951, the CWLA held a series of national adoption workshops and conferences. What the organization discovered in these national meetings was that while the profession of social welfare was retreating from social reform and caseworkers were being criticized for complacency towards the poor, individual child welfare agencies were reforming traditional adoption practices. No single factor can account for all the changes that occurred at the local level in different parts of the country. While pressure from would-be adoptive parents challenged social workers to alter their policies, at the macrolevel a deep humanitarianism, spawned by a revulsion of the atrocities of World War II, Allied propaganda espousing the cause of democracy and attacking illiberal regimes, demographic shifts in population as over one million African Americans moved out of the South to Northern and Western cities, and a consequent liberalization of race relations, deeply affected adoption agencies' policies. Nowhere were these changes more noticeable than in agencies' definition of the "adoptable" child. Before World War II, social workers refused to accept children with physical and mental handicaps in the belief that adoptive parents desired only "perfect" children. In the postwar era, social workers began to abandon the idea of the unadoptable child and broadened the definition of adoptability to include "any child . . . who needs a family and who can develop in it, and for whom a family can be found that can accept the child with its physical or mental capacities." With the enlarged definition of adoptability, social workers for the first time initiated serious efforts to place disabled, minority, older, and foreign-born children in adoptive homes.[63]

The new definition of the adoptable child was first brought to the attention of the nation's social workers in 1947 when Belle Wolkomir, the supervisor of the intake department of the Jewish Child Care Association of New York, reported on the agency's successful placement of "unwanted children whose heredity showed considerable pathology." Wolkomir announced that the great majority of children "made excellent and physical and social progress, and when placed in skillfully selected homes adapted to their needs became 'adoptable' after a period of boarding care." At the CWLA's 1948 Conference on Adoption the issue surfaced again. Adoption case workers manifested such intense interest in the subject that CWLA officials took the initiative and held a workshop the next year devoted entirely to examining the principles and special problems involved in adoption of children with mental or physical disabilities. Soon thereafter, a CWLA survey of 90 member agencies revealed that whereas in 1948, 80 percent looked for the "perfect" child for adoptive placement, in 1951 only 47 percent required that the child be free from disabilities. By 1955, Marshall Field, CWLA president, issued a press release hailing the "peaceful revolution" then under way in adoption. Field cited as evidence of "a new trend, a shift in the wind, a broadening in our approach," the successful placement of disabled children and "children with histories of mental illness in their families."[64]

With the CWLA taking the lead, minorities, especially dependent

African American children, soon felt the effects of the profession's expanded definition of "adoptable." The war years represented a turning point in opening up America's child welfare system to the idea of placing black children for adoption. Progress was slow: northern cities such as Philadelphia and Cleveland continued to maintain inadequate segregated child welfare institutions, and neither provided adoption services for African American children. But in 1939 the New York State Charities Aid Association for the first time extended adoption services to African American children, annually placing eighteen to twenty children during World War II. Additional factors that paved the way for the expansion of adoption services to nonwhites included black militancy against continuing wartime segregation and discrimination, a sharp increase in the number of nonwhite out-of wedlock births, and federal and state action and court rulings in favor of equal rights. In 1948, the journal *Child Welfare* reported: "We find over the country a growing conviction, translated in practice, that the color of a child's skin, the texture of his hair, or the slant of his eyes in no way affects his basic needs or the relation of his welfare to that of the total community." Years before *Brown v. Board of Education* (1954) and more than a decade before the civil rights movement, many of the nation's adoption agencies began placing an increasing number of African American children for adoption. In 1949, Lois Wildy, Illinois Children's Home and Aid Society's director of casework, proudly informed her colleagues that since 1944 adoption placements of black children had averaged twenty-five a year. Over the next decade, many agencies found themselves with more black children than could be placed locally, and they began intense mass-media publicity campaigns and programs specially designed to recruit black adoptive parents.[65]

The end of World War II witnessed the first phase of an upsurge of intercountry adoption (ICA). Between 1946 and 1953, American citizens and organizations such as the American Branch of International Social Services brought to the United States 5,814 foreign-born orphans and abandoned children for adoption, many of whom were from war-torn Greece, Germany, and Japan. Military laws enacted in 1947 permitted armed forces personnel to adopt German children, and a highly publicized campaign to adopt Japanese children orphaned by the atomic bomb met with great success. Between the end of the Korean War in 1953 and 1962, what adoption researchers Howard Altstein and Rita J. Simon label the second phase of ICA began, a period that ended only recently. In this phase, "for the first time in history, relatively large numbers of Western couples, mostly in the United States, were adopting children who were racially and culturally different from themselves." Almost one-third of the 15,000 children adopted during this period and 65 percent of the additional 32,000 foreign-born children adopted by American citizens in the following decade (1966–1976), came from Asia, primarily the Republic of Korea. Consequently, Korean children became the largest group of foreign adoptees within America and the United States the leading receiver of foreign children in the world.[66]

Social workers noted that the couples adopting foreign children often did not fit the standard profile of adoptive parents, having been rejected by local agencies because of age or lack of available children. But they were impressed by their "amazing understanding, ingenuity, patience, and sensitivity." They urged their colleagues to reexamine "the criteria we have established for suitable adoptive parents to see if a more flexible attitude should be accepted towards such factors as age, housing, income, families with children." Not only would increased flexibility result in finding more homes for hard-to-place children, but it might also "dispel some of the criticism heaped upon social workers by the public."[67]

By the early 1960s, American adoption was riding high, a popular and respected institution. Moreover, after a century of trial and error and strong advocacy by the U.S. Children's Bureau and the CWLA, there existed a strong public and professional consensus on child welfare policy and principles of adoption law. From the basic modern social work belief that all children have a right to a family and that the child's interests are paramount, five major attributes of adoption in America had been developed.[68]

First, the states, through their legal processes, create or expand a family. Through the 1960s, modern adoption in the United States was mainly a matter governed by state laws, not federal ones. State laws govern all the circumstances of legal adoptions, from who may be adopted through the issuance of new birth certificates. Second, as a result of the cultural preeminence of "blood" kinship, the state or adoption agency must get informed and voluntary consent to the adoption from the natural parents. Without that consent or a court order citing grounds to dispense with parental consent—abandonment, neglect, or abuse—children cannot be separated from their family of origin. Third, after obtaining consent, the adoption must meet "the best interests of the child" doctrine. At a minimum, this doctrine is defined by a judicial finding that the adopters are likely to be suitable parents and that the adoption will promote the child's welfare. In determining what is "the best interests of the child," the courts usually rely on the judgment of professional social workers who conduct background investigations of the parties involved. Fourth, adoptive relationships are permanent. All the child's prior connections to the biological family are severed, and the adoptive family replaces the original one. When the court issues a decree of adoption, the natural parents are divested of all legal rights and obligations to the child, and the child is freed from all legal obligations of obedience in respect to them. Consequently, adoptive parents are deemed exclusively responsible for the child. Fifth, adoption records are sealed and access is denied to everyone, except upon a judicial finding of "good cause."

It is with this last attribute of modern adoption—sealed records —that a history of secrecy and disclosure in adoption must begin. But what exactly are "adoption records"? Where are they located? And what kinds of information do they contain?

The Origins of Adoption Records

All adoption records contain, in the parlance of modern social work, *identifying* and *nonidentifying* information. Identifying information, so called because its possession could enable adopted persons to contact their family of origin, usually consists of the names and addresses of the biological parents, and siblings if any, at the time that parental rights were terminated. It might also include the name of the child before placement. Nonidentifying information is data that would not allow the adopted person to locate the biological parents. These facts include the date, time, and place of birth; the medical history of the adopted person; the biological parents' ethnicity, occupation, religious background, medical record, and educational level; and the method by which parental rights were terminated: voluntary or court-ordered.[1] Because adoption has been for most of its history a matter for the state, not the federal, government, the amount of family information in an adoptee's records will vary greatly depending on where and when the person was born.

Although it is commonly imagined that adoption records are a single, tangible, entity—a thick file folder crammed with data and located at an adoption agency—the reality is much more complicated. There are in fact three sources of family information about an adopted child: the records of the court that approved the final adoption (including preliminary proceedings, if any), the state repository for birth certificates, and the case files of the adoption agency.[2] Today's adoption activists might be surprised by the paucity of information in adoption records, especially in the earliest created ones, court records.

With the enactment of the Massachusetts Adoption Act of 1851 and its imitation by twenty-five states in the next quarter-century, there arose the first adoption court records. The family information contained in those first records was meager, despite the statutory requirements that judges inquire into the suitability of adoptive parents and that the adoption serve the best interests of the child. In general, magistrates made only perfunctory investigations. Certainly, the statutes did not require detailed background studies or long probationary periods to observe adoptive parents' conduct. Initially, judges merely asked the parties to the adoption a few questions. Did the natural parents consent to the adoption? Were the adoptive parents capable of supporting the child, and were they of the same religion as the child? If old enough—ten to fourteen years of age in most jurisdictions—did the child consent to the adoption as well?[3]

By the 1920s, judicial adoption proceedings had hardly changed. Adoptive parents now appeared in court accompanied by their attorneys. Only if a natural parent contested an adoption was it likely that he or she would be interviewed by a judge. In a few states, such as Illinois, mothers of illegitimate children were represented in court by a guardian *ad litem,* appointed to defend the interests of persons incapacitated by infancy. More commonly, magistrates simply scrutinized written adoption petitions and natural parents' consent forms, and asked a question or two. But whatever form the judicial proceedings took, they were quick. Typically, adoption proceedings were begun and completed the same day the court received the petition, sometimes in less than an hour. Even as late as the 1920s, 67 percent of the adoption petitions in Massachusetts and nearly 50 percent of the adoption petitions in Illinois were approved in one day. A rare verbatim account that has survived of an adoption proceeding in 1936 in Illinois' Cook County Court gives the flavor of these hearings (Mr. T. is the lawyer for the adopting parents, and Mr. C. the adopting father):

> *Mr. T.:* If the Court please, this is the petition of C——, Roy C. and Margaret M. C. to adopt P. R. R., a minor. Mr. and Mrs. C. are petitioning to adopt this child, now one and one-half years of age. The child has previously been adopted. You will note attached to the

petition for adoption a certified copy of a decree which was en-
tered in the Stephenson County Court on April 29, setting aside
the previous adoption. This was set aside in open court on juris-
dictional grounds.
The Court: Yes.
Mr. T.: Mr. and Mrs. C. are well able to take care of this child and
bring it up.
The Court: Yes. You have no children of your own?
Mr. C.: No, we have not.
The Court: You understand when you adopt this child, you must
raise it and provide for it during its minority?
Mr. C.: Yes.
The Court: And that the child will have the same rights of inheri-
tance as a natural born child?
Mr. C.: Yes.
The Court: All right.[4]

As this verbatim account reveals, the record of court proceedings
contained little social information about the family.

A better source of family information was the adoption petition
presented to the court, but it varied greatly from state to state. In
many states, the adoption statute merely mandated who was permitted to adopt, but did not specify what the petition was to contain.
Other states, such as Pennsylvania and Ohio, required the adoption
petition to include, in addition to the names of the petitioners, a
minimal amount of identifying information: the name and age of the
child and the names and addresses of the natural parents, if living.
The petition in these states also required a few items of nonidentifying information, such as the name by which the child was to be
known and a description of any property belonging to the child.
Adoptees searching for family information would find little of interest
in these adoption petitions.[5]

There were a number of reasons why the legal records were so
sparse. Judges were predisposed to favor adoptions, believing that
adoptive parents acted from altruistic and humanitarian motives and
that adoption in general was in the best interests of the state. Consequently, judges felt no compulsion to investigate adoption petitions
thoroughly. As one magistrate put it: "It is not the duty of the courts
to bring the microscope to bear upon such a case in order that every
slight defect may be magnified, so that a reason may be found for

declaring invalid the proceedings under a beneficial statute of this character." Because many of the children were illegitimate, there was also a general sense about adoption proceedings that "few, if any, questions, should be asked concerning such children." Moreover, most adoptive parents preferred anonymity and did not want to be investigated. Finally, some courts were simply derelict in their responsibilities. As late as 1936 in Cook County, Illinois, one researcher found that adoption petitions were incomplete because "the attitude of the court and of the lawyers practicing in these cases [was] reactionary from the point of child welfare workers."[6]

Although adoption proceedings were carried on with discretion—judges heard cases in chambers and issued adoption decrees quickly—the legal proceedings were not confidential. On the contrary, they were recorded by the court clerk and available for public inspection. The first wave of adoption statutes during the second half of the nineteenth century had no provision whatsoever for the confidentiality of the court proceedings. It was Progressive Era child welfare reformers who introduced the idea that adoption court proceedings should be closed from public scrutiny. Progressive reformers became involved in making adoption court proceedings confidential through their interest in lowering America's high rate of infant mortality, especially in the nation's cities, where illegitimacy was high.

The U.S. Children's Bureau took the lead in 1915 by commissioning a massive three-part series entitled *Illegitimacy as a Child Welfare Problem* (1920). It also sponsored in 1919 and 1920 a series of regional conferences that brought the best minds in child welfare together to discuss the legal handicaps facing children born out of wedlock and to formulate broad principles of treatment and legislation. The Children's Bureau initiatives were joined by a spate of book-length surveys, statistical studies, policy discussions, and articles on illegitimacy and unmarried mothers that emanated from children's organizations such as the Boston's Children's Aid Society and the Juvenile Protective Association and from social welfare periodicals like *Survey* and the Child Welfare League of America *Bulletin*. Between 1910 and 1920 social workers heard nineteen papers presented at the National Conference of Charities and Correction on the topic, ranging from feeblemindedness among unmarried mothers to the necessity of reforming illegitimacy statutes.[7]

Social workers' initial research documented the existence of tens of thousands of illegitimate children born to single unmarried women who were legally denied birth control information and contraceptive devices and who were frequently unable to secure abortions. They also uncovered a shocking statistic: infants born out of wedlock were subject to a mortality rate two to three times higher than infants of legitimate birth. They discovered that the primary reason for death was the early separation, often within a month after birth, of the mother from her child. Moreover, social workers found that unwed mothers were separated from the infant for preventable reasons: poverty, desertion, or the stigma of illegitimacy. According to the researchers, the unwed mother, when faced with what she perceived as insurmountable difficulties, often solved her dilemma by abandoning her baby to child-placing agencies run by amateur social workers or to commercial baby farms, which would place the infants for adoption.[8]

In a move typical of Progressive reformers' solution to urban problems, professional social workers called on the states to regulate adoptions. In 1917, they persuaded legislators to enact the Children's Code of Minnesota with the hope that investigation of adoptions would thwart unwed mothers from unnecessarily relinquishing their babies and, if relinquished, the children would be protected from abuse. Most important for the issues of secrecy and disclosure, the law stipulated that the court records "shall not be open to inspection or copy by other persons than the parties in interest and their attorneys and representatives of the State board of control," unless by a court order. Court clerks, who were often the ultimate arbitrators of how to interpret this phrase, permitted everyone involved in the adoption, including natural parents, to view the court adoption records.[9]

Although many states revised their statutes to require investigations of adoptions and probationary periods for children, few states in the years before and after the Great Depression included Minnesota's clause regarding confidentiality. Before 1939, only five states joined Minnesota in safeguarding the court records of adoption proceedings from public inspection; and only two others, Massachusetts and Texas, protected the social investigations of the court.[10]

The origins for the inclusion of confidentiality clauses in state leg-

islation had little to do with preventing natural parents, adult adoptees, and adoptive parents from viewing their adoption records; they
were never the initial target of the legislation. The wording of the
statutes, contemporary statements from state legislators, and existent
commentary by social workers indicate that the laws' original purpose was to keep the *public* from viewing the records, not those who
had a personal stake in the adoption proceeding. The Children's Code
of Wisconsin, for example, justified the confidentiality clause of its
1929 revision of the adoption statute on the basis that "curious and
unscrupulous persons formerly might secure and disclose much information with regard to illegitimacy and other circumstances connected with adoption matters." Likewise, California legislators successfully introduced a bill to place adoption records in a "secret file"
because of several cases "where unscrupulous persons have obtained
access to the adoption records and blackmailed the adopted parents
by threatening to tell the child it was adopted."[11]

By the end of 1941, an additional sixteen states enacted legislation
making adoption court records confidential, while two others provided for limited protection. Social workers' successful advocacy for
a 1941 amendment to the Social Security Act provided an important
impetus for the new laws. The amendment mandated that "a State
plan for aid to dependent children . . . must provide safeguards which
restrict the use or disclosure of information concerning applicants
and recipients to purposes directly connected with the administration
of aid to dependent children." It was aimed specifically at making
public welfare, not adoption, records confidential. Social workers
pressed for the amendment's passage for a number of reasons. They
hoped that by establishing the principle of confidentiality they would
foster a more constructive relationship with clients, protect the civil
liberties of indigent persons, and gain for their professional communications a degree of legal privilege commensurate with that
granted lawyers and doctors. Thus, although safeguarding adoption
records was not the original intent of social workers' lobbying efforts,
by the end of 1941, twenty-four states had enacted legislation safeguarding all or part of the court records of adoption from public
inspection.[12] Summing up the trend in 1941, a U.S. Children's Bureau
researcher noted: "with the growing appreciation of the need for protecting adoption records from curious eyes, an increasing number of

adoption laws have included provisions to keep the records confidential and available only to persons having legitimate reasons for knowing their contents."[13]

Keeping those directly connected to the adoption from viewing the record of the adoption court proceedings had never been the original impulse for closing them: rather, keeping a snooping and unscrupulous public from embarrassing or blackmailing adoptive parents (and, indirectly, social workers' professional interests) had been responsible for the confidentiality clauses. But eventually, in a few states during the 1930s, the wording of the adoption statute was altered to prevent natural parents from viewing the records of the adoption court proceeding. In 1939, Mary Ruth Colby, speaking for the Social Service Division of the U.S. Children's Bureau, generally approved this development, but at the same time she reaffirmed the standard social work policy of disclosure for those directly involved in the adoption process: "We have about concluded that the only persons who should have access to adoption records without specific approval of the court are the adoptive parents, the child when he becomes of age, and representatives of the State Department responsible for investigation of the adoption." Furthermore, the alterations of a few state adoption statutes' wording should not obscure the far more significant fact that before World War II twenty-three states failed to provide *any* statutory protection for the confidentiality of the records, thus making the court proceedings of adoptions legally open for viewing by any state resident. In 1942 Jean Paton, the founder of the adoption rights movement, simply looked up her adoption at the Probate Court in Detroit and discovered her natural mother's full name. "There was no rigmarole then," Paton observed. "You were allowed to see your own paper in a kindly procedure." In addition, in another twenty-odd states, where confidentiality clauses existed, the statutes' language explicitly exempted "parties in interest"— meaning everyone directly connected to the adoption, including natural parents—or "parties of record"—adoptive parents and adoptees—from the prohibition of inspecting adoption records. Court clerks understood the meaning of the law. When a social worker proposed that a Minnesota court clerk interpret the clause in a manner that ran counter to the common understanding that natural parents were to be considered a "party in interest," he resisted, saying,

"Who could be more of a party in interest than the own mother?" Moreover, even if the state legislators' intent had been to interpret the confidentiality clause strictly, the enforcement of these statutes was lax. Many courts failed to develop methods of filing adoption records to ensure their confidentiality. Adoption records were often filed with other court papers, allowing attorneys and other people easy access to them.[14]

Before World War II, legislators responsible for enacting the laws to protect the confidentiality of adoption court proceedings deliberately constructed them with two classes of people in mind: those with and those without legitimate reasons for viewing their contents. Except in a few states, all those connected directly with an adoption were considered to have legitimate reasons for viewing the court adoption records. Nowhere in the laws, legislative proceedings, or professional social work writings was the idea voiced that adoptees should be prevented from gaining access to the information in their own legal files.

Most important is what state adoption statutes did not do: they did not mention adoption agency case files, nor did they restrict access to them. A typical clause in a state statute governing confidentiality, for example, referred only to "the files and records of the court in adoption proceedings," which meant in practice, "all petitions, exhibits, reports, notes of testimony, [and] decrees." It was these court records that were sealed and could be opened only if a petitioner demonstrated to a judge "good cause." The legislators never defined "good cause." In the context of the times, however, reflected in the language of the statutes, it is likely that judges would have interpreted "good cause" broadly and would have routinely granted adoptees permission to view their adoption court records. It is significant that for forty years, roughly from 1930 to 1970, judges rarely had to rule on the issue of what circumstances constituted "good cause," because adult adoptees and natural parents who wished to receive information about their family of origin or child could easily gain access to that data from a variety of sources, including bureaus of vital statistics and adoption agencies. But the "good cause" requirement was a time bomb that would explode in the faces of adult adoptees and natural parents in the 1970s, as they were forced to file lawsuits to view their adoption records and as judges had to interpret the law in a completely different social and demographic milieu from its original setting.[15]

Those most intimately involved in adoption, however, would be disappointed in the meager amount of family information they might find in court records of adoption proceedings. Although the quantity of information in court proceedings varied from state to state, in all too many cases the discrepancy between the law and its execution was manifest. One must always be wary of believing that laws on the books reflect reality. Shifting the responsibility for investigating adoption petitions from judges to state departments of social welfare or private adoption agencies after 1917 reduced the problem of inadequate social investigations but did not eliminate it. A 1926 study of one Ohio county, for example, found that in 57 percent of the adoption cases examined no reports had been filed. Another study of adoptions in Cook County, Illinois, involving 496 petitions acted upon during the first half of 1936, revealed that even the minimal identifying information required on an adoption petition was ignored or subverted by the court. Where the petition asked for the name and address of the parents of the child, the address frequently given was simply "unknown" or "Chicago." When asked for reasons for the adoption the most frequent, formulaic response was that the adoptive parents love children and the natural parents were unable to maintain and educate the child. Children's Bureau official Mary Ruth Colby deplored the lack of uniformity and information that characterized adoption reports made to the court. After touring a number of states in 1938, she noted that "it seemed particularly unfortunate that the reports on approved cases were oftentimes too brief to give the court any interpretation" of the suitability of the adoption. Adult adoptees searching for family information would learn little from such adoption petitions and reports filed with the court. They would have better luck in discovering their family roots by looking up their birth certificates.[16]

The birth certificate is an important source for adoptees searching for family information. But for most of recorded history, there were no birth certificates as we commonly understand them; indeed, there was little use for them before the twentieth century. Births did not go unrecorded, however. In seventeenth-century Europe, the task of collecting vital statistics fell to church officials, who were supposed to record in parish registers the ecclesiastical ceremonies of baptisms, church weddings, and burials. Their negligence in fulfilling their duty has been the bane of contemporary historical demographers. In colonial America, Virginia emulated England's example and in 1619 required parish ministers to keep a register of all burials, christenings, and church weddings. The Puritans, however, believing in the separation of church and state, departed from English practice. In 1639, the Massachusetts General Court passed a law requiring town clerks, not church officials, to record the exact dates of the colony's births, deaths, and marriages. Other New England colonies soon followed suit, but the repeated issuance of regulations penalizing both town clerks and the next of kin for failing to register a birth or death suggests that in the New World as in the Old, compliance was haphazard. That inattention to collecting accurate statistics on births continued into the nineteenth century is well illustrated by the fact that the Secretary for the Commonwealth of Massachusetts reported in 1843 that Boston recorded only nineteen births among its population of 93,383.[17]

Ironically, the movement to collect accurate birth statistics in the United States evolved out of the need to record deaths more accurately. In 1850, an effort was made to bypass the states' haphazard collection of vital statistics by using the national census to derive more comprehensive mortality tables. This necessitated counting the number of children who were under one year of age. But this method failed to produced accurate results because, as Cressy L. Wilbur, chief statistician of the Bureau of the Census, observed, "vital events, such as births, marriages, and deaths, must be registered—that is *recorded*—immediately after occurrence" for maximum accuracy. Beginning with the Tenth Census in 1880, the federal government established registration areas for deaths in two states based on immediate registration. At the same time, interest in child mortality rates was intensifying, as American public health authorities and vital statisticians recognized that urban infant mortality was a public health problem demanding special measures. Without accurate birth registration statistics, however, it was impossible to calculate infant mortality rates. As late as 1896 the federal government continued to calculate infant mortality rates based on birth estimates, resulting in grossly inaccurate numbers.[18]

In 1902, the newly created Bureau of the Census, using an expanded registration area for deaths to include 10 states, the District of Columbia, and 153 cities outside the registration states, provided the first in-depth analysis of infant mortality rates. It confirmed less scientific estimates of an extraordinarily high rate of infant mortality in the United States. A decade later, however, the Children's Bureau noted that only 63 percent of the American population was covered by the Census Bureau's registration areas for deaths; without knowing the total number of infants born, an accurate infant death rate was impossible to calculate. Furthermore, as late as 1910, only 25 percent of the country was included in the registration area for births.[19]

Beginning in 1912, the Children's Bureau campaigned for mandatory 100 percent birth registration and the creation of birth certificates, both for reasons of statistical accuracy and as part of an effort to reduce infant mortality. Having a public record of a child's birth would alert public health authorities and private charitable agencies to families in need of medical care. In urging registration of births, Progressive reformers also acknowledged the passing of a simpler, rural way of life by stressing the increasing need for a birth certificate in modern, industrialized America. Proof of age, certified by a birth certificate, was becoming a necessity in legal cases involving inheritance, insurance, and titles; in the enforcement of laws relating to education and child labor; in voting, jury, and militia service; in admission to professions and many public offices; and in marriage. In 1911, New York City's birth registration department issued 101,197 certified copies of birth certificates for school or employment purposes. For Progressive reformers, the birth certificate had become an engine of child welfare reform: it would help save infants' lives, secure education for all children, and protect their working lives and legal rights.[20]

To achieve these ends, the Children's Bureau endorsed a Model Law of national birth registration prepared by the Bureau of the Census and various public organizations such as the American Public Health Association, the American Medical Association, the American Bar Association, and the American Statistical Association, which had been urging such a measure for many years. The first national standard birth certificate recommended by the Model Law for use by the states and employed by the Bureau of the Census from 1915 to 1917 was a six-by-seven-inch form that was to contain the following items: name and sex of child; place and date of birth; name, age, birthplace, residence, occupation, and race of both parents; whether the child was legitimate or illegitimate; the number of other children born to the mother and the number living; and the name of the attending midwife or physician. Progress in implementing the Model Law was slow but steady: by 1933, birth and death registration areas encompassed the entire nation.[21]

Birth registration for children born out of wedlock was a special problem for Progressive reformers. Studies revealed that infant mortality among children born out of wedlock was extraordinarily high. Child welfare reformers believed that one of the primary causes of the high mortality rate of illegitimate children was unwed mothers' efforts to avoid social stigma. Voicing a common sentiment among child welfare reformers, John A. Brown of the Indiana Board of State Charities observed that "the natural impulse of such mothers is to hide their shame from the world." Unwed mothers avoided prenatal care and brought their children into the world undernourished and sickly because of a desire to hide their pregnancy. Censure and disgrace also caused unwed mothers to evade registering their children's births, which in turn prevented competent medical authorities from providing postnatal care. The link between the social stigma of illegitimacy and infant mortality was even more direct: to escape the shame of pregnancy, unwed mothers relinquished or abandoned their babies to foundling hospitals where, research revealed, from 51 to over 90 percent died from malnutrition or infectious diseases within the first year. The moral outrage at the unnecessary death of babies is well captured in the despairing comment of one researcher that "it can matter but little to the individual infant whether it is murdered outright or is placed in a foundling hospital—death comes only a little sooner in one case than in the other."[22]

Between 1915 and 1922, when a Uniform Law of illegitimacy was agreed upon by the Commission on Uniform State Laws, Progressive reformers debated and proposed numerous measures to reduce infant mortality among children born out of wedlock and to shield mother and child from the taint of illegitimacy by reforming the law governing birth registration. To relieve the community of unnecessary expense, child welfare activists and legal reformers sought to establish the paternity of the child and hold the father equally responsible for support. Child welfare reformers such as those in the American Association for Study and Prevention of Infant Mortality recommended that the state should "assume a special responsibility" and both monitor and instruct unwed mothers in pre- and postnatal care, including six months to a year of compulsory breast feeding. They advocated legislation to require physicians and nurses to report unwed mothers to local boards of health and favored a law permitting expectant mothers to assume a fictitious name before giving birth "in order not to expose her identity."[23]

The proposal to alter birth registration forms and seal them from public view first emerged in the context of measures to reduce infant mortality by shielding the unwed mother from the stigma of illegitimacy. In a paper delivered to the American Public Health Association in 1916, Hastings H. Hart, a prominent Progressive reformer and director of the Department of Child-Helping of the Russell Sage Foundation, raised a series of questions: If unwed mothers were prone to evade birth registration, what could be done to encourage them to comply with registration? Should "certain facts be omitted" from the birth registration form, such as the mother's real name? Should the name of the father be sought and become part of the record? Should the birth records of a child born out of wedlock be "protected by the seal of secrecy?" Or should birth registrars make no distinction between illegitimate and legitimate births?

Hart's answers to these questions became the foundation for birth registration officials' practices. Hart contended that it was essential that the *same* facts governing illegitimate and legitimate births be recorded. He recognized that recording the real name and address of the unwed mother was a hardship, but explained it was necessary "both for the welfare of the child and for protection of the community." Hart believed that the way to protect the unwed mother was not by falsifying the birth record and "destroying all trace of the parentage of the child, but by imposing the seal of confidence upon the custodians of the record." The unwed mother's reputation would be shielded from public opprobrium by enacting a law making birth records confidential and by conferring the same type of privileged relationship on birth registration officers that attorneys enjoyed with their clients.[24]

Hart and other child welfare activists' chief objection to distor the birth record by lying about the unwed mother's identity was that it would prevent children from later discovering their past. "Everyone who is accustomed to deal with illegitimate children," Hart noted, "is familiar with the eager desire which such children have, when they grow up, to know the facts as to their parentage, and many cases are on record where these facts have become important for the welfare of the child." Other reformers agreed. At a regional conference, held under the auspices of the Children's Bureau in 1919, to consider the problem of illegitimacy, Louise de Koven Bowen, president of Chicago's Juvenile Protective Association, remarked on the "curious tendency on the part of young persons to dwell upon their parentage." She related instances "where persons have spent large sums of money and much time in the vain endeavor to learn of their parents." Bowen cited a case in which a girl had committed suicide because she remained in doubt about the identity of her parents. The solution Bowen proposed was "to place at the child's disposal information regarding his parentage, regardless as to whether it is good or bad."[25] Hart, Bowen, and other child welfare reformers would make birth records confidential, but permit children access to them when they became adults. It was never the original intention of Progressive reformers to prevent children born out of wedlock, or adopted children, from viewing their own birth records.

Progressive reformers balked at altering birth records to protect the reputation of unwed mothers. However, they had no qualms about modifying them to remove the stigma of illegitimacy from children. The rights of the child were paramount as the Reverend Robert F. Keegan, Secretary for Charities to the Archbishop of New York, reminded his colleagues at the 1919 New York Conference on Illegitimacy. At a similar conference in Chicago, Ernst Freund, the noted professor of jurisprudence at the University of Chicago, declared that "every effort should be made by the law to relieve the child of the stigma that attaches to illegitimate birth." It was unjust that children born out of wedlock were handicapped by the circumstances of their birth. Not even the sacredness of statistical accuracy should stand in the way. The interests of children, Freund declared, should take precedence over "the abstract desirability of complete data for registration or statistical purposes." Chief among child welfare reformers' goals was the encouragement of state legislation "guaranteeing to children born out of wedlock the rights naturally belonging to children born in wedlock." Child welfare reformers concentrated their effort on removing the stigma of illegitimacy from these children by reforming the centuries-old "bastardy" laws.[26]

Colonial Americans initially followed the English common law, which defined bastards—both children born out of wedlock and adulterine offspring—as *filius nullius,* the child and heir of no one. The common law denied these children family membership rights and the right to inherit property. Thus, the children had no legal relationship with their parents and the parents had no legal rights or duties to the child, though by custom mothers exercised custody. By the eve of the American Revolution, the colonists had modified the common law's emphasis on punishing sin and focused instead on limiting the public costs of illegitimacy. By the first half of the nineteenth century, Americans became increasingly reluctant to stigmatize children as illegitimate and "contrary to the common law, proceeded from the conviction that the parents' sins should not be visited on the innocent issue." The result of this humanitarian sentiment was a national movement to liberalize bastardy laws and protect the welfare of illegitimate children. Subsequent statutes and judicial decisions provided illegitimate children with their own set of guaranteed rights and responsibilities. The unwed mother became the child's legal guardian, responsible for support and education; the child gained the right to inherit from his or her mother. The revolution in American domestic law stalled by 1850, but in the early twentieth century Progressive reformers began questioning once again the morality and legality of stigmatizing children born out of wedlock.[27]

Inspired by Norway's 1915 Castberg law, which embodied the principle that legitimate and illegitimate children had equal rights before the law, a small number of Progressive child welfare reformers in the United States sought to "decriminalize" illegitimacy and eradicate the differences between legitimacy and illegitimacy. North Dakota took the lead in 1917 by enacting a law declaring that every child was "the legitimate child of its natural parents and as such is entitled to support and education, to the same extent as if it had been born in lawful wedlock. It shall inherit from its natural parents and from their kindred heir lineal and collateral." In the same year, Minnesota passed a law that sought to secure for children born out of wedlock "the nearest approximation to the care, support, and education that they would be entitled to receive if born of lawful marriage." Arizona in 1921 passed similar legislation. But such radical reform of the illegitimacy laws ultimately foundered in other states because of conservative fears that paternity laws favoring men and the right to inherit from the father would be undermined, and that society's respect for monogamy would be weakened.[28]

Although Progressive reformers failed to revise illegitimacy laws dealing with paternity and inheritance, they were able to institute two changes to the birth registration forms of children born out of wedlock, which ultimately had a profound effect on the ability of adult adoptees to uncover information about themselves and their families. Concerned that birth records never be used "in any way" to endanger "the child's future happiness," the first legal revision child welfare reformers unanimously championed was to make birth records confidential. Like the laws mandating the confidentiality of court records of adoption proceedings, the primary purpose of providing for the confidentiality of birth records was to prevent the *public*, not the child born out of wedlock, from viewing the record. Children's Bureau researchers Emma O. Lundberg and Katharine F. Lenroot wrote approvingly of laws permitting access to birth records by persons who could show a valid interest in the information. Conversely they noted that experience had shown that where laws were not in force they were needed to prevent "the use for malicious purposes of records relating to births out of wedlock."[29]

The second change that child welfare reformers advocated was the elimination of the word "illegitimate" from all public documents, including birth records. To reduce the stigma of illegitimacy, reformers fervently believed, it was "of vital importance to the individual child that transcripts of birth records used for school, employment, and other purposes should contain no information which will indicate birth status." A start had been made in achieving this reform when New York in 1916 and Minnesota in 1917 pioneered in legislating against the inclusion of the term on birth records. At the Chicago Conference on Illegitimacy in 1920, Professor Freund urged that "reference to illegitimate birth should disappear from certificates, from the records of adoption proceedings—from all records, in fact, other than those of proceedings in which the fact of illegitimate birth . . . are the direct issue." By the early 1930s, states had passed a variety of laws to eliminate any mention of illegitimacy on all birth records or to modify certified copies or transcripts of birth certificates to reflect only the name and age of the child.[30]

In Illinois, North Dakota, and the District of Columbia, legislators went so far as to enact a law mandating that all identifying information concerning the unwed mother and child be omitted from the birth certificate. Agnes K. Hanna, Director of the Social Science Division of the U.S. Children's Bureau, denounced this "mistaken idea of protecting the mother and her child" and lamented that "as a result, many children born in these states are truly no one's, and no means are available for satisfying their desire in later years to know something of their own people." Similarly, Helen C. Huffman, an analyst at the National Division of Vital Statistics of the U.S. Public Health Service, denounced the practice of a few state registrars who used ink eradicator on the original birth certificate to conceal the child's birth status, and "in doing so they destroyed for many children the only source of information concerning identity." Birth certificates had to be accurate and be preserved, as Maud Morlock, Consultant in Services for Unmarried Mothers at the Social Service Division of the U.S. Children's Bureau, observed, "for every person has a right to know who he is and who his people were."[31]

Accordingly, as late as 1949, child welfare reformers wanted accurate birth statistics both for their own sake and for the sake of the child. It was important and expected that blood ties be reunified. Child welfare specialists anticipated that children born out of wedlock would naturally inquire about their family origins when grown and believed that there was something inherently right about preserving an accurate account of the past. The idea that access to their own birth certificates should be denied to children born out of wedlock was never proposed and would have been totally foreign to child welfare reformers before the Second World War.

But making birth records confidential and eliminating the word "illegitimate" from birth certificates did not obviate the stigma of adoption from these documents. For adopted children, there still remained the problem of birth certificates. Although Minnesota's 1917 Children's Code was the first law to stipulate that when the court approved an adoption, the decree could reflect a change in the child's name, birth certificates still carried the names of the adopted child's natural parents.[32] How then could the public—in the guise of school officials and employers—be prevented from discovering the child's adoptive and possibly illegitimate status?

In 1929, Carl Heisterman, a Children's Bureau legal researcher, was one of the first persons to hit upon the idea that within a decade would revolutionize the issue of birth certificates and adopted children. Heisterman suggested that an adopted child should be issued a second birth certificate reflecting his or her new name. Such a procedure, Heisterman stated, had many advantages. It would "facilitate determining the child's identity in connection with its education and employment and it would eliminate embarrassing situations under many other contingencies where a birth certificate is required."[33]

It was left, however, to two enterprising registrars of vital statistics, not federal officials, social workers, or adoptive parents, to put forth a concrete plan of issuing new birth certificates to adopted children. The topic was first broached publicly at the 1930 annual meeting of the vital statistics section of the American Public Health Association. During the meeting, Sheldon L. Howard, Illinois State Registrar of Vital Statistics, and Henry B. Hemenway, Medical Assistant Registrar at the Vital Statistics Division of the Illinois Department of Public Health, presented a paper advocating several amendments to the Model Law. In support of their proposals, Howard and Hemenway articulated a need to increase the statistical accuracy in birth records, widen the professional influence of registrars, and promote the welfare of illegitimate and adopted children. No longer conceiving of themselves as mere statisticians, Howard and Hemenway described registrars of vital statistics as "guardians and trustees of the interests of the people," especially in relation to birth records. The two registrars characterized their professional brethren as "missionaries, who should bring about the rectification of the existing evils" in the birth registration of children born out of wedlock. The "evils" Howard and Hemenway were referring to were the disclosure of illegitimacy on birth certificates. They agonized over the psychological damage such information might inflict on the child. Reflecting the increasing incorporation of psychological concepts by social workers and mental health officials into professional discourse, Howard and Hemenway worried that the revelation of a person's illegitimate status to public officials was "likely to permanently impair otherwise peaceful mental conditions and happy lives." They called on registrars to reform the Model Law in order to "insure for these children immunity from unnecessary embarrassment, pain, or disgrace, from the time of the launching of their individual careers—their advent into school or employment."[34]

Howard and Hemenway were referring specifically to the section of the Model Law concerning adopted children, which stopped short of offering sufficient protection from the stigma of illegitimacy or adoption. As written, it merely stated that after the court had issued the adoption decree, it might also order that "the name of the child be changed according to the prayer of the petition." Howard and Hemenway proposed that the Model Law be amended so that when the name of the child was changed the clerk of the court would forward the adoption decree to the state registrar of vital statistics. Upon receiving the decree, the state registrar would "make a new record of the birth in the new name, and with the name or names of the adopting parent or parents." The registrar would then "cause to be sealed and filed the original certificate of birth with the decree of the court." The birth record was to be sealed from the prying eyes of the public, not from those directly involved in the adoption, who were to be permitted to view them. Howard and Hemenway specifically recommended that the "sealed package shall only be opened upon the demand of said child, or his natural or adopting parents, or by order of a court of record." Vital statisticians shared the basic assumptions of Progressive child welfare reformers that the birth record would be sealed to preserve family information *for* those connected to the adoption, not to prevent them from viewing such data.[35]

With adult adoptees increasingly requesting birth certificates in order to verify their age for employment, Social Security benefits, and draft registration, state legislatures responded positively to the registrars' recommendations. By 1941, thirty-five states had enacted legislation instructing the registrar of vital statistics to issue a new birth certificate using the new name of the child and those of the adopting parents in place of the original one. In addition, Illinois and North Carolina legislators attempted to mitigate the embarrassment of adoptive status by enacting laws permitting the alteration of original birth certificates. They authorized registrars to change birth certificates so they would not state that the child was adopted or born out of wedlock. Colorado legislators enacted a law authorizing registrars to issue a "certificate of identification," or birth registration card, in lieu of a birth certificate. The Public Health Service's National Division of Vital Statistics championed the birth registration card because it did not disclose any facts concerning birth out of wedlock, adoption, or irrelevant medical facts. By 1948, however, nearly every state embraced the registrars' original recommendation of issuing a new birth certificate upon receiving a court-ordered decree of adoption.[36]

There is no evidence that child welfare or public health officials ever intended that issuing new birth certificates to adopted children would prevent them from gaining access to their original one. On the contrary, they specifically recommended that the birth records of adopted children should "be seen by no one except the adopted person when of age or upon court order." This policy, which provided adoptees with the right to view their original birth certificate, was staunchly affirmed by Children's Bureau officials in 1949, who worked out guidelines for a nationwide directive on the confidential nature of birth records with members of the American Association of Registration Executives and the Council on Vital Records and Statistics. They declared that the right to inspect or secure a certified copy of the original birth certificate "should be restricted to the registrant, if of legal age; or upon court order." Access was widened slightly in the case of the new birth certificate. In addition to "the registrant," the Children's Bureau gave the adoptive parents and social and health agencies the right to inspect or secure a certified copy of the new birth certificate.[37]

As late as the immediate postwar era, child welfare and public health officials justified the confidentiality of adoptees' birth records for the sake of the child's identity and welfare. In describing the new birth registration system for adopted children, Helen C. Huffman, an analyst at the National Division of Vital Statistics of the U.S. Public Health Service, applauded keeping old and new birth certificates together because "too frequently in the past we have neglected the child's right to a document linking his original and adoptive identity." It was Huffman's opinion that the new system was designed to help, not hinder, adoptees who sought knowledge of their original families and was a boon to those who went "through life feeling a great need to know the names of their natural parents."[38]

Child welfare and public health officials also justified making birth records confidential to protect adopted children from the public, primarily school and government officials, employers, and advertisers. Increasingly detailed birth certificates contained medical and social information, such as the results of a mother's test for syphilis, identification of an infant's physical disabilities, and illegitimacy—"facts which were never intended for public view." Forcing citizens to reveal intimate details about themselves or their families could be damaging to a person's self-esteem and his or her chances of getting a job or entering military service. It was exactly these unintended and unwelcome consequences of revealing a birth certificate that the new birth registration system for adopted children was designed to foil.[39]

In addition to preserving information pertaining to an adopted person's identity and preventing the public from learning embarrassing information, Children's Bureau officials adduced two novel justifications for enveloping adoption birth records in secrecy. The first grew out of the familiar goal of protecting the adopted child from the threat of a new category of social stigma. After World War II, in the wake of the baby boom and prosperity, Americans moved to suburbia and created a family-centered culture that stressed early marriage, large families, and domesticity. Responding to the pronatalism of the age, Children's Bureau officials deemed it desirable to suppress the fact that the adopted child's parents were perhaps unknown. In this ideological context, true orphanhood—the loss of both parents—was a more terrifying burden to bear in a society where the highest ideal was membership in a biological family. Children's Bureau officials also began to justify keeping birth records secret by invoking the need to protect adoptive parents from the possible interference of natural parents. They recommended that both sets of parents remain unknown to each other. Such a concern reflected a long-standing fear of social workers, but 1949 was the first year that Children's Bureau or public health officials had justified confidentiality of birth certificates for reasons other than the welfare of the adopted child.[40]

Although legally permitted to view their original birth certificates, adult adoptees who did so might be terribly disappointed at the meager information contained there. Indeed, some found no record whatsoever. Before 1930, state birth registration was incomplete, especially in rural areas where informal methods of recording births, such as in the family Bible, baptismal or church records, midwife reports, and personal papers, predominated. Thus, it was quite possible that adoptees would find no birth certificate on file in the state vital records department. Those who were successful in locating their birth certificates might discover that the stigma of illegitimacy had made the documents an unreliable source of family information. State laws governing paternity in cases of illegitimacy shielded men from being identified. A survey of birth registration laws by the Children's Bureau in 1919 revealed that six states prohibited recording the father's name when children were born out of wedlock. In four other states, the name of the father could be entered only with his consent, which was often impossible to obtain. Two other states and the District of Columbia held that no record should be made of either the mother's or father's name. Adult adoptees might find their birth certificates unenlightening in other ways as well. The stigma of illegitimacy caused many women to give fictitious names and addresses. William H. Guilfoy, Registrar of Records of the New York City Department of Health, testified to a pattern of behavior that was common among unwed mothers: "Quite a number of persons in trouble come to the City of New York and enter our institutions and give false names, and . . . those names are on record as their true names." In some cases, adoptees might find they had no birth certificate because sympathetic doctors, in violation of the law, "forgot" to send in certificates of birth for children born out of wedlock. As J. Prentice Murphy, a prominent Progressive era social worker observed, "a very large number of children of such parents are never officially born."[41]

Still, what must be emphasized is that during the first half of the twentieth century, adult adoptees had legal access to their birth certificates, just as they had legal access to the court records of their adoption proceedings. If a child born in wedlock was subsequently adopted, as many children before World War II were, the birth certificate was a valuable document, containing crucial facts needed for tracing one's family roots. If born out of wedlock—and if the birth had been registered in the mother's real name and not eradicated by a "compassionate" registrar—the adopted child would at least have evidence of the date of birth, mother's name, and the name of the physician or midwife. Not much to go on, but at least some family information. Thus the irony of both court proceedings and birth certificates: although they were legally accessible, they often contained little personal or family information.

The situation was remarkably different for twentieth-century adoption agency case records, however. They were the richest source of personal and family information and contained an extensive array of legal, social, and medical information, which increased as the twentieth century wore on.

A modern case record usually "contains recorded notes, correspondence, copies of pertinent forms, and other written materials concerning delivery of service to a client" filed in a special folder.[42] But the first child-placing institutions barely kept any records. Adoption case records in particular and social work record-keeping in general evolved in response to the haphazard and negligent child-placing methods associated with the first generation of children's aid societies in antebellum America, especially Charles Loring Brace's Children's Aid Society (CAS or Aid Society) in New York.

As a matter of personal philosophy, Brace eschewed a written contract of apprenticeship between the CAS and the family, thus eliminating the one tangible record of the transaction. In other ways, too, the CAS's child-placing methods was not conducive to record-keeping. During the CAS's pioneer days, Brace and his agents sometimes failed to keep any records in their eagerness to find homes for the children. En route to their Western destinations with their charges, for example, CAS agents would occasionally permit passengers to take a child. Thus, as the ship *Isaac Newton* made its way up the Hudson to Albany en route to Michigan in 1856, CAS agent E. F. Smith noted that "a lady from Rochester had selected a little boy for her sister." Smith neglected to record the name of the child, the woman who took the youth, or her sister. Similarly, a year later, CAS agent C. C. Tracy related how the train had stopped at Prairie Ronde, a tiny village in Michigan, when a "traveller on his way to his home, chancing to stop at the tavern, with no previous thought of adopting a boy, was so much taken with a round-faced chubby little fellow of ten, an orphan, the 'Willi' of the company, that he secured him on the spot." In reporting these incidents, CAS agents found nothing amiss. What counted was the result, not the process: securing parents for a child. Fortunately, giving children away on the spur of the moment was relatively rare and its incidence decreased over time.[43]

Yet even the CAS standard placement procedure generated little permanent paperwork. It consisted of a CAS agent and the children, usually numbering between five and thirty, arriving in a town after advertising some six weeks in advance of their imminent appearance. Addressing a crowd in a train depot, town hall, or church, the agent announced the organization's mission and a few details of the children's lives. A town committee made up of its leading citizens quickly reviewed and evaluated the applications and references submitted by local families. Most times, the process took less than an afternoon. In conformity with the screening committee's judgment, the CAS agent then placed the children with the approved families. Thus, all the CAS's child-placement decisions were made by non-CAS personnel, and all the small amount of accompanying paperwork was kept by local citizens.[44]

Rather than indenture contracts and completed application forms kept on file, the CAS's record-keeping consisted of maintaining an office journal, agents' reports, and correspondence with the families and children. The office journal provided a short description of the child's stay with the Aid Society, but often lacked detailed information concerning his or her personal or family history. The following office journal entries illustrate the brevity and vagueness of CAS record-keeping:

> H. J. D——. Father died six years ago; mother drinks; don't know where she is. The last time I saw her was in the street, drunk; spoke to her, called her "mother," and she didn't know me. Has carried trunks at Erie depot, Jersey City; slept in saloon with the same; makes sometimes 6d and then 4s per day. Sent by Mr. V——, missionary. Sent to a farmer, S. B——, C—— County, New York.

> A—— M——, a stubborn girl, difficult to manage, brought here by her father with the request that we take her under our protection. She behaved with propriety while here, and was sent to an excellent home.

The agents' reports, while more specific about names and the location of the new family, contained little else. For example, the Reverend

Mr. Van Meter wrote to Brace on January 15, 1856, reporting how the latest batch of placements had turned out:

> Emile Caret is with Deacon Sperry, Tremont, Taswell Co., Ill. Mr. S. is a farmer, and a member of the Baptist Church. He is one of the best men in the land.

> Caroline Leek is with Mr. R. R. Payne, Galesbury, Ill., and they are pleased.

> Isabella and John Lee were placed at a good home eight miles from here [Peoria, Ill.], in the family of an Episcopal Minister.

For the first twenty-five years, Brace relied exclusively on correspondence to supervise the children placed out. To facilitate the oversight of his charges, Brace invited receiving families and the children to write him about home conditions. He even provided the younger children with prestamped envelopes as an incentive for them to write to the Aid Society immediately upon being placed. By 1871, an extensive correspondence existed. The CAS was receiving annually some two thousand letters from foster parents and children, while the Aid Society's assistant secretary, Josiah Macy, was mailing out some eight to ten thousand letters. Brace put the children's letters to good use. He reprinted the most positive ones in the CAS *Annual Reports*, trumpeting the success of its system of child-placing. Despite the copious correspondence, however, there were tremendous gaps in the information recorded. A 1922 study of the Aid Society's first two decades revealed the inadequacy of relying on correspondence to supervise the children. It showed that in nearly 40 percent of its placements in 1865 the CAS had recorded literally no information concerning the children after placement; a decade later, the figure had improved slightly, to 36 percent.[45]

During the last quarter of the nineteenth century, a new generation of child welfare reformers condemned the CAS's failure to keep records. This led to the development of extensive written adoption case records, which came to be considered essential for ensuring sound child placement. These Progressive child welfare reformers built upon and reinforced the practice of late-nineteenth-century charity organization societies, which began keeping detailed records of their investigations of the poor to prevent fraud and to direct them to the proper agencies for relief and service. Typical of the advice offered was a suggestion from F. M. Gregg, Illinois Children's Home and Aid Society assistant general superintendent, to his colleagues at the 1892 National Conference on Charities and Correction. He suggested that they keep a "Children's Register." In it, Gregg instructed, child-savers were to record the child's "name, date and place of birth, age, names of parents, when adopted, time spent in the Temporary Home, when and where placed in a permanent home, color and nationality." Another book, which Gregg called a "Family Register," would keep track of all the families applying for children. A third book, a "Register of Final Settlement," would keep "all of the names of all children adopted, indentured, or placed by special contract." The importance of maintaining written records was underscored in 1909 when, at the first White House Conference on the Care of Dependent Children, child welfare reformers passed a resolution urging that "every child caring agency should secure information concerning the character and circumstances of the parents and near relatives of each child in whose behalf application is made, through personal investigation of its own representative" and make a permanent record of it. By 1918, social work training manuals, which Children's Bureau officials strongly endorsed, recommended that when a child was admitted to an agency "all possible facts, reports, letters, photographs and legal documents bearing upon the case should be collected, arranged systematically, and filed for future reference."[46]

Maintaining family histories, or "case records," as they were beginning to be called, became a central task of social workers during the first quarter of the twentieth century. This development was central to the rise of professional social work. In 1917, Mary E. Richmond, the founder of modern social work and director of the Russell Sage Foundation's Charity Organization Department, wrote *Social Diagnosis*, the influential textbook that established the process and rationale of differential casework, a social work skill and technique that promised to enhance social workers' professional status. By "differential casework" Richmond meant that the social worker should think in terms of individual cases and not resort to universal laws of human conduct, which invariably failed to account for the individual's social situation. Social workers were to shun statistical averages, moralistic pronouncements, and mechanical interviewing: each client was different, each problem had multiple and complex causes, and social workers had to ground their policies in empirical observation.[47]

The key to differential casework was social diagnosis, which Richmond defined as "the attempt to make as exact a definition as possible of the situation and personality of a human being in some social need ... in relation to the other human beings upon whom he in any way depends or who depend upon him, and in relation to the social institutions of his community." Social diagnosis involved a threefold process: investigation or gathering of evidence; the critical examination of facts; and, finally, the interpretation and definition of the social problem. Crucial to the new profession of social work was the collection of facts and their correct interpretation. Richmond urged social workers to redouble their efforts and collect "social evidence," which she defined as "any and all facts as to personal or family history which, taken together, indicate the nature of a given client's difficulties and the means to their solution."[48]

Richmond was speaking to the converted. All over the nation, social workers were inventing forms and assiduously filling in the blanks. By the time the first state (Minnesota, as part of its 1917 Children's Code) mandated that child-placing institutions keep a record of their activities, there had already existed for two years a social work manual, *Elements of Record Keeping for Child Helping Organizations,* published by the Russell Sage Foundation's Department of Child-Helping, devoted to instructing and standardizing child-placing record-keeping. *Elements* discussed the purposes and gave multiple examples of case record forms drawn from a variety of child-placing institutions, revealing the wide range of information social workers gathered on prospective adopted children and their families. Within five years of its publication, Children's Bureau officials were recommending the book to social workers, noting that it "contained a great deal of very valuable information in regard to ... what forms are the best adapted to the work of child-caring agencies." Thus it is not surprising that compared to court proceedings and birth certificates, an adopted person would find the most complete identifying and nonidentifying family information in the case records of child-placing institutions.[49]

An examination of the adoption case records of the Children's Home Society of Washington (CHSW), which conform for the most part to those displayed in the Russell Sage manual, illustrates this point. In the following discussion of adoption case records I use the CHSW's records where applicable, but I also include other types of documents not necessarily found in CHSW case records.

The number of documents and the amount of family information in the CHSW adoption case records increased dramatically during the first quarter of the twentieth century. In the first decade of its existence, roughly before 1907, CHSW case record information was spare by modern standards, numbering three or four documents; in addition there might be some brief, miscellaneous correspondence, usually between the CHSW's State Superintendent and a natural parent. But in the two decades after 1907, CHSW forms grew more numerous, more complex, and by any standard contained an enormous amount of family information. While the typical CHSW case record in the 1920s and 1930s contained five or six different forms, other child-placing institutions might have used more.

Typically, the first document most likely to be found in any adoption case record would be a 3½-by-6-inch preprinted face sheet containing blanks for the child's name and other identifying data. The purpose of the face sheet was to provide social workers with a convenient form that contained "certain objective social facts of a more or less permanent character."[50]

After 1907, the CHSW's face sheet was usually followed by the family history card. In addition to the child's name, sex, date of birth, physical and mental condition, birth status (legitimate or illegitimate), and whether relinquished by a court or parents, CHSW adoption workers were required to fill in the father's and mother's name, age, occupation, nationality, religion, medical history, and cause of death, if deceased. There was also space for the case worker to fill in the names and addresses of siblings and other relatives.[51]

Immediately following the family history card could be found a third document, the story sheet. Whereas the first two documents provided the essential facts concerning the child and family, the story sheet recorded all the details of the client's personal visits, interviews, and telephone calls; the results of the agency's investigations; and the social worker's personal observations—the analysis that gave the facts significance. The purpose of the story sheet was to facilitate the treatment of the client, sharpen the critical skills of the caseworker, and ultimately contribute to the general betterment of society. For social workers, it "was the most important part of the record." Until the 1940s, social workers followed Mary Richmond's recommendation to use a method of recording that became known as process recording, "a chronological account both of the essential processing used and of the observations upon which these processes [are] based." After World War II, social workers abandoned this method of recording in favor of one that was less time consuming and costly. But while process recording was in use, social workers filled case records with every conceivable detail, resulting in story sheets averaging ten to fifteen single-spaced typed pages in length. Often these case records provided a detailed history of an adopted person's entire life.[52]

The fourth document most likely to be found in a CHSW adoption case record would be either a legal document or a CHSW preprinted form signed by the natural parent(s) giving the Society permanent custody of the child with the intent of adoption. In 1899, CHSW's Superintendent Harrison D. Brown lobbied and helped draft legislation authorizing the Washington State Superior Court to remove children from "improper and vicious surroundings" and commit them to the custody of a child-placing institution. After 1905, Washington State's Juvenile Court shared this function with the Superior Court. By interposing the state's judicial authority between the natural parents and the adoption agency, child-placing officials protected themselves from accusations that they were "taking" children from their natural parents. The importance of documenting the circumstances surrounding the child's separation lay in establishing that the child had been relinquished freely with the parents' consent or, alternatively, that state authorities had investigated the child's home circumstances and sanctioned the separation. During the first decade of the CHSW's existence, both the CHSW relinquishment form and the legal document transferring permanent custody of the child to the CHSW contained only the natural parents' and child's name and sex. After 1907, the CHSW relinquishment form expanded to include the natural parents' residence, nationality, and occupation and the child's birth date.[53]

The CHSW's relinquishment form also contained a section that shrouded the adoption in secrecy by prohibiting natural parents from searching for their children. Although other states during the early decades of the twentieth century prohibited divulging the identity of adoptive parents, there were many qualifications and exceptions to this policy. In 1900, for example, the superintendent of an Indiana orphan asylum who explicitly warned against revealing the identity of adoptive parents to natural parents also stated, "Yet there should be no ironclad rule. Circumstances should determine, in all cases of this character, whether or not the parents can be safely informed of the location of their children." He admitted that despite the "distinct understanding" that the natural parents are to have no further contact, "I frequently inform them where their children are placed, after they are well settled, provided I have good reason to believe that there will be no interference and the guardians themselves consent." Similarly, the CHSW's relinquishment form was qualified by the clause that parents could not seek the whereabouts of the child until he or she *"shall arrive at full age."* It was never the intention of CHSW officials to prevent the natural parents, if they so desired, from eventually reuniting with their grown children.[54]

In addition to these documents—face sheet, family history card, story sheet, and a form giving the CHSW permanent custody—a fifth document was commonly found in CHSW adoption case records: the adoptive parents' application form. On it, prospective adoptive parents provided the Society with their name, address, occupation, name of church, number of children, and whether or not they owned their own home. Applicants were asked whether they desired a boy or girl, what age, whether they were prepared to receive the child "at any time" by railroad or boat, and were asked the name of the person who would meet the child. At the bottom of the application, the family was asked how far it lived from a school and church. Other child-placing institutions, such as the Henry Watson Children's Aid Society and the Maryland Children's Aid Society, used more elaborate application forms, including a request for character references. Whether or not the child-placing institution approved the application, it sent the applicants a letter informing them of the decision.[55]

The visitor's report, another document commonly found in case records, indicates that in response to the charges that foster families mistreated and overworked CAS children, many second-generation child-placing institutions began to supervise children *after* they were placed with families, reporting their findings on preprinted forms. These "visitors" looked into the conditions of the child and the home and recommended whether or not the child should remain with the family. In 1915, the Boston Children's Aid Society, for example, reported that visitors saw the children an average of four to five times a year. The visitor's report would be of special interest to adult adopted persons because it often provided them with information, such as their health status, playing activities, and living conditions, from when they were very young and that they might have forgotten. In addition, if the visitor's report had been completed before an adoptive family moved away, it would provide adopted persons with details about the earlier geographical location of their homes and the type of dwelling they once occupied.[56]

Adoption case records not only reflected the new standards of child placement and social work professionalism; they also contained documents generated as a consequence of Progressive child welfare reformers' intense concern with preventing illness in children. Childsavers established milk stations for infants; neighborhood settlement houses ran new programs for children's health; local health clinics sprang up; schools began immunization programs; and the Children's Bureau became a mighty engine for educating the public on medical matters and promoting children's health. The attention to children's medical care by child-savers, physicians, public officials, and scientific experts spilled over into child-placing administration. By 1912, children admitted to child-placing institutions were routinely given physical examinations. The CHSW, for example, employed an examining physician and a head nurse, and engaged the services of a dozen other doctors. During one seven-month period, December 1912 to June 1913, one of the CHSW's physicians made 39 visits, examined 19 children for admission, and performed 20 adenoidectomies, 20 tonsillectomies, and 20 circumcisions.[57]

Another case record document was generated by social workers' response to the eugenics movement, which stigmatized adopted children born out of wedlock. Eugenicists claimed that "illegitimate" children were poor candidates for adoption because they carried the hereditary disease of feeblemindedness acquired from their unwed mothers. Social workers defended children born out of wedlock by minimizing the importance of heredity. Instead, they stressed the power of a loving home environment and employed psychometric tests to assure prospective adoptive parents that the children they received were mentally sound. As early as 1910, Edwin D. Solenberger, General Secretary of the Children's Aid Society of Pennsylvania, was urging his colleagues at the National Conference of Charities and Correction to subject "deficient, backward or delinquent" children to mental examinations "conducted by doctors and trained psychologists." In 1915, Boston Children's Aid Society officials reported that they administered "a mental examination where there is any indication of defect." Four years later, CHSW officials arranged with Dr. Stevenson Smith, Director of the Psychological Clinic of the Bailey Gatzert Foundation at the University of Washington, "to have all the children tested according to the latest scientific methods in order to obtain an accurate knowledge of their mental fitness for family life." By the late 1940s, fifteen states recognized the importance of psychological examinations for children prior to adoptive placement, while popular magazines assured prospective parents that "the 'danger' of adoption has been largely obviated by scientific advance."[58]

Although to our modern sensibility, record-keeping is a familiar and routine feature of modern American society, such was not the case in the early twentieth century. Whether or not to maintain records on dependent children entrusted to their care became a disputed issue between professional and amateur adoption workers. Private adoption agencies staffed by nonprofessional volunteers, such as Chicago's Cradle Society, scorned professional social workers' preoccupation with record-keeping. Horace Bridges, a member of the Board of Directors of the Cradle Society, gave a number of reasons why child-placing institutions should not keep records. First, he believed that because of the Cradle's limited resources, keeping records was a waste of time, money, and personnel. Second, Bridges doubted the value of keeping records. He emphasized the lack of any meaningful relationship between recording a child's family history and successfully placing him or her in a family, rhetorically asserting: "No amount of investigation of Thomas Lincoln and Nancy Hanks would have enabled any committee of social workers, psychologists, or sociologists to foresee the towering genius and nation-moulding achievements of Abraham Lincoln." Third, he contended that keeping records could "do no possible good either to mother or child." Given

The Cradle's belief that the unwed mother and child should be separated and that it was impossible to ascertain the paternity of the child, the only function of a child-placing institution was to place the child in a family. Record-keeping was simply superfluous and too costly.[59]

Career social workers could not have disagreed more, and as professionalism came to dominate the practice of social work their ideas prevailed. For them, case records were at the center of their professional identity. It was, in fact, their skill at interpreting the case record that permitted them to determine their clients' needs. Case records functioned as the data base from which social workers could provide accurate, effective treatment of clients, train new social workers, study social problems as a basis of social reform, and educate the public as to the value and purpose of social work.[60]

Most important for understanding the history of secrecy and disclosure in adoption, until the end of World War II, professional social workers shared the national culture's preference for biological kinship. Wanting to preserve the child's blood ties, they compiled detailed family histories because they believed that adopted children were entitled to that information when they grew up. Child-placing agencies recognized that in order to "secure the full protection to the child of his God-given rights we should take every reasonable step to conserve somewhere the information which may be of vital importance to him." Social workers asserted that it was wrong to deprive the child of this information, and they repeatedly deplored any failure to keep accurate records on dependent children. In 1923, the State Charities Aid Association of New York (SCAA), an influential adoption agency in the field of home-finding services, called attention to "a tragic instance" of a thirty-year-old man unable to obtain his natural mother's or father's name or his own birth date because the foundling asylum had failed to record them at the time of his placement. Similarly, social workers at the Illinois Children's Home and Aid Society denounced "the spectacle of men and women all over the country who seek in vain for information concerning the members of their family who were separated from them in childhood." In order to solve the problem, officials of the Pennsylvania Bureau of Children proclaimed, "it is better to write a thousand records that are not used than to fail to be able to supply a vital bit of family history when it is needed."[61]

The Great Depression caused dependent children to enter institutions in record numbers and deepened social workers' commitment to preserving biological kinship relationships through the mechanism of keeping family records. Grace Abbott, chief of the U.S. Children's Bureau, impressed upon social workers that the child-placing agency was sometimes the only link between a child and his or her family of origin. When agencies failed to record information, various members of a family could be lost to one another for all time. When that happened, the individual—usually the adopted child—often felt like a social outcast and "was invariably tormented by a longing to know about his people." Abbott agreed with the officials of other child-placing agencies and with professional adoption workers that children had legal and social rights that had to be protected, including, when grown up, "the right to know about himself."[62]

By the beginning of World War II, collecting family information for future use by adoption agency clients had become a social work ideal. Summing up a decade of social work experience in adoption, Ora Pendleton, executive secretary of the Children's Bureau of Philadelphia and vice-chairman of the Philadelphia Chapter of the American Association of Social Workers, underscored the agency's responsibility to preserve family information in case records. She noted that in addition to legal purposes, "that information may be desired at some future time either by the adopting parents or by the child who has been adopted." These people, Pendleton declared, "should have access to whatever part of it they need." Undoubtedly, there would be many adoptees who would never want this information. Nevertheless, Pendleton affirmed, "they are entitled to it if they do want it. The very knowledge that it can be made available to them is in itself a reassurance to them." In conformity with the increasingly psychiatric orientation of social casework and anticipating the adoption rights movement's emphasis on the therapeutic value of family knowledge, Pendleton observed, "many adopted children could perhaps have made a better adult adjustment if this need for knowledge about themselves and their own parents had not been frustrated." As late as 1946, at the National Conference of Social Work, Grace Louise Hubbard, a supervisor at the SCAA Child Placing and Adoption Committee, stressed the importance of preserving the "child's true heritage through complete records." She reminded her social work colleagues that "the identity of a child is his sacred right, and he should not be deprived of it either through indifference or through lack of realization of his concern with it."[63]

Underlying professional social workers' insistence on maintaining full and accurate case records for the adopted child was an ideological allegiance to a biological model of the family that glorified parenthood and the importance of maintaining "natural" families and counseled unmarried mothers to keep their "illegitimate" children. The leading professional adoption caseworker, Sophie van Senden Theis of the New York State Charities Aid Association, stressed that "family ties are strong and should be broken only after a thorough consideration of the psychological, social, and economic factors involved —and then not too easily." These injunctions to preserve "natural" families also found expression in the CWLA's 1932 "Standards for Institutions Caring for Dependent Children," which stated that "contacts with members of the child's own [i.e., natural] family should be maintained by correspondence and visits, safeguarded when necessary to protect the child and the foster [adoptive] family, and the tie between child and his own family should be fostered and encouraged." Thus, behind the impulse to fill case records with a child's family history was the hope of social workers everywhere that eventually all the members of the child's original family would be reunited. When that happy day occurred, social workers told each other, adoption agencies would be ready.[64]

For nearly half a century, social workers assumed that natural parents, adoptees, and adoptive parents would return to agencies to request family information, whether out of natural curiosity, as a matter of right, or from psychological need. In anticipation of the knock on the door, social work leaders exhorted their colleagues to collect every piece of information about adopted children and their original families that they could and enter it in the adoption case record. All evidence points to social workers' intention to convey this information to their clients. But were adoption experts correct in their expectations, and did they in fact release family information to clients? We need to look at what social workers did in actual practice and whether they lived up to the professional standard they created to disclose family information to all of the groups involved in the adoption process.

CHAPTER THREE . . . .

When Adoption Was No Secret

As Children's Bureau officials and professional social workers had predicted, adopted children, when grown, often returned to adoption agencies searching for their natural parents or wanting to know something about their family history. What adoption experts had not counted on, or at least failed to discuss publicly, was the possibility that natural parents and their relatives, siblings of the adopted child, and adoptive parents might also return to the adoption agency requesting information about family members.

The adoption case records of the Children's Home Society of Washington (CHSW) shed much light on this phenomenon. These records provide a portrait of the individuals who returned to the Society, their motivation, and the Society's policy and practice toward revealing the contents of adoption case records to former clients. Between 1895 and 1988, the most frequent seekers of information were adoptees. They constituted 47 percent of the sample of those who returned, followed by birth mothers (18 percent), adoptive parents (15.5 percent), siblings of adoptees (11.5 percent), birth fathers (4.0 percent), and blood relatives of the adopted child, such as grandparents or aunts and uncles (4.0 percent).[1]

Clients returned to the Society for different purposes. Adult adoptees returned for three main reasons: to obtain copies of their birth certificates, to receive family background and medical information, and to contact members of their natural family. One-fifth of the adult adoptees who contacted the Society did so to obtain copies of their birth certificates. Most of this group had never received one. This is not surprising, for as noted in the last chapter, birth certificates were not in wide use during the first decades of the twentieth century. Even if the state or county had issued one, it is unlikely that the natural parents would have turned it over to the CHSW. The onset of World War II, however, forced adult adoptees to secure birth certificates. In wartime, the foreign born were automatically considered a security risk. America's national defense plants, such as Boeing Aircraft and Kaiser Aluminum, demanded as a condition of employment that workers produce a birth certificate to prove their citizenship. In addition, eighteen-year-old adoptees had to register for the draft or prove their age when they enlisted in the military. Within a five-year period, 1940 to 1945, the requirements of employment or service in the armed forces caused numerous adult adoptees to contact the Society for copies of their birth certificates. Indeed, in that five-year period the CHSW was visited by nearly half (43 percent) of *all* adult adoptees who sought their birth certificates from the years 1895 to 1988. After World War II, most adoptees returning to the Society for birth certificates did so to establish their eligibility for Social Security or Medicare benefits. This occurred especially in the early 1960s, as those most likely not to have a birth certificate approached retirement age.[2]

Adult adoptees returned to the CHSW most often for nonidentifying information, such as background or medical history about themselves or their natural parents, or for identifying information, such as names and addresses of their natural parents in order to reunite with them. Slightly more than half of the adult adoptees returning to the Society requested nonidentifying family information. The median age of those requesting background or medical information was twenty-three, and almost two-thirds were women.[3] Typically, adoptees wanted to know whether an adoption had ever been formally legalized, how to acquire a copy of the adoption papers, or what their racial background or nationality was. In July 1952, Jack C. called at the Society wanting to know his nationality "because he fears he is part Negro (curly hair—people ask him)." Many adoptees voiced curiosity about their "early history" and wanted to know the circumstances leading up to their placement in the CHSW. In March 1934, for example, Josephine L. returned to the CHSW wanting to know if it was true, as a relative had informed her, that she was "a child of a bad woman." Others, usually on the threshold of marriage or parenthood and worried about possible genetic problems, inquired about their natural family's medical history. Typical was Mary T., age twenty-two, who wrote the Society asking for "a health record of childhood diseases contracted there." Similarly George C., twenty-six, sent the Society a letter in 1939 wanting to "know something about his own parents" because he was "contemplating marriage and wanted to be sure that there was no history of mental instability or syphilis that would prevent him from marrying."[4]

But a large percentage, some one-third of adult adoptees requesting family information and 27 percent of all adult adoptees who returned to the CHSW, asked for identifying information about their natural parents, usually their mothers or brothers and sisters.[5] Often these adult adoptees were like Sarah N., who returned to the Society in June 1928 with her husband, "very anxious to locate or get some trace of my family." Individuals like Sarah usually asked specifically for their mother's maiden name or the names and location of siblings. Another adoptee, Barbara M., requested in 1912 her early history in order to "locate her mother's grave and if possible any relatives she may have."[6]

Eight percent of adult adoptees who requested information expressed an interest in finding brothers or sisters. Of those adult adoptees searching for their siblings, the median age was twenty-two, with women making up 54 percent. The large number of adult adoptees searching for their brothers or sisters reflected the CHSW's pre–World War II policy of routinely splitting up siblings, even twins, and placing them in different homes. When Ada M.'s husband deserted the family, she placed her five children with the Society in July 1911. Over the next five years, the Society placed the children with families in four towns in eastern Washington and one in Oregon. Social work principles called for keeping siblings together "wherever possible," but in practice this was very difficult. Before World War II, a high proportion of adopted children were considered "older children," from four to six years old. In the 1920s, the average age of the children entering the Illinois Children's Home and Aid Society, for example, was six years old. Similarly, 68 percent of the 1,050 children admitted to the Children's Home Society of Florida were over five years of age. The median age of children placed in the CHSW before World War II was four and a half years. Few adoptive parents wanted "older" children, and fewer still wanted to adopt two of them. Occasionally, the CHSW's policy of separating siblings came to the attention of the press. In September 1957, Washington newspapers reported the meeting of twenty-one-year-old twins who had been separated by the Society at the age of eleven months. The ensuing negative publicity caused Elizabeth Bannister, head of the CHSW's adoption department, to circulate a memorandum detailing the circumstances surrounding the case. She pointed out that the Society had informed both sets of adoptive parents that the child was a twin "and in each case the family was not able financially, or for other reasons, to ask for both children," adding ruefully, "the Society did not have psychological consultation 20 years ago."[7]

After adult adoptees, women who had given up their children for adoption returned most frequently to the CHSW. These mothers' median age when relinquishing their child was twenty years, and they usually returned to the CHSW within three years of placing the child for adoption. Before the end of World War II, a dramatically high percentage of postadoption contact (PAC) mothers had been married at the time of the child's conception. Sixty-five percent of children relinquished by PAC mothers before 1946 were born in wedlock compared to virtually none afterwards. Most of these pre-1946 PAC mothers placed their children for adoption as a result of poverty caused by divorce or desertion. The advanced age of the children they relinquished—their median age was four-and-a-half years—permitted strong bonds to develop between mothers and children. Not surprisingly, all the mothers who contacted the Society wanted to know about their child's welfare: they asked about the baby's health or the nature of the adoptive parents or requested the child's photograph. Before 1946, an impressive 43 percent of the mothers who returned to the CHSW, as compared to 9.5 percent thereafter, either wanted their children returned or begged to know their whereabouts. Typical was Mary N., who had placed her child with the Society in 1918 and four years later could not "seem to forget my little girl and just wisht I had never given her up. I long for her. And wonder if she is well and happy."[8]

In most cases the contact between adoptive parents and the Society was unexpected, primarily because the Society rarely prepared or encouraged adoptive parents to seek postadoption contact. Nor did many adoptive parents, who preferred to remain anonymous and not be reminded of or forced to reveal the child's adoption, welcome the idea of returning to the agency. Without pressure from outside the home (employers, school authorities, haphazard birth registration) or from within (the child's illness, delinquency, or desire for information about the child's natural family), adoptive parents would never have returned to the Society. Given the social and psychological pressures discouraging contact, it is not surprising that only 15 percent of all adoptive parents contacted the Society.[9]

The adoptive parents who did return were looking for counsel, advice, and help. They asked Society officials for advice on how to tell their child about the adoption, how to obtain lost adoption papers, and how to find employment for the child. They asked caseworkers to intervene with school authorities, employers, and even with prospective spouses. In one remarkable case an adoptive mother who objected to her son Jack's impending marriage to a woman named Martha asked a CHSW caseworker to break up the couple. Though the caseworker refused, she counseled the boy about "the seriousness of marriage, but hesitated to mention Martha, fearing for the confidence Jack had in the Organization if he felt that they were making inquiries into his personal life." Nevertheless, on her own initiative she elicited damaging family information about Martha from local school authorities and turned it over to Jack's mother. Despite the Society caseworker's interference, however, Jack and Martha eventually married.[10]

Adoptive parents also asked Society officials to act as intermediaries between their adopted children and their natural parents. Prompted by their adopted daughter, one couple asked the Society to arrange a meeting with her natural mother. On another occasion, anxious adoptive parents asked the Society to find their child's sibling. Laura "has always mourned for her sister," the parents revealed, and they hoped that "she might find her and visit her." Such requests were not common. More typically, adoptive parents asked for help when their child manifested behavior problems, especially those due to difficulty in school, promiscuity, or in the words of one adoptive couple, "reverting to type." Similarly, it was not unusual for adoptive parents, fearing their children were headed for reform school or prison, to ask CHSW caseworkers to talk to them.[11]

In addition to requesting help, 42 percent of returning adoptive parents did so to obtain a birth certificate for their adopted children, which they usually never received from the Society. They typically wrote or visited the Society as the child approached young adulthood and embarked on a career or marriage. Many parents were in a hurry, and some were panic-stricken; having kept the child's adoption a secret, they hoped to obtain a birth certificate that would not reveal the facts about the child's birth.[12]

Another 42 percent of returning adoptive parents contacted the Society to receive their children's medical history and information about the social background of the natural parents. They were particularly interested in records of infant inoculation, childhood eye or stomach problems, and such inheritable conditions as diabetes or heart trouble. Because in the early decades of the century most people believed that mental illness such as "feeblemindedness" was inherited, adoptive parents also queried the Society about this issue. When Mrs. X.'s adopted daughter, Janice, was committed to a mental institution, for example, she wrote the CHSW requesting "all the information possible in regard to the girl's ancestry, especially her parents." Similarly, Mr. and Mrs. Y. asked the Society, after their son was sent to a special school, "if the mental deficiency was inherited" from their son's family. When requesting the child's social history, adoptive parents frequently asked for all the information in the file concerning the natural parents. They also made requests for specifics of the adopted child's past, including his or her nationality and religion, and the whereabouts of separated siblings.[13]

When former clients returned to the CHSW for family information or assistance in locating family members, Society officials initiated sincere efforts to accommodate their requests. Nevertheless, the Society's response varied enormously, depending on which clients were involved, what kind of information they desired, and when they made their inquiry. With some exceptions, as late as the mid-1950s Society officials and caseworkers exercised discretion while adhering to the social work ideal of disclosure.

That policy can even be seen in the way Society authorities treated natural parents who wanted their adopted children returned or requested information about the child they had relinquished. Even though the CHSW's relinquishment form explicitly prohibited natural parents from ever making contact with the children they placed for adoption, circumstances sometimes called for exceptions to be made. On rare occasions, officials informed natural parents of the adoptive parents' identity. In August 1910, the Society's Director, the Reverend Luther J. Covington, gave John M. the address of and a letter of introduction to the adoptive parents of John's daughter Mary, who had been placed with them a month earlier. Covington explained to the adoptive parents that because John had demonstrated his ability to provide for the child, he thought it best that Mary be returned to her original parents. Covington regretted that the adoptive parents had become attached to Mary but urged them to "come in at your convenience and I will see what we can do about giving you another girl." Returning children to their original parents and revealing the identities of adoptive parents to them was exceptional, however, and it is significant that in those few cases the Society confided in natural *fathers*. Even though a few fathers hired attorneys to demand their rights and some mothers tearfully begged for the return of their children, Society officials refused to bow to legal threats or emotion. In general, CHSW officials refused to divulge the child's whereabouts to natural parents.[14]

However, Society officials actively cooperated with natural parents' requests for facts about their child's welfare. They invariably provided them with optimistic reports of the adopted child's development and progress in school, but suggested it would be unfair for the natural parents to interfere with adoptive parents, who had invested so much time and energy in raising the child. Nor were these status reports simply routine and outdated summaries of the case record. At times, Society caseworkers visited the adoptive parents' home, checked on the child's welfare, and even requested the child's photograph for the natural mother.[15]

The most notable aspect of the Society's policy toward natural parents before World War II is the openness with which it responded when they requested the whereabouts of their *grown* children. When dealing with a request about adoptees, Society officials seemed to believe that biological kinship was of supreme importance and consequently acted as though they had a responsibility to reunite natural parents with their grown children. Sometimes, Society caseworkers facilitated meetings by searching for the adult children of natural parents. For example, the Society received a letter in February 1929 from a California county department of social welfare requesting the whereabouts of a boy the Society had placed for adoption. Mrs. Mary O., the boy's natural mother, had placed the child with the Society in 1897 when he was four years old. Now, thirty-two years later, Mary contacted her local welfare agency because "her mind turn[ed] constantly to the thought of this son," and she wondered where he was. A Society caseworker, Miss T., initiated a search for the man. Miss T. first called the hotel where he had been last reported staying but was informed that he was no longer registered there. Next, she called the local credit association and consulted an old city directory to find where he had last been employed, but to no avail. She then tracked down the man's ex–business partner, who gave her his current address. Before forwarding the information to California, Miss T. decided to write directly to the young man to make sure he was Mrs. O.'s son. The trail ends at this point. Perhaps Miss T. never received a reply to her letter. Two years later, in June 1931, Mrs. O. wrote directly to the Society requesting information about her son. A week later, Society Director Robert B. Ralls informed Mrs. O. of her son's last reported address and closed the letter with the "sincere hope that you will be able to locate him."[16]

More commonly, however, the Society responded to natural mothers by serving as a kind of passive adoption disclosure registry. Case workers would inform natural parents that they would keep their letters of inquiry on file and if their child contacted the Society they would "be very happy to put him in touch with his mother."[17] At other times, the Society volunteered to act as a confidential intermediary between natural and adoptive parents. In June 1935, when Mrs. W. requested contact with her twenty-year-old daughter, CHSW Director Ralls wrote the adoptive parents asking if they would permit a visit. After explaining that Mrs. W. had improved her financial position and wanted to aid her daughter, he articulated the Society's role: "We are telling you this so that you may make your own decision in the matter. This letter is merely to inform you of the facts of the case and not to urge you to one course or another. We will abide by your decision and will accordingly notify the mother." Ralls then assured the adoptive parents that the mother "does not know where Mary was placed and there is no way of her obtaining that information, so if you decide that you do not wish to communicate with her, we will write her to that effect and the matter will be closed." In this case, the adoptive parents declined to permit the mother to visit.[18]

The importance of biological kinship that the Society felt extended even after the death of the child. For instance, in 1909, a mother, deserted by her husband, placed her eleven-year-old son with the Society. Two years later, the boy was hospitalized and died after an unsuccessful appendectomy. A case worker attempted to locate the mother so she could attend the child's funeral, but failed to find her in time.[19]

The Society's policy of providing mothers with nonidentifying information, such as details about the welfare of their child or acting as a passive adoption disclosure registry, did not violate state law. The confidentiality clauses of state statutes before World War II made no reference to adoption agency records. For much of the twentieth century, it has been entirely within the discretion of social workers whether or not to reveal family information in agency records. And as the CHSW records reveal, as late as the mid-1970s, Society adoption caseworkers repeatedly released nonidentifying family information to adult adoptees. As one CHSW adoption worker put it in 1929, "it is the policy of the Organization to give all information possible to wards which is felt to be to their interests." In 1940, Emily Brown, Director of Children's Services, provided the most explicit statement of the CHSW's guidelines on divulging family information. Responding to a query by the registrar of Idaho's Department of Public Welfare concerning "our policy of telling children information about their own parents," Brown stated that "I think we would rarely withhold information of an authentic nature . . . I do feel that the child has a right to the information we have about his parents. When we accept children for adoption, we try to remind the parents that this situation may arise years later." Society officials maintained this policy even when they mistakenly believed that it violated state law.[20]

Adult adoptees were the primary beneficiaries of the CHSW's policy of freely divulging family information. Indeed, as late as 1968, Society caseworkers gave *identifying* as well as nonidentifying family information to adoptees upon request. When a young adoptee in

1930 "called at the office to find out about himself," Director Ralls instructed a staff member "to give him any information I could find in the file which I did." The staff member noted in her files that "the boy went away very happy." Similarly, when the wife of an adopted person wrote the Society in the same year requesting information for her husband, who "would like very much to know about his own people and what his real name is," Ralls sent him his natural mother's name, his birthdate, his given name, the date of his relinquishment, the name of the family with whom he was first placed, and the date of placement. Similar examples could easily be given. Adult adoptees sometimes even received identifying information when they requested only a birth certificate. Surely Robert O. must have been startled when, in response to his request for a copy of his birth certificate in 1941, the Society not only told him how to secure one from the Bureau of Vital Statistics, but also informed him that he had two sisters who would like to hear from him![21]

Society caseworkers eagerly assisted reunions of siblings who had been separated when young, though they made a sharp distinction between adult and minor siblings. When adoptees requested information about the location of their adult siblings, Society officials sent it to them immediately.[22] If the Society did not possess the information requested, caseworkers responded sympathetically. When Doreen K. inquired about her brother Lester in 1924, District Supervisor Charles S. Revelle was unable to inform her of his location, though he did provide her with the name and address of Lester's adoptive parents. Revelle's reply summarized the Society's policy and illustrates the cooperative spirit with which it responded to requests for family information: "We have been hoping that as this boy grew up, he would do as you have done; namely inquire at this office concerning his relatives. Many do this but so far we have not heard from him . . . You may be sure that if we get any information regarding his present whereabouts, we will immediately communicate with you."[23]

Society officials refused, however, to divulge any information about siblings who were still living with adoptive parents. In such instances, it played the role of a confidential intermediary, acting as a neutral third party between the adoptive parents and the adoptee seeking the sibling by contacting the adoptive parents to obtain permission before releasing any information.[24] In March 1953, Jane C. wrote the Society asking for the location of her brothers. The adoption worker called Jane and explained that one brother was adopted and the other, though placed with a family, was not, adding that her unadopted brother was aware of her interest but had decided not to get in touch with her. The CHSW worker promised to keep her address and phone number on file in case the brother changed his mind. Three years later, Jane wrote again, this time to announce that she was in touch with her adopted brother but not the other. CHSW case worker Evelyn Tibbals then recontacted this brother's foster parents and urged that a meeting "might be safe since the mother is deceased and the father is living in London." Perhaps thinking she had been too strong an advocate of reunion, Tibbals reasserted in the case record the Society's position of neutrality: "We are not giving the sister any encouragement at this time and there was no pressure on the family to accede to this request." The foster parents refused contact, and the Society acquiesced.[25]

Yet for all of its willingness to release family information and arrange meetings, the Society's policy toward adoptees was not one of "open records." The term is anachronistic before the era of the adoption rights movement. Although social work experts asserted the child's right to family information, they never envisioned that adoptees should be allowed to read their own files. Nor were they prepared to reveal everything in the record. Even the most progressive child welfare reformers assumed that under certain circumstances professional social workers should *withhold* family information. Grace Abbott, the Children's Bureau chief, counseled social workers that "no person should presume to withhold [family] information from the child," but quickly added that "he need not be given every unpleasant detail, but neither should he be told anything untrue."[26]

The Society's caseworkers adhered to professional social work principles by devising various strategies to limit the kind of information clients received. They tried to prevent curious adoptees from discovering "unpleasant" truths about their natural families. Social workers sought to protect parents, especially unwed mothers who desired secrecy, from being discovered by the children they had placed with the Society. CHSW caseworkers sometimes tried to stall or discourage young adoptees—usually those eighteen to twenty years of age—

who were searching for their natural parents or siblings because of the potential embarrassment. For example, in 1936, when Jack S., an inmate of Joliet Prison, requested information about his family, Society caseworker Nicoline C. Kidahl asked him to consider his decision carefully. She reminded him that his three brothers were unaware of his imprisonment and posed a rhetorical question: "Do you honestly feel you should be entitled to probably cause sorrow to three boys unnecessarily?" Ever the neutral "go-between," Kidahl nevertheless wrote the adoptive parents of two of his brothers and reported back to Jack that the letters had been returned unclaimed and she had been unable to locate the third family.[27]

The most common tactic Society caseworkers used to prevent some adoptees from finding out "unpleasant" truths and the one recommended by adoption experts was simply not to tell them. Throughout most of its existence, Society workers omitted telling a small number of adoptees about the circumstances of their birth (that is, that they were illegitimate), their parents' medical background (that there was a history of insanity or venereal disease), or their parents' racial background (African American or American Indian). A sincere wish to spare the individual painful emotions or, as they saw it, from social stigma, motivated these omissions. In 1939, when Lance R. and his fiancée returned to the Society to inquire whether there was insanity in his family, adoption worker Emily Brown did not tell him that his parents had been classified as "mentally subnormal." Nor did she tell him of his father's American Indian ancestry. Lance's mother and grandmother had given the Society that information, and Brown considered it "purely subjective and unnecessary." In an era of strong prejudice against American Indians, Brown believed that informing Lance of his reputed Indian father "could do no good and might do a lot of harm," especially since he "shows absolutely no Indian characteristics." Ultimately, Lance was never told because Brown felt it was "unnecessary to pass this bit of information along, as I don't consider it 'information.'"[28] Similarly, caseworker Mary Lehn did not tell nineteen-year-old Gloria D., an adopted woman searching for her natural parents, that her mother was confined in an institution for incorrigible women, nor that her father was in prison for sodomizing her nine-year-old sister. Instead, Lehn told Gloria only "the positive things I knew, leaving out the very negative which are certainly in the record." Nevertheless, Lehn was beset by doubts and wondered whether she was doing the right thing in withholding information. She voiced her doubts to a social worker at Medical Lake Custodial School, who "was absolutely horrified that I would consider telling Gloria about her mother. She said that the mother was such an unattractive, low mentality sort of person that a teen-age girl would simply be crushed meeting her." Undoubtedly, Lehn was reassured by this outsider's professional opinion.[29] In emphasizing the strategies of adoption workers for withholding what they considered unpleasant truths from adoptees, we must not lose sight of the far more significant point that before the mid-1960s they gave *identifying* family history to most clients who requested it and that the number of clients from whom they withheld information was small.

Adoptive parents were also the beneficiaries of the Society's liberal disclosure policy. Although never formally codified during the first half of the twentieth century, the CHSW's disclosure policy toward providing adoptive parents with information about their child can be reconstructed from case records and Society correspondence. From these sources, it is clear that Society caseworkers were instructed to cooperate and help adoptive parents who contacted the agency with a request for a birth certificate, advice, or intervention, or medical and social history. As one adoptive mother reminded CHSW officials: "The Society told me [that] at any time I wished to know more about the child they would gladly let me know as they had all the records." Consequently, when adoptive parents requested a birth certificate for their child, Society caseworkers promptly gave them the information necessary for acquiring one. Many adoptive parents were visibly relieved after 1939 when they were told that the Washington State Department of Birth Registration would issue them a birth certificate that made no reference to the adoption, bearing only the names of the adoptive parents and the new name of the child. In addition to help in procuring birth certificates, Society officials counseled adoptive parents about how to tell their children about the adoption and how to obtain lost adoption papers. Society caseworkers also promptly came to the aid of adoptive parents who requested help getting their adult child a job or a marriage partner. Moreover, Society officials, at the behest of adoptive parents, intervened with school officials and often counseled troubled adopted youths. When an adoptive father wrote complaining that his daughter was "necking with some soldier in Tacoma," he received a reply from a CHSW caseworker inviting him to the Seattle office, where she would "be glad to talk to him about his difficulties and if this [was] impossible, that our visitor in his area could see him there."[30]

Society officials willingly complied with adoptive parents' requests for medical and social information. They diligently searched case records for adopted children's medical ailments and dutifully reported their findings to adoptive parents. When adoptive parents requested the social history of their child's natural parents, Society officials responded by giving them identifying and nonidentifying information. Thus, when Mrs. A. wrote a letter requesting the social history of her adopted son, Henry, for example, a Society caseworker replied by sending her the first and last name and address of the boy's father as well as the names of his brothers and sisters. Similarly, Society officials gave adoptive parents information pertaining to their child's nationality and religion. Often adoptive parents' initial request for social history also expressed a desire to locate their child's natural family. Caseworkers cooperated with the adoptive parents' request by acting as neutral intermediaries to facilitate meetings between adopted children and their natural parents.[31]

How representative of other adoption agencies' was the CHSW's disclosure policy? Scattered anecdotal evidence in popular magazines between World War I and World War II suggests that adoption agencies' disclosure policy toward adoptive parents was fairly open and widespread. As one informed commentator in 1919 reported, "The best child-placing organizations wish the prospective parents to be as fully informed as possible as to the child's history. Not only is this history usually of great assistance . . . in the intelligent bringing up of the child, but in after life, when the child realizes that he is adopted, he should be allowed to know the facts concerning his forebears." Similarly, some twenty years later, the *New York Times Magazine* reported that it was standard practice for adoption agencies to review the child's history with the adoptive parents, including "his health, his psychometric tests, and as much as is known of his heredity. Parents are told everything about background except the identity of the child's natural parents."[32]

Several social work studies done in the 1930s and 1940s surveying adoption agencies' disclosure policies establish that from 50 to 70 percent of them observed a disclosure policy that encouraged giving adoptive parents much of the medical and social history in a case record. A 1937 survey of 30 child-placing organizations, for example, found that they were evenly divided between telling prospective adoptive parents as little as possible of a child's background, particularly material of an unfavorable nature, and revealing everything except the natural parents' identity. A decade later, a larger survey of 55 CWLA member adoption agencies found that 70 percent told adoptive parents everything in the case record except identifying information. These studies indicate that the CHSW's open disclosure policy was typical of a large majority of child-placing agencies before the 1950s, although its practice of revealing identifying information to adoptive parents appears to be more liberal than that of most other institutions.[33]

Adoption agencies instituted a fairly open disclosure policy toward adoptive parents' requests for medical and social history for a number of reasons. During the early decades of the twentieth century, it was not a difficult task: there was not much family information to give to adoptive parents, and it rarely contained extensive medical or social background information. In addition, before World War II, in many adoption agencies a majority of adopted children were older children with memories of their parents, so that in many cases adoption workers were simply telling adoptive parents what the adopted child already knew. Thus, adoption agencies were not the only source of information about the child's natural parents, alleviating the pressure on them to disclose negative information. Also, adhering to an ideal of full disclosure to adoptive parents was consistent with other social work ideals to provide natural mothers and adult adoptees with family information upon request.

Adoption officials believed that adoptive parents needed the information to fulfill a number of parental tasks. These included planning for the child's future, responding intelligently to behavior problems, and "sharing with the child his birthright of knowledge about himself when the occasion arises." Child-placing officials, influenced by the turn-of-the-century eugenics movement, were especially sensitive to the need to give adoptive parents medical and social history if there was any hint of mental illness in the child's background. As Amy

Watson, chair of the Philadelphia Conference on Parenthood, cautioned, "No child that is of diseased and no child of feeble-minded parents should be placed in any home for adoption until the [adoptive] parents know the full facts of the case." In 1932, the Child Welfare League of America codified this ideal: "Children with special handicaps of a physical nature or related to personality or behavior, and those whose heredity suggests that difficult problems may arise, should be placed for adoption only when the adoptive parents thoroughly understand the child's condition and needs."[34]

The CWLA's standard of full disclosure to adoptive parents went publicly unchallenged until the publication in 1936 of Eleanor Garrigue Gallagher's book *The Adopted Child*. Gallagher, a volunteer adoption worker, criticized adoption agencies' liberal disclosure policies and advocated instead that child-placing institutions withhold from adoptive parents all information about the child's natural family. Gallagher thought that adoptive parents who could honestly plead "we know nothing of your social background nor who your father or mother were, nor why you were not brought up by them but given to us for adoption" were "fortunate indeed." In Gallagher's view, adopted children were better off not knowing anything about their origins than having their curiosity aroused by fragments of unreliable testimony that social workers had collected from unmarried mothers, relatives, and neighbors. She recommended that when the child asked for information about his or her family, the adoptive parents should simply answer, "We do not know and you can never know," assuring her readers that the child would accept this statement "as he accepts many things about which he has a normal curiosity that cannot be satisfied." For Gallagher, if adoption caseworkers did not tell the adoptive parents anything about the child's natural parents, the child could not be scarred by false or wrong information.[35]

In responding to Gallagher, professional social workers reasserted their commitment to the ideal of full disclosure to adoptive parents. They universally condemned Gallagher, especially for her advice to withhold from adoptive parents information about their child's past. In a typical book review, Sophie van Senden Theis, the country's foremost authority on adoption at the time and then secretary of the Child Placing and Adoption Committee of the New York State Charities Aid Association, rejected Gallagher's concept of child welfare and concluded that the book held "no value for social workers." Other social workers, in direct opposition to Gallagher's position, advocated giving parents information about their adopted children. Writing in the *Bulletin* of the Child Welfare League of America, George J. Mohr, president of the American Orthopsychiatric Association, stated that there was "no alternative but to fully advise prospective adoptive parents of all favorable and unfavorable known factors that might influence the subsequent development of the child." By 1945, providing adoptive parents with family history was axiomatic. Maud Morlock, chief of the Social Service Division of the Children's Bureau, provided ample evidence of this statement when responding to a request for advice from The Cradle Society concerning the "fundamental principles" of disclosing family information to adoptive parents. Morlock asserted that adoptive parents were "entitled to all pertinent information about the child . . . There would seem to be no question over the matter of either their right or the need to know about the child they are adopting." Morlock went on to compare the disclosure of family information "to the purchase of an automobile. Few people would think of buying a car, particularly a second-hand car, if they did not know the history of its previous use." She insisted that "the essential facts of the child's background" should be "accurate and objective" and include "some details about members of his family, their cultural pattern, education, interests, physical and mental health, etc." Finally, adoptive parents "should also know why it seemed wise to the natural parents to entrust the care of the child to others."[36]

As part of their open-disclosure policy, professional social workers believed it their responsibility to ensure that adoptive parents tell their children of the adoption. The history of "telling," or adoption revelation, sheds considerable light on caseworkers' attitudes toward openness in adoption, their motivations for insisting that adoptive parents tell their children of the adoption, and the methods by which they transmitted this information to their clients. In addition, the history of telling provides a revealing window on how this information was transmitted to adoptive parents and, in the few accounts that exist, what adoptive children thought of the message.

Throughout the twentieth century, there never was a time when professional adoption workers advised parents not to tell their children of their adoption. Child-placing experts routinely recommended that all adopted children be informed "when very young" or when they "reached an age of understanding." Although adoption workers rarely gave a specific age, the *New York Times Magazine* in 1940 reported that "the established practice nowadays [is] to tell a child of his adoption, before he's 5." Throughout the twentieth century, social workers originated and adhered to these theoretical considerations. Indeed, as early as 1927, the Pennsylvania Children's Home Society (PCHS) refused to consent to an adoption if the prospective adoptive parents were unwilling to promise to tell the child of it. By 1954, the PCHS's practice had become virtually universal. In that year, a nationwide survey of 270 adoption agencies revealed that all but six made a promise to tell a requirement for prospective adoptive parents.[37]

Experts in the field of child-placing advocated this course of action for a variety of reasons. There was the very practical consideration dictated by demographic factors: a large number of the children placed for adoption in the early twentieth century were older children with memories of their original parents and siblings, so they already knew they were adopted. As CHSW caseworker Marian Elliot looked back at pre–World War II placements, she observed that "a child who had been placed well beyond infancy . . . had a memory of his natural mother." Even if the Society had wanted to enforce strict confidentiality, "it could not be handled in the same way since all parties had so much knowledge of the situation."[38]

Most frequently, however, adoption workers urged disclosure on the part of adoptive parents for the pragmatic reason of sparing the child the psychological trauma of finding out about their adoption from neighbors or schoolmates, who might convey such information either unknowingly or maliciously. The traumatic effect of early revelation of adoption to an unsuspecting child was thought to be twofold. First, as a result of the eugenics movement, adoption had been stigmatized in the popular mind by association with feeblemindedness, illegitimacy, and social inferiority. The power that the stigma of adoption had to affect young minds was dramatized in popular fiction. *Harper's Monthly Magazine,* for example, published a short story in which nine-year-old Margaret overheard children gossiping about a schoolmate who was unaware of her adoptive status. One of the children declared, "She is *nothing but an adopted!*" Another child chimed in, "It's just like a disgrace, isn't it?" A third child observed, "Think o' kissin' your mother good night an' it's not bein' your mother?" The author, however, wants to emphasize the psychological shock to Margaret, who mistakenly believes that her schoolmates were discussing her. As Margaret listened, "the terror within her was growing more terrible every moment. Then came shame. Like the evilest of the evil Things it had been lurking in the background waiting its turn—it was its turn now. Margaret sat up in the grass, *ashamed* . . . She could feel something burning her on her forehead —it was 'Adopted' branded there."[39]

The second trauma that social workers predicted when parents failed to tell their children of their adoption was the child's realization that his family life was based on a falsehood. Downplaying the stigma of adoption, Ida R. Parker, associate director of the Massachusetts Research Bureau on Social Case Work and author of one of the first studies of adoption practices, concluded that it was "not the fact of adoption which is so disturbing to the individual, but the manner in which the knowledge is acquired." Ora Pendleton, assistant executive secretary of the Children's Bureau of Philadelphia, summed up the wisdom of 1920s adoption practice by observing that "it is the discovery of the hidden thing that is devastating." Cautionary tales under the heading of "The Pitfalls in Adoption" were printed in professional social work journals detailing how a young woman who discovered at her college commencement that she was not her adoptive parents' biological child "packed her bag and left without their knowledge." The message was again clear: social workers must instruct adoptive parents to tell their children of their adoption at an early age.[40]

In addition to informing adoptive parents of their responsibility to tell their children of their adoption at an early age, adoption workers disseminated true-life accounts that stressed the happy results of telling the child of his adoptive status. The stories, usually a paragraph in length, were printed in the child-placing institution's quarterly "homefinder" magazine. Typically, they revolved around an anxious adoptive couple reluctant to reveal the adoption for fear of losing the child's affection. After much doubt and hesitation, however, they overcame their anxiety and were rewarded by the child's fervent declaration of undying devotion. In 1911, the Children's Home Society of California, for example, printed the story of a seven-year-old girl who, when informed by her nervous mother that she was adopted, responded happily, "You are just the mama I should have chosen." Similarly, the New York State Charities Aid Association reported that upon hearing the news of her adoption a twelve-year-old girl "seemed to grasp the situation instantly. She went up and kissed her [adoptive] parents without saying a word and has never referred to the matter since." The Illinois Children's Home and Aid Society printed a response from a father of two adopted girls to the question of how to tell children of their adoption and yet retain their affection. The adoptive father replied, "We never had any trouble about that. It was no secret, and as we never hesitated to speak of it people forgot the wonder of it, and it passed as a matter of course." His answer, like the adoptive children's testimony, was meant to reassure adoptive parents, encourage disclosure, and minimize the negative consequences of telling. The idea that loving repetition of the word "adoption" would take the edge off the stigma would become a staple of adoption workers' advice.[41]

Increasingly, adoption experts encased their belief that the child should be told early and often within the idea of "the chosen baby," a motif that would dominate advice to adoptive parents until the mid-1960s and that still can be found in present-day adoption self-help books. As early as 1916, the Illinois Children's Home and Aid Society was using the "chosen baby" theme in short stories in its newsletter to advise adoptive parents. Typically in these stories, the mother informed the youngster that "an adopted child means a chosen child . . . you were chosen out of all the world full of babies. We didn't have to take you. We took you and kept you because we loved you, and wanted you." Inevitably, the story would have the child one-upping a playmate by declaring proudly that he had been chosen while his friend's parents had to take him. In another version, reported by the Children's Bureau in 1927, the adoptive mother explained "to her tiny charge that she had been especially fortunate in being able to select and adopt a child rather than having to accept one that just came." The account went on to point out that the adoptive mother was laying the groundwork for a more detailed explanation "when the child was old enough to grasp fully the meaning of the information." Similarly, in 1929 the Children's Bureau chief, Grace Abbott, advised an adoptive mother that "a very happy relationship can be kept by explaining to him that you chose him for your little boy, and that means that he is just exactly what you wanted, etc., that he has been with you always, and is just as truly yours as though he had been born your child."[42]

Until the 1940s, there was a remarkable consensus on the psychological principles underlying telling. Adoption experts never attributed their advice about telling or the resulting trauma of not telling to a particular school of psychology or psychotherapy. One searches vainly in the adoption literature for some explicit mention of Freud's theory of child psychosexual development or, for that matter, John Watson's environmental behaviorism or Arnold Gesell's theory of normative child development. Indeed, until the 1940s, there were few, if any, explicit references to Freudian concepts. Before that time, it was rare for professional social work articles or advice literature for parents regarding adoption to mention Oedipal conflicts, unconscious motivation, family romance fantasies, defense mechanisms, repression, or personality disorders. Nor did the literature of telling indicate that the sudden revelation of the child's adoption would lead to long-term pathology, condemning the child to serious dysfunction as an adult.[43]

Although adoption experts did not invoke the names of famous psychologists or psychoanalysts, the advice they disseminated to adoptive parents on telling reflected an underlying psychology of what can be called commonsense behaviorism. Adoption experts' admonishment to parents to reiterate frequently the word "adoption" in loving and positive tones, for example, echoed the educational psychologist Edward L. Thorndike's and the behaviorist psychologist John Watson's belief that "learning occurred because a random act that caused pleasurable sensations would tend to be repeated." Similarly, the resulting trauma children experienced from the unexpected revelation of their adoption—the product of an unpleasant external environmental stimulus—could result in adoptive children's rejecting their deceptive adoptive parents. But adoption workers were not radical behaviorists: they did not deny that internal emotions or cognitive structures also came into play. Sudden revelation of adoption, a source of social stigma, they felt could cause deep personal shame.[44]

Behaviorism held a great attraction for adoption workers because it stressed environmental factors over genetic ones and implied optimism about the plasticity of human nature. Such ideas were useful to adoption workers in fending off proponents of the eugenics movement. While never denying the role of heredity, adoption experts worked tirelessly to emphasize the importance of a loving home environment and embraced psychometric testing for infants to persuade prospective adoptive parents that their children were "normal." Behaviorism's democratic and hopeful implications that all children were capable of developing into healthy, productive human beings regardless of genetic endowment strongly appealed to adoption workers.[45]

During the first half of the twentieth century, researchers from outside the social work profession incorporated psychoanalytic insights into their analysis of telling, but their conclusions and recommendations merely reinforced adoption experts' commonsense behavioristic advice. For example, in the early twentieth century, the mental hygiene movement provided the impetus for child guidance centers to study and treat maladjusted children. The first center, the Juvenile Psychopathic Institute of Chicago, was founded in 1909 by the psychiatrist William Healy, and initially focused on treating juvenile delinquents, sociopaths, and conduct-disordered children. In 1917, Healy predicted "disastrous" consequences from a child's finding out about his adoption from someone other than his adoptive parents. When the child had the slightest suspicion of "anomalous parentage," repression occurred, resulting in mental conflicts and a "grave psychic shock," which manifested itself in antisocial attitudes and misconduct. When knowledge of a child's adoption became public, Healy recommended that the family go so far as to move away from the neighborhood "for the sake of prevention of harm." The best protection was to tell the child the truth of his adoption for "the openness of statement never does as much harm as concealment." When adoption workers read Healy's work they had only to ignore the Freudian concept of repression to have their behavioristic understanding of telling reinforced.[46]

Similarly, the work of Sidney Tarachow, a member of the Medical and Research Department of the New York Neurological Institute, confirmed rather than challenged adoption workers' understanding of the negative consequences of not telling. In 1937, Tarachow began to research the psychological problems resulting from the sudden revelation of adoption. Taking as his sample an "unselected group [of] 250 admissions to the New York State Training School for Boys," Tarachow discussed seven cases of sudden revelation of adoption. He found that before the youngsters unexpectedly found out about their adoption, they had entertained doubts about their parentage that had led to fantasies about their finding or communicating with their natural parents. The confirmation of the boys' doubts resulted in a major trauma, which manifested itself in their resenting the adoptive parents and deserting the home. Tarachow also warned that the hostility and resentment generated by the sudden revelation of the child's adoption might be expressed by antisocial behavior toward the adoptive parents or society. But he also reassured adoptive parents that none of the runaways harbored any conscious motive to seek out and find their natural parents.[47]

Four years later, in an article that was later widely disseminated as a Children's Bureau publication, Robert Knight, Chief of the Psychotherapy Department of the Menninger Clinic, observed that "psychiatrists are not consulted as often as they should be by prospective adoptive parents who presume that anyone can rear a child." To remedy this oversight Knight offered advice to parents on how to raise an adoptive child, including when and how to tell the child of the adoption. Knight's advice, however, hardly differed from conventional social work wisdom. He urged that the child be told "as soon as he can comprehend the statement" with pleasurable connotations around age four and recommended the use of the "chosen baby" theme to convey the information. Where Knight diverged from the usual social work prescription was in his psychoanalytic rationale for telling. Although, like adoption workers, he believed that it was impossible to keep the secret from adopted children—they would inevitably hear about the adoption from well-meaning relatives or malicious playmates—Knight used Freud's family romance theory to warn adoptive parents that their children would inevitably fantasize and ask about a second set of parents. But aside from taking note of the use of one of Freud's psychoanalytic concepts, adoption workers could read Knight without significantly changing their psychological frame of reference or the content of their advice to adoptive parents.[48]

The compatibility of adoption experts' behavioristic understanding of telling and psychoanalytic studies is not surprising. On the one hand, there was a paucity of psychoanalytic literature on telling. On the other hand, the few articles that were published relied heavily on pre-existing social work knowledge: witness the recommendation of all the psychiatrists that the child be told at an early age, the traumatic consequences of failing to do so, and the general approval of the "chosen baby" theme. Moreover, the psychiatric literature did not challenge adoption workers' fundamental beliefs about telling. Adoption experts and popularizers could easily ignore or overlook under lying psychoanalytic concepts like repression, fantasy, and family romance theory and instead find their basic understanding of telling confirmed.

Still, despite the agreement by social workers and psychoanalysts on the advisability of telling, parents were unsure exactly how and what to tell their adopted children, in part because advice was not readily available. Postadoption services did not exist before the 1950s, and little contact existed between the agency and adoptive parents once the adoption was legalized and the six-month to one-year probationary period expired. And because independent adoptions were common, many parents did not receive adoption agencies' quarterly newsletters. Psychoanalytic articles about telling appeared only in esoteric professional journals. Other sources of information about adoption and specifically about telling scarcely existed. Before the late 1930s, self-help books about adoption were totally unknown.

During the interwar years, adoptive parents had to rely on infrequent articles on telling appearing in mass-circulation magazines and increasingly on radio advice programs. In 1920, there appeared in the *Delineator* magazine one of the first accounts addressing the issue. The article repeated adoption experts' advice to tell their children "the truth from the beginning." It also recounted, in the words of Carolyn Conant Van Blarcom, an adult adopted person looking back on her life, the perils of failing to tell, which included intense psychological conflicts leading to a nervous breakdown. A year later, an article in *Sunset* emphasized the rewards of telling at an early age. Specifically addressed to adoptive mothers, it advised them to encase the telling in a story where a boy whose parents died when he was a baby is chosen by a lady after a long search. At age five, the lady tells the child that the little boy was him. She is rewarded: "He was elated with the thought that in spite of the tremendous competition he had been selected" and shortly thereafter is heard bragging to a playmate " 'your mother *had to take you;* but mine'—proudly—'*chose* me.' " Similarly, in 1928, *Children: The Magazine for Parents* published a short piece by Francis Lockridge on how to adopt a child, which included a paragraph on the issue of telling. Citing adoption experts, Lockridge advised adoptive parents to tell the child of the adoption at an early age and to do so "naturally, simply, even casually." Lockridge warned that "tragedy may follow in the wake of concealment." When adoptive parents wrote the Children's Bureau requesting advice on how to tell their children of their adoption, officials directed them to the Van Blarcom and Lockridge articles. Few, if any, other mass-circulation or women's magazine mentioned the issue.[49]

As radio programs grew in popularity in the late 1920s and 1930s, the Children's Bureau used the new medium to answer questions about adoption, including telling. Similarly, occasional fifteen-minute radio programs, such as "Dr. Crumbine and Cheerio," advised adoptive parents always to tell their children of the adoption and to emphasize that they had been especially chosen. But few radio programs emulated the pioneering efforts of "Dr. Crumbine and Cheerio" to advise adoptive parents. The popularity of adoptions in the 1930s, numbering some 16,000 children annually, magnified the need for information about telling.[50]

The rapid increase in adoptions, coupled with a dearth of information on when and how to tell children of their adoption, created a demand for popular literature to guide new adoptive parents. The result was the publication in the 1930s of several commercial books addressed for the first time to adoptive parents. Dr. Valentina P. Wasson of New York City, the parent of two adopted children, resolved her own anxiety about telling by writing the text of a children's picture book, the adoption classic *The Chosen Baby.* It told the story of "a Man and his Wife" who were happily married but had no children. They called "a Home which helps people to adopt babies" and asked "the Lady at the Home" to help them find one. They went to the Home and said to the Lady: "We wish so much to choose a baby. We want to have a lovely, healthy baby boy." The caseworker did a home study. After a long time, she called and offered them a choice of three babies. The prospective adoptive couple came to the agency and, after rejecting the first infant, chose the second, stating, "This is our Chosen Baby. We won't have to look any further." The next day they took the baby home. In the foreword, Sophie van Senden Theis, the leading authority on adoption in America, enthusiastically recommended Wasson's book to adoptive parents "who wish to make the first explanation of adoption as happy as it is true." During the 1940s *The Chosen Baby* became a best-selling classic, helped along by the support of the Children's Bureau, which recommended it to social workers and adoptive parents.[51]

Although Wasson had provided adoptive parents with a convenient way to convey the information about adoption to the child, the book contained no advice as to the age at which the story should be read to the child or how many times it should be told. Nor did Wasson's book provide adoptive parents with an understanding of how the tale would likely affect the child. These issues were addressed in 1939 by a University of North Carolina sociology professor, Lee Brooks, and his wife, Evelyn C. Brooks, in their *Adventuring in Adoption*, one of the earliest self-help adoption guides. Themselves adoptive parents, the Brookses' objective was to provide a book "for adoptive families . . . interested in a nontechnical discussion of adoption." The Brookses recommended telling the child "as soon as he could talk." At this stage, the adoptive parents should introduce repeatedly the idea that the child was "especially selected." The Brookses also urged the adoptive parents to use frequently the terms "adopted" and "adoption" to demystify their meaning and to guard the child from the stigmatizing tones of visiting adults who chanced to use the word in a disparaging manner in the child's presence. A bright child, they cautioned, would understand the implication of such remarks and come to feel "different, set apart, or possibly inferior." Regarding the method of telling, the Brookses counseled adoptive parents not to plan elaborately for the right moment. Instead, they should take advantage of a child's chance question or comment to defuse an inherently emotional situation and provide the information gradually "in small doses, as the child indicates a readiness and need for it." The child's assimilation of the idea of adoption would gradually increase, "very much as sex understanding is a cumulative process." The Brookses assured adoptive parents that it was useless to withhold this information from the child, who usually found out anyhow. An attempt to conceal such knowledge "must create a barrier and a lack of knowledge as well as needless worry and repression."[52]

By the early 1940s, articles in popular magazines and newspapers joined children's books and self-help guides in advising adoptive parents when and how to tell their children they were adopted. Written by adoption agency officials, journalists who reported the latest information from adoption experts, and adoptive parents who related first-person experiences of their successful efforts at telling, these articles appeared in such mass-market periodicals as *Good Housekeeping, Hygeia, Parents Magazine,* and the *New York Times Magazine.* The articles echoed earlier information and themes about telling: it was impossible to hide the fact of adoption; because children would eventually discover the truth, it was imperative to tell the child at an early age to avoid the shock of disclosure, unspecified psychological damage in the future, or destruction of the child's sense of security. Adoptive parents should emphasize that adoption was something to be proud of: the child was chosen, while other parents had no choice. Child-placing agencies, such as New York's State Charity Aid Association, recommended that parents use Wasson's *Chosen Baby* book. Authors began to embroider the "chosen baby" theme with numerous details for adoptive parents to use. Thus, in the October 1942 issue of *Hygeia,* Douglas E. Lawson provided adoptive parents with the following elaborate script to tell their adopted child:

> You know, a lot of parents plan the kind of baby they want. Then they start its growth and trust to luck. Well, when it comes, it doesn't look like what they ordered at all. It's wrinkled and red-faced and mostly ears or mouth. But what can they do about it? They just have to be good sports and pretend that there never was such a perfectly beautiful baby before. But that's what happens to folks who have to order sight-unseen. Now in your case, we saw a lot of children. We looked them over and suddenly we actually saw just exactly what we wanted—right size, right sex, right sound and everything! So we took you, because we loved you and needed you. We could have had our choice of just hundreds of children, but you were just what we wanted. So, the fact that you weren't ours right at first gave us a chance to choose. That's why we—and you—have something to be proud of.[53]

At the end of World War II the professional and popular consensus about the importance of telling children of their adoption was widely disseminated in Dr. Benjamin Spock's best-selling handbook for parents, *Baby and Child Care*. Although historians have often noted how Spock skillfully popularized Freudian principles without using psychoanalytic terminology, the section on adoption and telling is surprisingly free of Freudianism. Instead, Spock, synthesizing the existing professional adoption literature, highlighted the futility of keeping the adoption a secret, the psychological shock of unexpectedly discovering the adoption, the necessity of telling, the utility of the "chosen baby" theme, and the need to repeat the facts of adoption at different stages of the child's development. Where Spock differed from earlier adoption experts was that he stressed doing what was "natural" and kept his advice vague. To the question "At what age should the child be told of the adoption?" Spock answered that "the news shouldn't be saved for *any* definite age." However, this indeterminate advice, which was meant to put parents at ease, inevitably contributed to their anxiety. In a formula that would be repeated frequently in later adoption self-help books, Spock advised parents neither to keep the adoption a secret nor to overstress it. Constant reiteration of the word "adoption" would reveal the parents' insecurity and might cause the child to wonder what was wrong with being adopted. But how could adoptive parents be sure that they were not discussing the issue too much? Spock provided no specific guidelines, but suggested that if parents accepted adoption as naturally as they accepted the color of the child's hair everything would turn out all right. When the new 1958 edition of *Baby and Child Care* appeared, Spock's publishers ensured that copies would come to adoptive parents' attention by providing the Child Welfare League of America with an unlimited supply of free copies for its member adoption agencies.[54]

Strikingly absent from all the popular and expert advice on telling was the voice of the adopted person. It is a revealing commentary on this group's marginalized status that the first book recording their experiences was entitled *The Adopted Break Silence* and did not appear until the mid-1950s. It is almost as if social workers and other professionals acted on the aphorism "A child should be seen but not heard." Although social workers professed they had only the best interests of the child at heart, they rarely asked adopted children or adult adoptees what they thought about their experience. Instead, they interviewed adoptive parents, studied familial relationships, and made logical assumptions about the consequences of not telling.[55]

Still, before the appearance of *The Adopted Break Silence,* a few firsthand accounts by adoptees about the experience of growing up adopted or what they thought about being told about their adoption had appeared in popular periodicals. One rare account by an anonymous female adoptee turned up in a 1920 issue of *American Magazine.* The woman related how she had been adopted as an infant by an unmarried woman schoolteacher, aged fifty, who lived on a farm. Apparently her adoptive mother had followed the advice of social workers to tell the child early and often. Speaking of that experience, the woman observed: "She must have begun, when I was still a baby, to talk to me about my coming to live with her; for I cannot *remember* ever being told, or even experiencing any shock of realization that I was not her child." As she grew older, the woman refused to hide the truth. When the subject of her parents came up she remembered, "I learned it was easiest to come right out with 'I was adopted' and have it over with." One aspect of the adoption, however, was particularly troubling. Her mother repeatedly warned her not to "get in and ride with a stranger . . . And if anyone you don't know ever speaks to you downtown, run right away." Pressing for an explanation for her anxiety, the woman wrested from her mother the admission that "she worried for fear some of my own relatives might 'steal' me. This awful idea inflamed my childish imagination and I recall many times waking from a nightmare in which I was being bodily carried off." Heeding her mother's advice, the woman ruefully recounted that she turned down many invitations from good-hearted strangers who offered her rides on snowy winter school days. But she concluded that this was "the only instance . . . where my mother's good sense was in any way perverted."[56]

Thirteen years later, another adopted person, Martha Vansant, published an account in the popular magazine *American Mercury* that confirmed social workers' advice about the efficacy of telling at an early age and the harsh consequences of not telling. Vansant's purpose in writing was to discover whether being told about the adoption at an early age had a significant effect on how successful one's life turned out. For her sample, she used the lives of a number of adoptees she personally knew as a youth. She arrived at two conclusions. First, the adopted children who were successful in later life were "those who in childhood were treated as rational beings who could safely be told that they were adopted." As she said about her own adoptive parents: "They had the sense to tell me about my real origin so early that I took it quite for granted, and never felt that there was anything odd about my situation." Second, in contrast, there were those adopted children whose lives ended in failure. Vansant recounted the lives of three such adoptees: one became a prostitute, another a bum, and the third committed suicide. These misfortunes, Vansant believed, were the direct result of hearing the news of their adoption late in life from controlling or vindictive adoptive parents, who had kept the adoption a secret for fear of losing the child's love.[57]

Thus, during the first half of the twentieth century, there existed among legislators, vital statisticians, and social workers a consensus both in policy and practice of openness in disclosing information to those most intimately connected to adoption. By law, court proceedings of adoption and birth certificates had been made confidential, but the intent of the law had been to exclude the public and protect the privacy and self-esteem of adoptive parents and adoptees. Before World War II adoptive parents, adoptees, and even natural parents were legally permitted to obtain information about the adoption and birth from the courts and bureaus of vital statistics. Initially, the power of the state to define certain public records as confidential served the interests of everyone connected to the adoption. During this period, the confidentiality of adoption agency records scarcely arose as an issue. Professional social workers created case records, collected family information, and with discretion conveyed it to adult adoptees and adoptive parents (and to a lesser degree natural mothers).

There was no debate within professional social work circles on whether or not to disclose most of the case record to clients. The debate that did infrequently arise was between professional and amateur social workers. The professionals, imbued with the importance of biological kinship and professional social work standards, argued that the information belonged to adoptees and adoptive parents by right and that it was the social workers' responsibility to collect and provide it when asked. In contrast, the amateurs made it a principle not to preserve family information or convey it to adoptive parents.

In addition, for practical and pragmatic reasons, professional social workers also insisted that adoptive parents reveal the fact of adoption to their children and ensured that such information was widely dis-seminated in professional and popular literature. From the few ac-counts that exist, adult adoptees agreed with the policy of telling early and often.

After World War II, however, disclosure in adoption gave way to secrecy. How and why this development occurred is a surprisingly complicated tale embedded in the changing world of postwar America.

The Ephemeral Age of Secrecy

Although by World War II, the majority of states had made court records of adoption proceedings and birth certificates confidential, they were not secret. The distinction between confidentiality and secrecy is crucial to understanding why natural parents and adult adoptees have been refused access to their adoption records. Progressive and liberal reformers used the power of the state to confer confidentiality on adoption records. Their aim was to protect the privacy of groups they deemed deserving of such protection and to prevent the public from viewing information that was not its concern. Although secrecy originated in the nineteenth century and initially affected only natural parents, it was only after World War II that state officials and social workers invoked this principle to prevent adoptees from accessing the information about themselves in adoption court records, birth certificates, and adoption agency case records.

The process by which confidentiality was transmuted into secrecy was complex. Those state bureaucrats and social workers who had the power to provide or deny access to adoption records acted from numerous intentions, including a desire to defend the adoptive process, protect the privacy of unwed mothers, increase their own influence and power, and bolster social work professionalism; these motivations in turn reflected profound changes in client demography and an intellectual paradigm shift in social work. The result was that after World War II secrecy became pervasive, preventing everyone directly involved in adoption from gaining access to family information about their own lives.

The origins of secrecy in adoption emerged in the mid-nineteenth century, but initially secrecy was invoked against only natural parents in general and mothers in particular. It had been axiomatic since Charles Loring Brace founded the Children's Aid Society (CAS) in 1853 that natural parents should never be told the child's location or the names of the adoptive parents. Brace despised "vile parents," whom he blamed for the children's dependency and delinquency and reviled for their "stupidity and ignorance" when they failed to be "talked out or driven into saving their own children." Once the CAS gained control of the child, Brace did everything he could to prevent a family from reuniting. He introduced the principle of secrecy in placing out children to prevent what he perceived as neglectful or abusive or Catholic parents—Brace made no distinction between the three categories—from reuniting with their children.[1]

A well-publicized 1875 case illustrates the CAS's religious bias and use of secrecy to prevent families from reuniting. A Catholic father, temporarily ill, placed his two children with the American Female Guardian Society and Home for the Friendless (AFGS), who in turn had placed them out. When the father requested the children be returned, an AFGS official, Mrs. C. Spaulding, warned one of the foster families of the original parent's inquiry. "As we dread Catholic influence more than the bite of the rattle-snake, for that only destroys the body while the other destroys the immortal soul, too precious to be lost; if you have become attached to the dear boy, save him from the power of the fell-destroyer, and the conscious approving smile of your Heavenly father will be your award." Spaulding recommended that the foster family hide the child or send him away for a year until he was legally old enough to choose his parents for himself. She forwarded the letter to one of the CAS's chief visitors, John Macy, who tacitly approved hiding the child to prevent him from falling into the hands of the Catholic father.[2]

Brace also made it a policy to caution children not to contact their relatives after placement. But in many instances, they did anyway. After all, for much of the nineteenth century Brace was placing young adolescents in families. These children had clear memories of their parents and siblings. Consequently, many children corresponded with or visited their relatives after placement. Similarly, parents often sought out their children. As one child welfare reformer remarked, "Fathers and mothers crossed half the continent to find their children taken by questionable authority." Although in practice it was difficult to keep parents separated from their children or to keep adolescents from returning to their families of origin, the principle of shrouding the separation of children in secrecy and preventing biological families from knowing their children's whereabouts was Brace's legacy to the theory and practice of adoption, eventually becoming a tenet of professional social work.[3]

Progressive Era professional social workers incorporated the injunction of secrecy between natural and adoptive parents into the adoption case records they created. The Children's Home Society of Washington's (CHSW) relinquishment form, for example, contained a section prohibiting natural parents from searching for their children. Natural parents were asked to sign a statement promising to "not seek to discover the whereabouts of said child or the parties who may have 'him' or to molest or to deprive them of said child." The natural parent(s) also promised to "never visit or attempt to visit said child" and relinquished all rights, services, and claims to the child until he or she "shall arrive at full age." After 1907, the CHSW's expanded relinquishment form still required the natural parents to promise not "to take said child or induce it to leave the family where it may be placed by said Society." Similarly, the Cleveland Protestant Orphan Asylum required parents to sign an agreement that they were "to have no knowledge of the residence or name of the family with whom the child is placed."[4]

Child welfare experts gave several reasons for shrouding the adoption process in secrecy. In 1900 the superintendent of an Indiana orphan asylum asserted that it was not safe "to inform parents, particularly mothers where their children are placed." Fear that the natural parents or relatives would reclaim the child or blackmail the adoptive parents fueled the policy of secrecy. Child welfare reformers also worried that natural parents would corrupt the children. S. J. Hathway complained of the ill effects that followed when parents successfully found their children. "Just as the child begins to give promise of becoming a good citizen, the vicious and depraved relatives, in spite of all that can be done to conceal his whereabouts, will seek him out, entice him away, and so back he goes to vile associates in the dregs of society—a lost life." Similarly, Henry W. Thurston, superintendent of the Illinois Children's Home and Aid Society, cautioned that when a child had been taken by court order from "immoral, cruel, or persistently drunken relatives" the best interests of the child demanded that an adoptive home be found "at such a distance from its own home that interference from its unworthy relatives shall be unlikely."[5]

As child-placing gained in popularity, second generation child welfare reformers added another reason for secrecy: the adoption process itself. A few adoption officials worried that adoptive parents might become so annoyed at natural parents' meddling with the child "that they would return him to the institution again." More commonly, they worried that families interested in adopting children would be deterred from doing so if the parents or relatives could easily find their children. Their fears were confirmed by actual cases, such as that of a Minnesota couple who refused to adopt a little girl on the grounds that it was "unsafe to take a child who had older brothers or sisters who may in the future attempt to look her up." Child-placing authorities agreed. The need to reassure adoptive parents was necessary, according to Homer Folks, Secretary of the New York State Charities Aid Association, because they would not desire a child from "one or both of whose parents are living and who may reclaim the child, either when it has taken a fast hold of their affections or when it has reached a wage-earning capacity." Thus, the Illinois Children's Home and Aid Society made it a practice to choose a home "at a sufficient distance from the place where the child is taken from and its location is not divulged, in order that the child and his foster parents may not be disturbed in the new relationship by the child's former record or by the interference of relatives." The practice worked. As one researcher noted, adoptive parents were more easily recruited because "it is less likely that the natural parents will tamper with them."[6]

The preservation of the adoption process became one of the states' justifications for denying natural parents (and later adult adoptees) access to adoption case records. The law followed social work practice, and the legal precedent was set in New York. In August 1925, the front page of the *New York Times* reported that Mrs. Margaret Henderson, a nurse, had filed suit against the Spence Alumnae Society (SAS) to force the adoption agency to return her four-year-old son, David, whom she had relinquished six months earlier. Two years earlier, Mrs. Henderson had left her husband and four other children in Edinburgh, Scotland, and came to America, where she hoped to establish herself and then send for her family. Falling on hard times, Mrs. Henderson turned over David for adoption to the Spence Alumnae Society. Six months later, Mrs. Henderson returned to the SAS and requested her boy back. SAS officials refused to divulge the identity of the adoptive parents or return the boy, stating that Mrs. Henderson had voluntarily given up all claim to the child. Mrs. Henderson countered that SAS officials had told her that she could retrieve her son at any time within six months of the relinquishment. As a result of this impasse, Mrs. Henderson sued the SAS for fraud and false representation.[7]

The case took more than a year to wend its way through the courts, and at one point a New York State Superior Court justice ordered SAS authorities to produce the child in court. This action prompted a letter to the editor strongly defending the principle of secrecy in adoption. H. H. R. wrote: "What every woman taking a child for adoption wants to know is what is the danger of some relative showing up in later years when she has made the child her own and to take him away from her. This is the universal question asked every day—it is the haunting fear of every child in a foster home old enough to understand. The greatest protection they both have is the secrecy maintained by the society that brought them together and acts as an intermediary." New York's Court of Appeals agreed with H. H. R.'s logic. It ruled in favor of the SAS, stating that the agency was not required to give out the name and address of the adoptive parents because "secrecy is the foundation underlying all adoptions and if this secrecy is not to continue this great work must suffer."[8]

In the 1930s, state legislators closed off another avenue of access to family information for natural parents. In an effort to prevent them from viewing the court records of adoption proceedings and learning the identity of the adoptive parents, some states, like Minnesota and Ohio, revised the wording of the section of the adoption law governing confidentiality. The initial adoption laws of these states contained exceptions to the prohibition of viewing the adoption records: they were closed for viewing except to "the parties in interest" to the adoption. As noted earlier, court clerks often interpreted this phrase to permit even natural parents to view the court proceedings. To prevent this from happening, states like Ohio changed the wording of the statute from the "parties in interest" to the "parties of record." As a result, natural parents were no longer "a party of record" because their parental rights had been terminated before the placement of the child for adoption. By definition, natural parents were not a party to the adoption proceeding, and thus were legally denied access to the records unless the court ruled otherwise.[9]

In 1938 the Child Welfare League of America codified New York's Court of Appeals judgment and adoption agencies' increasingly common practice, advising members in its "Minimum Safeguards in Adoption" that "the identity of the adopting parents should be kept from the natural parents."[10] Nevertheless, before World War II, adoption agencies in general and the Children's Home Society of Washington in particular continued to release nonidentifying information to natural mothers and helped facilitate meetings between them and their grown adopted children. But all this changed in the postwar period. Social workers' attitudes became more rigid and less forthcoming, while adoption agencies' policies of disclosure and cooperation gave way to secrecy and legalism. Once again, the adoption case records and administrative files of the CHSW can provide a revealing close-up view of this process.

When the CHSW's disclosure policy became more inflexible, natural parents were the first to be affected. The evolution of the Society's new restrictive policy is illustrated by the way it responded, over a period of fourteen years, to three mothers who requested photographs of the children they had given up for adoption. In 1955, a distraught mother implored CHSW adoption worker Ruth B. Moscrip for a snapshot of her child. Without hesitation, Moscrip sent her one. Almost a decade later, when another mother made the same request, a different caseworker suggested she first discuss the matter with a psychiatrist. Initially, the doctor favored complying with the request, but then changed his mind because he "could see many reasons why it would not be a good idea for [Miss B.] to have a picture of her baby." The Society acquiesced in the psychiatrist's advice and refused to make the photograph available. Finally, in 1969, the Society simply stopped making any effort to accommodate natural mothers. When the by now familiar request for a photograph arrived a CHSW caseworker notified the mother that "we have a policy of 'no pictures.' "[11]

In other ways, too, the CHSW brought down a curtain of secrecy when dealing with natural parents. Departing from the Society's earlier policy of disclosure, CHSW officials flatly refused to act as intermediaries between natural and adoptive parents. In turning down one such appeal in 1955, a Society caseworker admonished a mother that "we do not harass adopting parents in any way." What once had been considered a right was now viewed as a threat. Not only did the Society increasingly restrict the amount of information released to natural mothers, but in a few cases it also began to falsify the data. Society adoption workers occasionally lied to mothers about the adopting family's social status or the child's health or the child's placement status. In the 1950s one mother was told that her child had been adopted by a college-educated, professional couple rather than, as actually happened, a blue-collar couple with high school educations. Another was assured that her child was in good health when in reality the baby was hospitalized with a serious congenital disease. A third mother was informed that her child had been placed for adoption when the child was still in the Society's custody.[12]

Society caseworkers believed that such deception was for the good of their clients. In 1958, as caseworker Charlotte Landau stated in justifying her lie to a mother about her child's status and adoptive parents, "I felt it was important, for the girl's peace of mind, that we tell her the baby was placed, as I feel if she believes it is placed she will be able to come to peace about it, whereas this way [i.e., telling her the truth, that the child was not yet placed] it would only continue to trouble her." By the late 1960s, not only were some natural mothers receiving less information then before about their children from adoption workers, but there was a strong possibility that the information they did receive had been falsified to avoid upsetting them. In 1969, when Society officials revised its adoption manual's section on "Post-Adoption Services and Service on Closed Cases," natural mothers were not even mentioned.[13]

In the postwar era, the CHSW also began an increasingly restrictive disclosure policy toward adult adoptees. Among some Society officials and caseworkers one can detect a hardening of attitude, a lessening of sympathy, toward adult adoptees who returned to the Society searching for family members. Society adoption workers began making decisions that were totally at odds with their earlier liberal disclosure policy. In 1958, for example, Bill R. returned to the Society to search for his brothers. Adoption supervisor Emily Brown tersely noted that "he knew about one brother, Robert, but apparently not about the other, Edward, and he was not told about him." When Wanda M. wanted to locate her parents and asked for her father's name, a CHSW caseworker lied and told her the Society did not know it. In 1969, for the first time, Society officials invoked state law to justify their refusal to divulge family information to adult adoptees.[14]

There is no evidence that the Society's policy toward adoptive parents became more restrictive in the postwar era. However, during this period many other adoption agencies changed their policy of freely disclosing family history to adoptive parents and became more cautious and restrictive about what information they divulged to them.

What accounts for the Society and a majority of other adoption agencies changing their attitude and policy on releasing information to natural mothers and adult adoptees? Previous researchers of this question made no distinction between confidentiality and secrecy. They seemed unaware that when state court proceedings of adoption and birth certificates were made confidential, the intent and practice of the law was not to prevent adult adoptees from gaining access to the records, and that before World War II adoption agency case records were not included in the statute. As advocates for open adoption records, they have not probed very deeply into the question of why adoption records became cloaked in secrecy. These researchers noted simply that reformers attempted to prevent stigmatizing information about adoption and illegitimacy from falling into public hands and acted to protect adoptive parents, and the adoption process itself, from interference by natural parents. At best and with many qualifications, these explanations are accurate only when discussing one group involved in the adoption, natural parents.[15]

The answer to the question of why secrecy was imposed on adoption case records in the second half of the twentieth century cannot be reduced to the altruism of child-welfare reformers or the self-interest of adoptive parents. In fact, the answer lies in a combination of factors, including the changing demographics of adoption agencies' clientele, adoption caseworkers' often uncritical embrace of psychoanalytic theory, and social workers' increasing professionalism. Not all these factors were operating simultaneously, but each had an effect. For example, changes in the age and marital status of natural mothers contributed to adoption agencies' turn to a policy of secrecy, but these factors played no role in the decision to deny family information from case records to adult adoptees and adoptive parents.

Adding to the difficulty of pinpointing both the onset and the causes of a policy of secrecy in adoption case records is the fact that social workers used different aspects of psychoanalytic theory to justify denying different parties to the adoption access to case records. They invoked Freud's Oedipus complex to deny natural mothers access; Freud's family romance fantasy to prevent adult adoptees from seeing their files; and a general theory of neurosis to restrict disclosure to adoptive parents. Yet social workers did not blindly accept the conclusions of all psychoanalytic studies. They resisted, and even criticized, psychoanalysts' advice that adoptive parents should not tell their children of their adoption at a young age because of unresolved Oedipal conflicts. But they fully accepted psychoanalytic advice recommending that they stop using the concept of the "chosen child" in adoption revelation.

In addition, social workers' increasing use of secrecy in the postwar era was spurred on and reinforced by their never-ending quest for professionalism, which saw them initially invoke the need for secrecy at the behest of clients or in defense of their clients' privacy. Consequently, social workers did not tend to view secrecy as restrictive or onerous, because unwed mothers had originally demanded it as a condition for using state-licensed adoption agencies, and social workers themselves had invoked it to protect welfare recipients.

Underlying the postwar movement toward secrecy in adoption case records was the changing demographic composition of natural parents, which mirrored the nation's explosion in illegitimacy. At the CHSW, for example, a majority of the pre–World War II natural mothers were married or divorced, worked outside the home, and had relinquished their children because they were unable to support them. In the postwar era, they were younger and predominantly single; the vast majority of their children were born out of wedlock and relinquished within days of their birth. Before the Second World War, only 35 percent of the children entering the CHSW were born out of wedlock; in the postwar era the percentage climbed to nearly 95 percent. Postwar unwed mothers' youth, their children's illegitimacy, and the quick separation of mother and child (as caseworkers increasingly followed British psychiatrist John Bowlby's advice on how to avoid "maternal deprivation") seemed to erode their special claim to receive family information. Caseworkers began interpreting the "best interests of the child" as consistent with separating parents and child rather than keeping them together.[16]

Unwed mothers' demand for privacy became the prime reason for the Society's increasing receptiveness to a policy of secrecy. Desperately wanting to start a new life, fearful that the stigma of bearing an illegitimate child would destroy their chances for marriage, single mothers dreaded public revelation of their pregnancy and the familial and public obloquy that was sure to follow. Consequently, unwed mothers insisted on secrecy as the sine qua non for patronizing a licensed adoption agency. Despite this, professional social workers rarely heeded their plea for secrecy during the first three decades of the twentieth century. Although Mary Richmond, the founder of modern American social work, emphasized the importance of the principle of confidentiality between social worker and client, for a number of reasons her adherents did not give it high priority. References to confidentiality in early codes of ethics guiding social workers' professional behavior were vaguely worded and lacked focus. Social workers' primary allegiance was to protect the laws and morals of the community and to investigate clients' problems, not to protect the individual rights of clients or their confidences. Mary Richmond's casework methodology, moreover, was incompatible with respecting client confidentiality. To gain insight into the client's problems, Richmond urged social workers to "break through the narrow circle of the client's own view of his situation" by interviewing a multitude of outside sources, including relatives, physicians, policemen, hospitals, employers, friends, teachers, clergymen, neighbors, and landlords. As social workers increasingly filled case records with countless details of their clients' lives, Richmond's casework methodology inevitably exposed unwed mothers' situation to family members and outsiders. Because the stigma of unwed motherhood was so strong, the result was predictable. Unwed mothers deliberately avoided state-licensed adoption agencies, staffed as they were with professional social workers, and they flouted state laws that prohibited the removal of a child from its mother during the first six months of life. Instead, in large numbers, they patronized private adoption agencies such as The Cradle Society, run by amateurs, because they asked no questions, kept no records, and refused to disclose any information to adoptive parents.[17]

Child Welfare League of America officials believed that any policy that encouraged private, unlicensed adoptions was neither in the best interests of the child nor advanced the professional interests of adoption caseworkers. Consequently, as a response to potential clients' preference for private, nonregulated adoptions, League officials began in the late 1930s to consider accommodating the increasingly upscale unwed mothers' demands for secrecy. A caseworker in one of the CWLA's member agencies suggested that a more flexible policy toward unwed mothers might attract more clients. If adoption agencies protected their identity, she wrote, "there might be less hesitance on the part of the mother about approaching a regular agency. More mothers of middle class families and those of higher educational and cultural advantages would turn to the accredited children's agencies for placement of their children if they could feel certain that their confidences would be respected and no publicity of any sort attached to the proceedings . . . Privacy and an appreciation of their own inner feelings of sufferings is what these mothers are looking for." After World War II, professional social workers would increasingly respect unwed mothers' wishes for secrecy, expropriating this aspect of unregulated adoptions, like those conducted by The Cradle Society, and trumpeting it as one of the benefits of patronizing accredited adoption agencies. Later, when under attack by adoption rights activists, CWLA officials would refuse to change its policy on sealed adoption records, viewing it as a violation of the contract entered into with unwed mothers to keep their identities secret. Few people, whether activists or adoption professionals, recalled that it was unwed mothers themselves who had originally demanded secrecy or that adoption professionals agreed to the policy because it was both good for business and based on the principles of sound social work.[18]

Adoption agencies almost immediately began to view secrecy as a professional attribute that provided them with a competitive edge over unlicensed private adoptions. In their uphill battle to sway public opinion in general and adoptive parents in particular of the benefits of regulated adoptions, agencies actively touted the advantages of secrecy. As early as 1944, California's Department of Social Welfare identified as one benefit of using an accredited agency its "ability to conceal the identities of the natural parents and the adopting parents from each other, thereby eliminating the possibility of the natural parents interfering or causing embarrassment to the child at a later date." Similarly, Maud Morlock, a consultant at the U.S. Children's Bureau, advised prospective adoptive parents to use licensed adoption agencies because their identity could be concealed from an unwed mother, thereby protecting the future security of the adoptive home. Failure to use an accredited agency, it was said, inevitably brought disaster. This theme was emphasized during the pronatalist 1950s, when childless couples, frustrated by the red tape of social agencies, were drawn to unregulated adoption agencies. Mass market magazines never tired of describing the dangers associated with not using accredited adoption agencies. In one article, the Carpenter family let slip where they lived to their newly adopted baby's natural mother and her relatives. "It was no time at all before they were insisting on visiting him, taking him presents and interfering with the Carpenters' management of him. The result, and the endless complications involved, can only be imagined." The moral of the story: "This would have been quite impossible in a professionally managed adoption."[19]

Equally important for understanding the CHSW's newly restrictive policies was social work's embrace during and after World War II of psychoanalytic theory to guide casework with unwed mothers. This was a new development and represented a significant paradigm shift in social work practice. As mentioned earlier, during the first quarter of the twentieth century, under the influence of Mary Richmond's differential casework, social workers' analysis of adoption, unwed mothers, and the problem of illegitimacy had recourse to a common-sense behaviorism, which stressed the underlying causes of nature and nurture, of heredity and environment, including the responsibility of the father and the community for the child. Social workers emphasized the need to use community resources and kin to keep mothers and their children together and recommended adoption only as a last resort. But between 1928 and 1935, social work's methodology began to shift, with momentous consequences, from Richmond's behaviorist-environmental perspective to a more psychoanalytic orientation using the work of Sigmund Freud, Otto Rank, and Alfred Adler.[20]

Still, it was not until the spectacular success of psychoanalysis in treating American soldiers for neuroses and psychosomatic disorders during World War II that psychoanalytic theory began to dominate casework treating the problem of illegitimacy. During the war, social workers began to take their cues from psychoanalytic studies of unwed mothers, which depicted them as neurotic at best, psychotic at worst. One investigation of sixteen unmarried mothers in 1941, citing the work of the Freudian psychoanalyst Helene Deutsch, concluded that "these pregnancies represent hysterical dissociation states in which the girls act out their incest phantasies as an expression of the Oedipus situation." Another study of fifty-four unwed mothers by James Cattell, an experimental psychiatrist at the New York State Psychiatric Institute, found the following distribution of diagnoses among its subjects: "character disorder, 30; neurotic reaction, 7 (anxiety, depressive, and conversion); schizophrenia, 17 (pseudoneurotic, 7; other types, 10)." But it was the prolific Florence Clothier, a psychiatrist affiliated with Boston's New England Home for Little Wanderers, who brought the more technical psychiatric research to the attention of social workers. In a series of articles appearing between 1941 and 1955, Clothier repeatedly stated that unmarried motherhood represented "a distorted and unrealistic way out of inner difficulties—common adolescent phantasies (rape, prostitution, and immaculate conception or parthenogenesis) and is comparable to neurotic symptoms on the one hand and delinquent behavior on the other."[21]

It is doubtful whether social workers in general or CHSW adoption caseworkers read the works of Freud, Deutsch, Cattell, or Clothier. More than likely they acquired their psychoanalytic perspective on a hit-or-miss basis. There is still much truth in the 1930 observation of Children's Aid Society of Pennsylvania's staff member Jessie Taft that "rarely does a social case worker adopt a complete, well-rounded psychology on which to base her work with human beings. Rather, she tends to pick up a dynamic concept here or there which profoundly affects her whole relation to her job. She goes ahead on the impetus of her new insight until it wanes, until fresh problems arise or different experience is undergone, and then other hypotheses are sought to broaden or alter her basic approach." During the 1950s it would have been almost impossible for social workers not to have picked up psychoanalytic concepts from its popularization in novels, news media, Hollywood movies, and mass circulation magazines such as *Time, Saturday Review,* and *Mademoiselle.*[22]

However they acquired knowledge of the latest psychoanalytic research, social workers medicalized the issue of illegitimacy by separating unwed mothers from the host of hereditary and environmental conditions that may have caused it and instead focused on individual psychopathology. As early as 1933 social workers used psychiatric concepts in nontechnical language to suggest that unwed mothers "seized every opportunity to escape from unreality" and began describing them in the professional literature as neurotic, emotionally immature, and irresponsible. By the mid-1940s, social workers confidently asserted that "we know that the unmarried mother is an unhappy and neurotic girl who seeks through the medium of an out-of-wedlock baby to find an answer to her own unconscious conflicts and needs. She is acting out an unconscious, infantile fantasy, the roots of which are unknown to us but the results of which constitute an urgent problem." By 1958, the psychoanalytic view of unmarried mothers had been incorporated into the CWLA's influential *Standards for Adoption Service,* which stated that unwed mothers "have serious personality disturbances [and] need help with their emotional problems."[23]

The logic of this diagnosis carried within it the prescription for treating unmarried mothers. Because the child was portrayed as a symptom of unwed mothers' neurotic drives, social workers believed that, with rare exceptions, unmarried mothers were incapable of providing sustained care and security for their babies. This led social workers such as the St. Louis Children's Aid Society's Ruth F. Brenner to question "whether mothers as emotionally immature as these have any interest in planning a sound future for their babies." Clothier had no doubts of unwed mothers' unfitness for parenthood. She claimed to have "never seen a school age, neurotic, unmarried mother who I thought would gain by keeping her baby, or who would be able to provide well for the baby." The inescapable conclusion social workers drew from the professional social work literature was that the best treatment was to separate the unmarried mother from her child.

Caseworkers were advised "to help the unmarried mother to see that she was using the baby as a symbol of neurotic need and that she did not have to keep it on that basis." As for those unwed mothers who wanted to keep their children or maintain contact with them, social workers echoed Helene Deutsch's observation that "the least mature among unmarried mothers are the very ones who often fight to keep their children."[24]

Publication of the British psychiatrist John Bowlby's influential monograph *Maternal Care and Mental Health* (1951) reassured social workers on their advocating the virtues of adoption in general and the early separation of mother and child in particular. Bowlby cited a mass of clinical evidence demonstrating the adverse effect early deprivation of maternal care had on the development of infants' character and mental health. He assumed that the unwed mother would neglect and reject her child. Consequently, he recommended "on psychiatric and social grounds" that "the baby should be adopted as early in his life as possible," specifying that the "first two months should become the rule."[25]

CHSW personnel adopted this psychoanalytic view of unmarried mothers. As late as 1971, the Society's Director of Social Services, Ben Eide, urged caseworkers to read Sarah Evan's "The Unwed Mother's Indecision about Her Baby as a Defense Mechanism," a 1958 article published with the imprimatur of the Child Welfare League of America. Evan stated as axiomatic two premises of psychoanalytic research concerning unmarried mothers. First, the pregnancy was "a fantasy fulfillment of Oedipal and pre-Oedipal strivings or a neurotic solution to such problems as loss of a loved person, or anxieties about one's sexuality." Second, the best solution for the majority of unwed mothers was to give the baby up. Evan argued that the unmarried mother's resistance to placing the child for adoption should be understood in "terms of the dynamics of defense and symptom formation." Therefore, the caseworker's job was to assist the client to recognize her defenses and help her work through them.[26]

CHSW adoption caseworkers read Evan and followed her recommendations. They helped unmarried women arrive, sometimes reluctantly, sometimes with ease, at a decision to relinquish their children to the Society. In difficult cases, they sought the advice of outside psychiatric consultants and accepted their diagnosis that unmarried mothers displayed "many characteristics of an adolescent character disorder with many hysterical features." In this milieu, it is not surprising that CHSW adoption workers began withholding photographs from unwed mothers and restricting their contact with their children and their children's adoptive parents.[27]

A somewhat different set of circumstances accounts for the Society's change in policy on releasing information to adult adoptees. Two interrelated factors may have been changing definitions of professionalism and increasing bureaucratization. Social workers during the Progressive Era advocated keeping adoption case records for professional reasons *and* because the child had a right to know his or her family history. After World War II, the CWLA's *Standards for Adoption Service* continued to recommend these twin objectives to member agencies, though the child's right to family information was clouded by the ambiguous injunction that the agency should preserve family history "which can be made available when needed." By 1969, however, Society officials had dropped the emphasis on providing family information to the client. Following Gordon Hamilton's authoritative *Principles of Social Case Recording*, they viewed case records only as illustrative of "the process in a particular adoption" and as an "aid to the supervisor in working with the social workers and to administration in reviewing and assessing the services of the agency." In practice, this meant that the Society emphasized keeping detailed records on the care given to unmarried mothers, the prospective adoptive parents' interview, and the child's placement, as well as specific administrative responsibilities such as fundraising, plant construction, and staff hiring and compensation. With the de emphasis on maintaining biological families, the Society's duty to preserve family information *for the child's future use* simply disappeared from the CHSW's mission.[28]

Psychoanalytic studies conducted on adopted children and adults also strongly influenced the Society's increasingly restrictive policy toward releasing family information after World War II. CHSW adoption workers began interpreting adult adoptees who searched for their parents of origin as "very disturbed young people" and "sick youths," a perspective grounded in the psychoanalytic concept of the family romance fantasy. First articulated by Sigmund Freud and then transmitted to psychiatric social workers by Otto Rank in his *Myth of the Birth of the Hero,* this concept received special emphasis in the psychology of adopted children developed by psychotherapists Helene Deutsch and Florence Clothier. According to Freud, the family romance is a common fantasy of most small children who, when sensing that their affection for their parents is "not being fully reciprocated" imagine they are a "step-child or an adopted child." Wishing to be free of his parents, the child develops a fantasy in which he is the child of "others, who, as a rule, are of higher social standing." The child's fantasy, however, of being adopted occurs only at the first, or asexual, stage of family romance development. When, during the "second (sexual) stage of the family romance," the child attains knowledge of the mother and father's sexual relationship, the family romance "undergoes a curious curtailment," and the child no longer fantasizes about being adopted. The child now exalts the father, based on the very earliest memory of an all-loving parent. As Freud observed, the child "is turning away from the father whom he knows today to the father in whom he believed in the earlier years of his childhood; and his fantasy is no more than the expression of regret that those happy days have gone." In other words, in normal child development, the fantasy of being adopted subsides quickly.[29]

Clothier wrote a series of articles between 1939 and 1943 that ignored Freud's second stage of the family romance and made the first, asexual stage of family romance fantasy central to the psychodynamics of the adopted child. Relying heavily on Deutsch and Rank, she postulated that the adopted child, who in fact had two sets of parents, did not experience the family romance as a fantasy. The adopted child's inability to use reality to neutralize fantasy, as nonadopted children did, served to strengthen and confirm the family romance. Clothier, for the first time in social work research, used the family romance concept to question the therapeutic benefit of providing adopted adults with identifying information. If reality could not dissipate fantasy, then telling an adopted person that "his father was such-and-such person" could not "in any way assuage his need of a real father." With this logic psychoanalysts and their social work adherents began to undermine the rationale for giving identifying information to adult adoptees.[30]

Although hesitating to draw definite conclusions until more clinical research was conducted, Clothier suggested that therapists consider the hypothesis that adopted children with behavior problems might be living out the family romance fantasy. By the 1950s, Clothier's tentative suggestion had evolved into a proven conclusion. Writing in 1953 and citing Deutsch's and Clothier's early articles, New York psychotherapist Viola W. Bernard asserted that the adopted child's inability to shake off the family romance fantasy was part of the "symptomatology of emotionally disturbed adoptive children." She concluded that "the most potent antidote to excessive and persistent pathological recourse to this escapist fantasy is a healthy, secure, satisfying relationship between the child and his adoptive parents." Social workers would interpret this tenet of psychoanalytic theory to mean that searching for natural parents was pathological and, by extension, represented the failure of the adoptive process. In 1958, CHSW adoption supervisor Evelyn Tibbals described to her staff several examples of adult adoptees searching for their "natural parents" and made clear her belief that "the troubled adult was a pretty unhappy, disturbed person."[31]

The difficulties that natural mothers and adult adoptees experienced in obtaining family information were exacerbated by social workers' growing adherence to the principle of client confidentiality and the importance of professional secrecy in general. In the 1930s, as casework dealt increasingly with emotional and psychological problems and unwed mothers increasingly demanded that their privacy be respected, social workers began to emphasize their responsibility not to reveal client-entrusted communications to other social agencies or caseworkers. Their views on confidentiality were first officially recognized in federal legislation with the passage of an amendment to the Social Security Act, mandating that the records of recipients of aid to dependent children be made confidential. Both the value and the precariousness of the principle of confidentiality were made evident to social workers with the passage in 1951 of the Jenner Amendment to the Social Security Act, which permitted state governments to open their hitherto confidential welfare records to public scrutiny. In Cold-War America, social workers invoked the principle of confidentiality to defend the civil liberties of some of their clients. Ironically, adoption workers applied the same principle to prevent unmarried mothers from obtaining information about their children and adult adoptees from learning about their original families.[32]

A decade later, Society officials codified all the new, restrictive policies that characterized its postwar response to adult adoptees who sought family information or desired to locate their natural parents into their "Adoption Manual" for CHSW caseworkers. Reflecting the newer policy of secrecy, the Society's guidelines for postadoption contact prohibited the release of identifying information and couched the justification in psychoanalytic language. It stated bluntly that "for reasons of confidentiality" no identifying information should be released to adult adoptees. The manual characterized an individual requesting identifying information as usually a person who "has had many unhappy past experiences and . . . is so intent upon finding the natural parent that he is not able to consider his request in a realistic or rational way." It advised the caseworker to discourage the adult adopted person's quest and suggested that "the person may be relieved by being stopped . . . but often he merely feels frustrated." Though not stated in the manual, the caseworker's next step was to refer the client to "a treatment agency," which probably meant seeing a psychiatrist. One can only imagine what adoption supervisor Lucille T. Kane thought when she suggested to Susan G., a woman who requested identifying information in 1956, that "she seek psychiatric help for this long standing problem" and Susan replied that "she had already talked to Psychiatrists who told her it would be a good thing if she could see her mother." The manual did note, however, that for the Susans of this world "who cannot accept that [they] have problems, referral to a treatment agency may not be appropriate."[33]

The 1968 CHSW adoption manual did not fundamentally change its policy of facilitating sibling meetings or acting as an intermediary between adult adoptees and natural parents. In 1971, however, the Society stopped releasing identifying information to adopted adults searching for their siblings. The decision was prompted by a female client's request for her adopted brother's whereabouts. At a staff meeting called specifically to discuss the issue, the question of whether to release the information provoked "considerable discussion." The staff members finally hammered out a consensus that "to divulge information of this type is not allowable by law." They left it to the Society's Director of Social Services, Ben Eide, to inform the sister punctiliously that "Washington State Law is quite specific (Revised Code of Washington 26.36.020 and 26.36.030) in stating agencies cannot release information from records without a court order." Eide enclosed a copy of the law and invited the woman to get a court order "which would force the agency to release the information you seek." By 1974, Society caseworkers such as Doris Gillespie routinely turned down requests by adult adoptees for identifying information about their biological families with what by then had become formulaic language: "Adoption records are sealed and our agency has no authority to reveal identifying information." The timing of the CHSW's restrictive policy and the growth in the early 1970s of the adoption rights movement was not coincidental. Frightened by the specter of their clients threatening social workers' paternalistic discretion and demanding their rights, CHSW caseworkers retreated behind a legal smoke screen.[34]

By the early 1950s, the increasing application of psychoanalytic concepts to child-placing also began to influence adoption agencies' generous disclosure policy to adoptive parents. Cast now within a psychoanalytic framework, social workers revived Eleanor Garrigue Gallagher's 1930s plea to withhold from prospective adoptive parents all information about the child's original family. The first indication of a change in attitude occurred in 1954 when psychiatric social worker Barbara Kohlsaat and psychiatrist Adelaide M. Johnson, both of the Mayo Clinic, argued in *Social Casework* that "because of the possibility of neurotic character traits in the adoptive parents, they and the child must be protected by keeping from them any knowledge about the child's background." On the one hand, the authors feared that adoptive parents, "hostilely envious of those who can bear children," would use negative information as a "cudgel" when angered by their child's misbehavior. On the other hand, Kohlsaat and Johnson asserted, any criticism of the adopted child's natural parents, especially if it had to do with illegitimacy, would prevent the resolution of the Oedipus complex and be devastating to the child's self-esteem. To avoid these problems, they recommended that all social information about the natural family be cleared through a few selected adoption agency supervisors, who would then certify the baby's adoptability to the caseworker. By insulating even the caseworker from any knowledge of the natural family's background, Kohlsaat and Johnson believed that the adoptive parents would accept the caseworker's attitude that "I know this to be a fine baby because my investigating chief and consultants have so agreed; that is enough for me." Kohlsaat and Johnson labeled prospective adoptive parents who demanded knowledge of the child's past as "very anxious, narcissistic, and unconsciously sadistic." Social workers justified their change in policy to ease adoptive parents' discomfort in discussing the issue, to relieve them of the burden of possessing information they were not "mature" enough to absorb, and to avoid stigmatizing the adopted child.[35]

Like Gallagher's idea to withhold information from adoptive parents, Kohlsaat and Johnson's views quickly drew fire. Three social workers responded to the Kohlsaat and Johnson article in a subsequent issue of *Social Casework*. One noted that the authors' basic assumption that adoptive parents were neurotic and could not be trusted was "alien to our long-standing belief in the basic integrity of people, and faith in the potential strength of the parent-child relationship." All objected strongly to the idea of completely withholding natural family information from adoptive parents. Yet all of the social workers advocated not full, but "selective and positive" disclosure of the original family's background because adoptive parents should not "be burdened with irrelevant history or particular psychopathology."[36]

The 1950s controversy over whether or not adoption workers should disclose natural family information to the adoptive parents revealed a new fissure dividing the social work profession. The dispute was no longer between total disclosure and total withholding. The debate had now shifted to the question of how much and what kind of family information should be withheld. The results of a 1954 CWLA survey of 257 adoption agencies confirmed this trend. Although agencies were still evenly divided on the question of disclosing family background information, in practice those agencies claiming "complete disclosure" qualified their answers by stating they gave only "selected background material" or left out "sordid or irrelevant details." No longer did adoption agencies view the social work ideal of fully conveying the child's family information to adoptive parents as obligatory. Even those agency authorities favoring full disclosure justified the practice only on pragmatic grounds, to forestall adoptive parents from returning to the agency or receiving false information from unreliable sources.[37]

Agency officials defended the practice of giving adoptive parents only favorable information about the natural parents because it would help them "to assist the child in building his own positive image later." Lela B. Costin, a prominent social worker, in a widely read and influential article advised adoption caseworkers to withhold from adoptive parents " 'pathological' background" information, if after careful scrutiny they determined that such data had "no significance for the child's future development." In addition, agency officials reasoned, the sharing of irrelevant or unverified information was of little benefit to the parent-child relationship and "may cause real damage in arousing anxiety and apprehension." One example was incest. Many agency officials believed that it was "doubtful that knowing about incest in the child's background [was] helpful to parents" and thus did not share such information with them. One unidentified agency official enunciated what was becoming the standard justification for withholding information from adoptive parents: "We should be honest, but when we don't tell, we know why we aren't telling. The agency bears a responsibility not to share things which will work harm upon a child. In that sense we are dishonest."[38]

Although both policies—full and selective disclosure—were applied on a case-by-case basis, adoption authorities were tilting toward not being "overmeticulous in presenting all the negatives." In January 1955, the CWLA sponsored a National Conference on Adoption at which Kohlsaat and Johnson's extreme view that "nothing should be told to adoptive parents regarding the child's background" resurfaced. After some conference participants disagreed, a consensus was reached that "agencies should select pertinent facts helpful to the adoptive parents and child" and withhold facts that were prejudicial or stigmatizing. The conference report noted that there was considerable disagreement on what information was "dangerous or not necessary to share." Ultimately, policy was left to the discretion of the adoption agencies, which increasingly chose to reveal to adoptive parents only favorable family information or none at all. The selective viewpoint was endorsed in the CWLA's revision of its 1959 *Standards,* which instructed member agencies not to give adoptive parents "information which is not relevant to the child's development and would only arouse anxiety."[39]

Self-help adoption manuals and newspapers in the 1950s transmitted agencies' new selective disclosure policies and even creatively provided a rationale. They suggested that without such "sordid details" adoptive parents could, "with true peace of mind," honestly plead ignorance when their children asked questions about their original families. If by chance the adoption agency conveyed to the adoptive parents a complete history of the natural parents, adoption experts such as Carl and Helen Doss advised them to *"forget everything that would not be helpful to your child."* If that advice was too extreme, Ernest and Francis Cady's *How to Adopt a Child* gave adoptive parents concrete examples of the type of information that should be withheld from children, including incest, fathers in prison, and "incorrigible" mothers. In the last case, the Cadys suggested that it might be more compassionate to the children to imply that their mother had died. *The New York Times Magazine* noted that although professional adoption workers did not approve of such falsehoods, some adoptive parents believed that it was "simpler and kinder to say that the natural parents were dead."[40]

In addition to social workers' increasing tendency to restrict the disclosure of family information, opposition to telling children of their adoption arose from an adoptive parent backlash and from psychoanalysts who sharply called into question social workers' long-held prescription for telling. Throughout the first half of the twentieth century, despite the strong consensus among professional social workers on the value of telling and the reiteration of their advice in the popular media, adoptive parents were extremely reluctant to convey this information to their children. As early as 1927, reports came back to child-placing institutions such as the Illinois Children's Home and Aid Society that adoptive parents were permitting their children "to grow up in ignorance of the fact of adoption." In 1931, two clients of the Children's Home Society of Washington confided to their caseworker that they had never told their ten-year-old adopted son that he was adopted and wished "it were possible for the boy never to be told the truth." During World War II, adoptive parents' failure to tell their children of their adoptive status was frequently revealed when boys needing birth certificates for induction into the army were referred to adoption agencies, much to their surprise and dismay.[41]

In the decades after the war, adoptive parents appeared to become more forthcoming about telling. A 1967 British study of fifty-two adoptive families found that, at one time or another, most children had been told of their adoption. Interviews revealed, however, that it was some external circumstance in the child's life—beginning school, applying for work, joining the armed forces, securing a passport, getting married, or hearing it from strangers—that "precipitated the adoptive parents into telling them of their adoptive status." Similarly, in 1971 two American researchers discovered in a follow-up study of one hundred adoptive families that 93 percent of the parents had informed their children of their adoption. Yet the study also revealed that "only 12 percent of the families had shared with their children the true facts of adoption as they knew them," that is, the family history of the natural parents.[42]

It became clear to social workers that trusting adoptive parents to inform the child of the adoption failed to produce the desired results. In the 1940s and early 1950s, adoption experts sought an explanation for the failure of adoptive parents to tell their children of their adoption. For answers, social workers turned naturally to the professional literature of the mental hygiene movement's child guidance clinics. In the 1930s these clinics focused on the emotional problems of parents, particularly mothers, and cited a multitude of alleged maternal attitudes—rejection, strictness, overprotection, overambition, overconcern, and favoritism—that were responsible for distorting the child's emotional adjustment. Relying on psychodynamic child-guidance literature, adoption experts began studying the underlying emotional dynamics of mother-child interaction. In one 1943 study of twenty-eight adoptive families, Dorothy Hutchinson of the New York School of Social Research investigated why adoptive parents failed to tell. She found that insecure, "less mature" adoptive parents, fearing the loss of the child's love, often postponed telling. Adoptive parents especially feared the questions the child would ask about his or her natural family. Although nearly all participants in Hutchinson's study agreed the child should be told of the adoption, most deliberately "forgot" the background information the adoption agency provided and preferred to tell the child they knew nothing about the natural parents.[43]

Such ideas concerning the importance for adoptive parents to conquer their anxieties were disseminated quickly to the public. Self-help adoption books, such as Francis Lockridge's *Adopting a Child,* cited Hutchinson's study and warned adoptive parents that the anxiety they generated from fearing that the child would discover his or her adoptive status would inevitably be conveyed to the child. Popularizers of adoption research, like British author Margaret Kornitzer, translated psychiatric jargon into more easily understood language. Explaining why adoptive parents "shrink from the whole business of telling," she cited their fear of upsetting the child, losing the child's love, or the child's desire to look for the natural parents.[44]

As the professional studies revealed and popular adoption literature explained, adoptive parents for a variety of reasons preferred not to tell their children of the adoption. In fact, they preferred to keep the adoption a secret from everyone—from relatives, neighbors, and strangers. They wanted desperately for their family's status to remain unknown in order to conform to America's cultural preference for "blood" families. Occasionally some adoptive parents revealed their real feelings about telling. In 1944, for example, *Reader's Digest,* the most popular magazine in America with a circulation of over eight million readers, published an account about adoption. It described a chance encounter on a beach between the author, Kathleen Norris, and a mother of two children, Ned and Tony. Norris is startled that Tony announces his adoptive status to strangers and eagerly repeats the story of how he was specially chosen by his parents. When Norris remarks that it must have been difficult to tell him, the adoptive mother answers that in truth she had concealed the fact of adoption for nine years until forced by a friend's inadvertent remark to reveal her son's true status just six months earlier. Later the adoptive mother confides to Norris a further layer of truth: Tony is her "own child. It's Ned who is adopted." Ned was a sickly child "and it would have killed" him "if I had told him he was adopted." The story ends with Norris extolling the sacrifice of the adoptive mother "to give her own son's place to the other boy, rather than break the adopted child's heart." The story's message is a confusing one. On the surface it affirms adoption experts' advice by having Tony proudly reiterate the chosen baby theme. But at another level it stigmatizes adoption as an inferior mode of kinship and mocks adoption workers' counsel. Ultimately the adoptive mother views adoption as shameful and chooses to perpetuate a hoax rather than tell the truth.[45]

Adoptive parents not only concealed from their children the fact of adoption, but some challenged social workers' advice to tell and voiced their opposition publicly in mass circulation magazines. One article, appearing in a 1959 issue of *McCall's* and entitled "To My Adopted Daughter: I Wish I Hadn't Told You," drew a formal protest from the Child Welfare League of America and 184 angry letters in response. The author, an adoptive mother, recited a litany of problems her twenty-one-year-old daughter had encountered throughout her life because she, the mother, had followed the standard advice of hospital authorities, "the psychologists, the welfare agencies, the knowledgeable caseworkers, and our good friend the doctor" to tell. These problems included the wounding remarks of adults and children, mental agony revolving around the question of identity and abandonment, an exaggerated sense of obligation, and feelings of inadequacy and guilt over an inability to express appreciation and gratitude. The adopted daughter's difficulties climaxed when her fiancé jilted her after she told him she was adopted. The mother concluded that she should have lied to her daughter because "the knowledge that one is adopted creates far more problems than the one it is supposed to solve."[46]

Adoptive parents' opposition to telling received support from a number of psychoanalysts who called into question both the efficacy of early and repeated telling and the chosen baby theme. The groundwork for the revolution in thinking about telling had been laid in the interwar years by psychiatrists William Healy, Sidney Tarachow, and Robert Knight, who first identified adoptees with particular psychological problems. Dr. Spock followed their lead and undoubtedly strengthened this negative perception by placing the section on adoption in his *Baby and Child Care* under the heading of "Special Problems."[47]

But it was the research of California psychoanalyst Marshall D. Schechter that triggered a twenty-year controversy over the issue of telling. Based on 120 children he saw in private practice between 1948 and 1953, Schechter reported in 1960 that by his calculation adopted children were overrepresented in his practice "a hundred-fold" compared with what could be expected in the general population. He suggested that adopted children's "neurotic and psychotic states" were due primarily to being told of their adoption "at the time of the Oedipal conflict." According to Schechter, informing the three-to six-year-old adopted child that he had a second set of parents prolonged and prevented the formation of a firm identity. Moreover, the child's "immature ego cannot cope with the knowledge of the rejection by its original parents," resulting in a "severe narcissistic injury." Schechter recommended postponing telling children of their adoption until the Oedipal phase was past and they had firmly identified with their parents.[48]

In the next three years, New York psychiatrist Lili E. Peller, in two papers presented to the Philadelphia Association for Psychoanalysis, agreed with Schechter's position and denounced adoption experts' advice on telling. Peller considered early and repeated telling "confusing and destructive" of the adopted child's identity. Repeated allusions to the child's adoption could lead only to one result: "it would convey to the child that he really is a stranger in the family." At what age should the adopted child be told? Because the family romance of having two sets of parents was an essential part of latency, the period during which sexuality becomes virtually dormant—from age five to puberty—Peller recommended that adoptive parents, perhaps assisted by a psychoanalytically trained authority figure, should convey the facts of adoption to the child when he or she reached the age of reason—ten to thirteen years. Although Peller conceded that the child should ultimately be told, she strongly advocated shrouding the adoption in secrecy. She criticized the idea of sending out announcements of the adoption and the practice of celebrating "adoption day" in the child's later years. Moreover, she praised the practice in some states of issuing new birth certificates that did not indicate the child was born to other parents.[49]

Peller also criticized that "unfortunate innovation," the chosen baby theme, though she was not the first person to denounce this tenet of telling. That distinction was reserved for Irene M. Josselyn, a psychiatrist at the Institute for Psychoanalysis in Chicago, who in 1955 first challenged the story. Josselyn questioned whether adoption workers should encourage parents to lie to their adopted children, since few parents actually had a choice of which child the agency offered them. Josselyn also pointed out that by emphasizing the chosen baby theme adoptive parents inadvertently forced the child to live up to standards of perfection, which bred resentment and insecurity. She counseled parents to use the chosen baby story only if they could "do it with a casualness, a touch of humor and an infrequency" that would not make it the focus of the adoptive relationship. Peller, too, considered the term "chosen baby" dishonest, frightening, and likely to induce insecurity in the child. Despite the positive message of being chosen specially by the adoptive parents, Peller claimed, the child realized that "he who has been chosen on account of certain values, while others were rejected, could in turn be rejected if he disappointed his parents." Unlike Josselyn, who implicitly sanctioned the chosen baby story by suggesting guidelines for its use, Peller's blanket condemnation of the story clearly left the impression that under no circumstances should adoption workers recommend it.[50]

Both Schechter and Peller strongly disapproved of telling children before they could comprehend the information about their adoption. But both agreed that children should eventually be told of the adoption, though they disagreed on the precise age, Schechter favoring the period after latency and Peller, age ten to thirteen. In several articles a decade later, Herbert Wieder, a psychoanalyst conducting research at the Adoption Study Center of the Brookdale Hospital Medical Center in Brooklyn, New York, would go one step further and practically advocate not telling, *ever.* Based on the findings of his clinical practice, Wieder denounced social workers' advice on telling for being empirically untested, urging instead that "the longer the communication can be put off the better." Wieder, like Schechter and Peller, rested his analysis on the classical Freudian doctrine of the family romance theory. His studies differed from earlier ones only in the vividness of his language. Wieder claimed that as adopted children listened to the adoption story, they came to believe that their adoptive mothers were rejecting them as "shameful, disgusting, or bad," a view that "revealed a self = baby = stool image of themselves which contributed to their tenuous level of self-esteem." Further, contended Wieder, after hearing of their adoption, his patients felt that their natural mothers had "cast them out to die," feelings that they then turned into fearful fantasies about abandonment. Calling the knowledge of adoption "a forceful pathogen in the mental life of young adopted children," Wieder concluded it caused a "deleterious effect on the adoptee's developmental processes, object relations, cognitive function and fantasy behavior."[51]

The studies by Schechter and Peller evoked an immediate critical response. By 1964, professionals outside the discipline of social work had strongly criticized the unscientific methodology and faulty theoretical underpinnings of the psychoanalytic advice to delay telling children of their adoption. Child psychiatrist James J. Lawton, Jr., and University of Minnesota clinical psychology instructor Seymour Z. Gross, for example, attacked the flawed statistical basis of the research by pointing out that case studies "lack generalizability, are open to bias, and allow too free rein of subjective impressions." They found Schechter's study scientifically untenable because of its failure to use a random sample of adopted children. They also demonstrated that Schechter and others ignored Freud's two-part formulation of the family romance by concentrating only on the first stage. Moreover, Lawton and Gross pointed out that Schechter's timing was wrong, since the final resolution of the Oedipal conflict occurred at or near puberty rather than the onset of the latency period. They concluded optimistically that "reasonably secure adoptive parents can tell the preschool child about his adoption without necessarily providing the stimuli for negative emotional reaction."[52]

Although adoption professionals prided themselves on reaching out to other disciplines such as pediatrics, psychiatry, and the law, few if any social workers in adoption embraced the psychoanalytic interpretation of telling. Adoption workers' position on the issue of delayed telling in the wake of Schechter's and Peller's articles can be gleaned from several articles that appeared in the Child Welfare League of America's house organ *Child Welfare,* the journal of professional social workers. In an article appearing in 1962, child psychiatrist Povl W. Toussieng agreed with Schechter that adopted children were overrepresented in the number of disturbed children he saw at the Menninger Clinic, but denied that the trauma resulted from telling. Instead, Toussieng attributed adopted children's emotional problems to the standard psychodynamic explanation: "an unconscious and unresolved aversion toward parenthood in one or both adoptive parents, particularly the mother." Uncharacteristically, the journal's editor, at the beginning of Toussieng's article, discredited Schechter's statistics on the overrepresentation of adopted children needing psychiatric care by noting he used the wrong population base for comparison. In addition, the editor, refusing to allow the article to stand alone, invited a response from Rita Dukette, Director of the Adoption Division, Illinois Children's Home and Aid Society. In the discussion that followed, Dukette criticized Toussieng for conflating agency and unlicensed placements in relation to the specific diagnoses of the children and for simplifying the complexities of the adoption process by ignoring such factors as the child's age at placement, sex, birth order, and existence of other siblings. Writing in *Child Welfare* two years later, psychologist Dorothy C. Krugman, consultant to six New York area child welfare agencies, attacked Schechter and Peller for reducing adopted children's emotional problems to the single factor of telling. Calling their methodology "disturbing," Krugman questioned the reliability of their findings when "scientific inquiry has taught us to be wary of attributing direct influence to the operation of a single variable."[53]

In the same year, 1964, the Child Welfare League of America gave its imprimatur to the rejection of delayed telling advice by reprinting an article from the *Encyclopedia of Mental Health* written by Viola W. Bernard, Clinical Professor of Psychiatry and Chief Psychiatric Consultant to a New York City adoption agency, the Louise Wise Services. Bernard affirmed all of the standard professional social workers' advice on telling. The child should be told of the adoption "as early as he starts to understand the language." Telling was a gradual process of communication over a period of time, not a single event. After reviewing the psychoanalytic studies on adoption revelation, Bernard rejected their recommendations to delay telling. She cited "preponderant expert opinion" that any "theoretical gains" from delayed telling were more than offset by damaging emotional problems. When the child sensed the "parental lies, half truths, and evasions" he would feel confusion, suspicion, and anxiety. If the child were to discover his adoption unexpectedly from others "his confidence in his parents may be shaken by feeling deceived, and the adoption is likely to be experienced not as an act of love but as a disaster." Rather than lie, Bernard recommended simplifying the truth to fit the young child's age level. Preeminent child welfare institutions such as the U.S. Children's Bureau followed the CWLA's lead and shaped its advice to adoptive parents about telling to conform with professional social work precepts.[54]

Bernard and other adoption experts based their rejection of psychoanalytic studies of telling on their methodological flaws. Aside from a 1967 British study, social workers had conducted little empirical research on adoption revelation. Were adoptive parents informing their children of their adoption? Earlier, anecdotal evidence suggested they were not, despite the adoption experts' advocacy of telling. Did early revelation of adoption cause adverse effects on adjustment later in life, as psychoanalysts claimed? How in fact did adopted children fare in later life? Although the CWLA had endorsed the traditional formula for telling by publishing Bernard's *Adoption,* that publication was not based on empirical research. In 1971, intending to remedy this oversight, the CWLA commissioned Benson Jaffee, associate professor of social work at the University of Washington, and David Fanshel, professor of social work at Columbia University, to investigate one hundred families who adopted children between 1931 and 1940. One of their major findings discounted the importance of adoption revelation in the adjustment of adoptees. Searching for a relationship between "adoptees' functioning and adjustment over the years and the particulars of how they were informed of their adoptive status," Jaffe and Fanshel found "no significant associations between outcome and the source, the timing, or the circumstances surrounding the initial revelation. Nor did the frequency with which the subject of adoption was discussed over the years or the amount or accuracy of information given the adoptees regarding their natural parents prove to be significantly correlated with how the adoptees subsequently fared." Although their findings affirmed neither position, adoption workers acted as if they now had empirical confirmation of the traditional interpretation of telling and could confidently reject the psychoanalysts' clinical findings.[55]

Nevertheless, adoption workers did not reject all psychoanalytic insights. They wholeheartedly accepted Peller's suggestion to discard the chosen baby theme, though her advice was no more methodologically sound than other psychoanalytic conclusions about telling. Their decision was based on their long-held sensitivity of the stigmatizing effects of language in adoption. During the Progressive Era, social workers waged a successful struggle in several state legislatures to substitute the phrase "born out of wedlock" for the terms "bastard" and "illegitimate." In 1955, Louise Richmond counseled parents telling children of their adoption to use the words "your first mother (or father)" or "your first parents" instead of "your real mother" or "your own mother" because the word "first" was both true and would not disturb the child.[56]

Ever alert for negative connotations of words associated with adoption, social workers had little difficulty accepting psychoanalytic advice to stop using the phrase "chosen baby." Bernard's 1964 guide for adoptive parents, *Adoption*, reprinted and widely disseminated by the CWLA, provided the first indication that social workers had decided to reject the "chosen baby" theme. Citing "psychological drawbacks," Bernard echoed Peller's objections to using the chosen baby story. It induced insecurity and anxiety: children might wonder, if they were "chosen" might they become "unchosen"? And if a child was chosen from among "others," what had happened to the others? Had the adopted child previously been rejected by other parents who chose someone else? Above all, Bernard stressed, the chosen baby story was untrue. Adoptive couples did not shop around and choose a baby from many children on display. If anything, they chose an agency.[57]

Popular adoption advice books quickly transmitted adoption experts' acceptance of the psychoanalytic interpretation of the chosen baby theme. This is well illustrated by a comparison of the 1951 and 1965 editions of Florence Rondell and Ruth Michaels's popular *The Adopted Family*, a slim, two-book set containing *The Family That Grew*, a story intended to be read to adopted children, and *You and Your Child*, a guide for adoptive parents. In the 1951 version of *The Family that Grew*, the child was told:

> Daddy had chosen Mommy for his wife. Mommy had chosen Daddy for her husband. And now both of them could choose you for their child.
>
> Choosing a child is called adopting a child, and the minute they saw you, they wanted to adopt you.

In contrast, the 1965 edition of *The Family That Grew* substituted in the first paragraph above the word "wanted" for "chosen" and "could choose" and reduced the second paragraph to the innocuous sentence "This is called adopting a child."[58] Similar changes occurred in the adoptive parents' guidebook that accompanied the storybook. Whereas in the 1951 edition Rondell and Michaels urged adoptive parents to use the words "chosen" and "adopted" together and interchangeably, the 1965 version echoed the adoption establishment's acceptance of the psychoanalytic interpretation and rejected the term "chosen."[59]

Adoption workers' rejection of the chosen baby theme was based more on logical consistency than empirical research. Conspicuously missing from their evaluation of the chosen baby story was the adopted person's viewpoint. In 1973, John Troseliotis remedied this oversight in his study of seventy Scottish adoptees. He found that "irrespective of what experts in this field may have to say, adoptees . . . said that stories about being 'selected', 'chosen', 'special', 'precious', 'needed,' etc. made them feel 'good inside' or 'proud' or 'pleased' or 'different and special.' " Troseliotis's findings had little effect on most professional and popular literature, which persisted in denouncing the chosen baby theme. The most dramatic evidence of the pervasiveness of the psychoanalytic interpretation of the chosen baby theme was evident in the 1977 edition of Wasson's best-selling *The Chosen Baby*. In the new edition, only the book's title echoed the original theme; all references in the text to adoptive parents choosing children had been silently removed.[60]

The CWLA's republication of Viola Bernard's 1964 *Adoption* and Jaffe and Fanshel's 1971 empirical repudiation of the harmful effects of early telling marked a watershed in social workers' leadership on the issue of adoption revelation. In contrast to the successful trend to envelop adoption case records in secrecy, social workers resisted psychoanalytic advice to do the same for telling. Instead, they continued to advise adoptive parents to tell their children of their adoption. But beginning in the early 1970s, the question of adoption revelation became a secondary concern as children previously considered unadoptable became adoptable and more controversial issues, such as transracial, intercountry, and special needs adoption, took precedence. The topic of adoption revelation fell by default to psychiatrists and popular writers, who researched and transmitted to the wider public the latest social science pronouncements on telling.

The result was a cacophony of advice. By the mid-1960s and continuing for the next fifteen years, conflicting notions about telling arose within the psychoanalytic profession and between psychoanalysts and social workers. As the debate shifted to demonstrating empirically whether adopted children were overrepresented in the psychiatric population, most psychoanalysts in this period, except for Wieder, stopped correlating adopted children's psychiatric problems with telling. Nevertheless, the psychoanalytic interpretation of telling remained influential in the popular media, even though it was criticized within the profession and rejected by the social work establishment. Alongside it, adoption experts' traditional advice to tell early and often persisted. Thus, both interpretations of telling confronted adoptive parents in the 1960s and 1970s as they searched for advice in popular magazines and adoption self-help books.[61]

The psychoanalytic interpretation of telling found its way into popular discourse almost immediately. In 1963, for example, a mother told the readers of *Parents' Magazine* that she sought professional help when her adopted daughter, Amy, began to have difficulties in the third grade. The psychiatrist connected Amy's lack of self-confidence in school with the questions she had been asking about her natural parents. He suggested that the adoptive parents were placing an unnecessary emotional burden on Amy by reiterating the story of her adoption. "There were times," the psychiatrist said, "when the truth could be unnecessarily cruel." Now, when Amy began inquiring about her natural parents and questioning her own self-worth, her mother feared revealing that Amy had been born out of wedlock. Instead, heeding the psychiatrist's advice, Amy's parents fabricated a story that the adoption resulted from her parents' death. The mother noted triumphantly the lie's effect: "There never was such an ecstatic orphan!" Soon after, Amy's schoolwork improved, her personality blossomed, and her friendships and interests multiplied. As for the future, the adoptive mother was sure that when Amy grew up she would forgive her adoptive parents for lying.[62]

Adoptive parents could find in self-help manuals similar advice to conceal the fact of adoption. Joseph G. Ansfield, an assistant professor of psychiatry at the Chicago Medical School and consultant to the Illinois Department of Mental Health, counseled parents in 1971 not to tell children of their adoption because the information would hurt them. Children in possession of the knowledge that they had been adopted, whether told lovingly or discovering it in an unexpected and traumatic manner, "may become depressed, angry, hurt, and embarrassed." Ansfield based his advice on his clinical practice with adolescent adopted children and his belief that the "so-called experts'" advice on telling was outdated and untested. He believed that the root of the adopted child's psychological problems was the invidious distinction society made between adopted and nonadopted children. He went so far as to suggest eliminating the word "adopted" from the language, because "all children should be loved for themselves, not merely because they are the physical extensions of their procreators."[63]

Because society stigmatized adoptees and because he believed that the later in their psychosexual development children discovered they were adopted the better, Ansfield made practical suggestions to conceal the knowledge of adoption. These included finding an adoption agency or a physician who would respect the parents' wishes to keep the adoption a secret, restricting radically the number of people who know of the adoption (including keeping the information from other adoptive parents and school officials), and storing adoption documents in a safety deposit box. Ansfield also suggested that the ideal time to adopt was when the prospective parents anticipated moving to a new community, because there would be "no need to inform the new friends, employers, or even relatives that the child is adopted." If, after all of these precautions, the child discovered that he was adopted, the adoptive parents should not deny it, but explain truthfully and logically the reasons for concealment. They should tell the child they had loved him too much to see him hurt and they "chose never to think of him as someone different, a second-class child, an inferior or an unfortunate genetic product, but they thought of him as their own flesh and blood." Ansfield clinched his argument by citing the "true feelings" of his adolescent patients about being adopted. He claimed "they are unhappy because they feel different, different because they are adopted, and what is more important they have been treated differently by their parents for this very reason."

During the mid-1960s and early 1970s, alongside popular psychoanalytic accounts advising adoptive parents not to tell could also be found advice that conformed to the traditional formula of telling. A Menninger Foundation psychoanalyst, for example, informed adoptive parents in *Time Magazine* that children should be told the facts of their adoption between the ages of four and seven. Similarly, members of the National Council of Adoptive Parents were assured in their newsletter, *National Adoptalk,* that children should be told of their adoption "as soon as the child can even begin to understand, probably about four years old" and were urged to repeat the information "from time to time" to ensure comprehension. Readers of Joan McNamara's popular *The Adoption Advisor* were also counseled to tell children frankly of their adoption at an early age. But McNamara cautioned not to overemphasize the telling because it would "emphasize the differences instead of making adoption seem natural" and would cause the child anxieties.[64]

By the mid-1970s, however, the cacophony of different interpretations about telling gave way to a single voice: openness not only in telling but in all aspects of adoption. The adoption rights movement would inaugurate a reassessment of the legitimacy of secrecy in all aspects of adoption and start a debate that is still unresolved today.

The Emergence of the Adoption Rights Movement

By World War II, adoption records were sealed. There was no protest, however, from adult adoptees or natural parents—no adoption rights movement (ARM)—for the simple reason that the records were accessible one way or another to those people involved in the adoption process who wanted them. The seeds of the ARM were sown only after the end of the war, when there was an enormous increase in the number of middle-class single mothers who relinquished for adoption their children born out of wedlock. By demanding secrecy from adoption agency officials, middle-class unwed mothers provided a new and compelling rationale for sealing the records in the first place. From keeping the public out, the rationale became keeping those most directly connected with adoption out. Thus, the sealing of adoption records and a steep rise in rates of illegitimacy among middle-class unwed mothers set the stage for the origins of the ARM. Without promises of secrecy given by adoption agency officials to these women, there would have been neither aggrieved adult adoptees nor official resistance to opening the records.

The convergence of these factors helps explain the timing of the ARM and why the demand to unseal adoption records began in the 1970s and not the 1950s or the 1930s. Most significant to the origins and subsequent progress of the adoption rights movement were its grassroots leaders, Jean Paton, born a generation too early, and especially the militant housewife Florence Anna Fisher and author Betty Jean Lifton. They were responsible not only for organizing the first adoption search groups, but also for convincing the public of the justice of their cause and overcoming the indifference or opposition of the adoption establishment. Crucial to achieving this latter task was a second group of spokespersons for the ARM, Arthur D. Sorosky, Annette Baran, and Reuben Pannor, who emerged in the early 1970s. These adoption researchers were responsible for providing the movement with its social science ideology. Their intellectual orientation led them to downplay Fisher's emphasis on adoptees' constitutional rights. Instead, Sorosky and associates medicalized the sealed adoption records issue. They made adoptees' identity conflicts central to the ARM by using the discourse of social science to demonstrate the therapeutic value of adoptees' genealogical searches and reunions. Finally, the mass media played a key role in making the ARM acceptable to American public opinion and eventually to the adoption establishment through exposure of the political secrets and cover-ups involved in the Watergate scandal, dissemination of the ARM's social science ideology, and broadcast of the TV miniseries *Roots.*

The "first" adoption rights movement can trace its origins to 1949. In that year, Jean M. Paton, a forty-one-year-old social worker and adoptee single-handedly pioneered the rights of adoptees. For some time, Paton had been dissatisfied with the legal and technical approaches that institutions took to solve problems of adoption. In an article submitted to *Mental Hygiene,* Paton singled out for condemnation adoption agencies and courts that refused to cooperate with adult adoptees and their natural parents in their searches. Paton's solution to this problem was novel. She did not appeal to the mass media to influence adoption agencies to open their records or mobilize public opinion to pressure legislatures or courts to repeal the laws sealing adoption records. Instead, because Paton was acutely sensitive to adoptees' powerlessness, she believed that they must not be dependent on social workers or public opinion for permission to search; they had to take responsibility for their own lives. They needed to create an institution independent of traditional authorities to facilitate searches for their parents or siblings or, in the case of natural mothers, for the children they had relinquished. To that end, Paton called for the creation of the first national, mutual-consent, voluntary adoption registry. Her "Mutual Registration" program would allow natural parents and adult adoptees to register identifying and nonidentifying information about themselves "together with a request that each be notified when both have registered and been matched." The mass media and the marshaling of public opinion were not only beside the point, but in Paton's mind they were counterproductive to the empowerment of adoptees.[1]

The editor of *Mental Hygiene* ultimately rejected Paton's article containing the idea of an adoption registry because he found the idea of adult adoptees and their original families re-establishing a relationship with each other too controversial, too vague, and too expensive. Moreover, he felt that the proper forum for debating the issue was the field of social work, not mental hygiene. The editor advised Paton that the question "must be answered by those who have had experience in the field of adoption"—that is, adoption workers and agencies, the very people and institutions that Paton rejected. Paton claimed that it was this editor's letter that was "as responsible as any single experience" for setting her off on her life's work. Henceforth, she dedicated herself to explaining the adoption experience to a wider public, providing a healthy self-image for adoptees, and helping to facilitate meetings between adult adoptees and their families of origin.[2]

Over the next four years, Paton quit her social work position, enrolled in "a hodgepodge of courses" at the University of Pennsylvania, and founded in 1953 the Life History Study Center as well as the first adoptee search organization, Orphan Voyage. The Center's initial goals were to make adoptees visible, give them a social identity, and overturn the belief that "the adult adopted [person] had nothing to say." To this end, Paton hit upon the idea of placing a notice for seven weeks in the personals column of the *Saturday Review of Literature* requesting persons adopted before 1932 to aid the Center in a research project. Initially, sixty-four adoptees responded, of whom forty subsequently filled out questionnaires. The source material contained in the forty questionnaires became the basis for the publication in 1954 of *The Adopted Break Silence*. For the first time, a book recorded verbatim the thoughts of adult adoptees on a multitude of subjects ranging from their attitudes toward being adopted to their attempts to locate their natural parents. Despite its small sample, *The Adopted Break Silence* is notable for its complexity: the community of adoptees was revealed as a diverse one that did not speak with a single voice.

Moreover, Paton provided readers with a number of conclusions, one of which claimed that adoptees had a psychological need to search for their natural parents.

Rebuffed by commercial publishers, Paton published the book privately. After a few favorable reviews, Paton recalled, "a great silence fell." Paton attributed this to the refusal of adoption workers to reexamine their policy of declining to disclose identifying information to clients who returned to the agency to search for their families of origin. For the rest of her life—and at this writing, she is alive and well—Paton continued to help adult adoptees and natural parents search for their relatives, championed the opening of adoption records, and published a newsletter promoting adoption rights and conveying the experiences of adoptees to a wider public.[3]

Paton's legacy was to give adoptees a voice, by collecting and publishing their life histories. When Paton began her research, both the mental and the experiential world of the adult adopted person was unknown. From the perspective of adoption agency policy, there were no *adult* adoptees. From the adoptees' perspective, their world was isolated and concealed a shameful secret, best kept from an unsympathetic public. Paton created and publicized a social entity: the adoption community, composed of adult adoptees who demanded recognition of and respect for their special circumstances. She was also prescient in identifying what was central to understanding the experience of ARM adherents: their frustration and anger over their inability to acquire knowledge of their natural parents. It is noteworthy that Paton's solution to facilitating adoptee searches was the establishment of a national mutual consent voluntary adoption registry, not the unsealing of adoption records. Perhaps Paton's belief that adoptees must not be dependent on social work or legislative institutions dictated the adoption registry solution. Or perhaps because Paton had little difficulty in finding her natural mother (she was fortunate enough to have gained access to her original birth certificate in 1942 before the law was interpreted to exclude adoptees) she never experienced the anger and frustration so common to later adoption rights advocates, such as Florence Anna Fisher and Betty Jean Lifton, whose efforts to find their natural parents were thwarted repeatedly. For whatever reason, Paton's enemy, at least initially, was never only the sealed records. Her vision was much wider.

Yet Paton's plea for rethinking adoptees' experience and for creating a national adoption registry was greeted by silence. Her one-woman crusade garnered hardly any national media attention, caused no adoption agencies to liberalize their disclosure policy, and induced no state legislatures to repeal their sealed adoption records statutes. The reasons for the movement's early lack of influence are not hard to identify. By isolating the adoption rights movement from public opinion and the political process, Paton ensured that by almost any standard the movement would have little effect outside a small circle of supporters. Moreover, the conservative, conformist 1950s was hardly a time for challenging conventional notions, whether in politics, social work, or family relations. As Paton herself later admitted, "I realized that I was going one way and the culture the other—toward sealed records."[4]

By the early 1970s, all this had changed. Three developments were responsible for the "second" adoption rights movement. First, there was a long-term precondition: the buildup in the two decades following the Second World War of a critical mass of adult adoptees who had grown up in a world of sealed adoption records. Unlike their pre–World War II counterparts, these adult adoptees were denied easy access to their adoption records. The thwarting of their desire to view their records was the tinder from which the ARM ignited.

Second, there was an intermediate precipitant: the existence of a radically different cultural milieu—the 1960s—characterized by grassroots protest movements, sexual experimentation and freedom, and the rise of rights-consciousness. The era began with the civil rights movement, the campaign against poverty, the Vietnam War, campus unrest and New Left student protesters, and the growth of a "counterculture" during the Kennedy and Johnson administrations. By the late 1960s and early 1970s "identity politics" overshadowed earlier liberal movements as various activist groups—including the Black Power, feminist, Indian rights, and Gay Liberation movements—organized to gain political legitimacy, economic power, and cultural authority. These movements were grounded in a vision of egalitarian, participatory democracy that questioned all existing systems of authority based on hierarchy, expertise, or wealth. The movements' democratic ethos sought to include all people in society, empower individuals through social participation, and create a loving community from atomistic and alienated youth. Often outrageous, exasperating, and heroic, these movements fundamentally challenged and transformed the nation's political and social institutions and racial and sexual mores. Their legacy was mixed. They ended legal segregation, broke down Southern voting restrictions, shortened the Vietnam War, stigmatized racism and sexism, and altered gender roles, resulting in a more egalitarian society. But the sixties' political and social movements also left the nation more ideologically polarized and fragmented than when the decade began.[5]

Of particular importance to the origins of the ARM was the sixties' youth culture's "sexual revolution," which successfully challenged many of the sexual taboos of the 1950s, including the stigma of illegitimacy. By the late sixties, having a child out of wedlock or being a child out of wedlock held none of the terrors of two decades earlier. Indeed, in the youth counterculture's philosophy, unrepressed sexuality "represented both a personal act of liberation and a form of radical politics." By the beginning of the seventies, many adult adoptees viewed their adoptive status in terms of liberation and rights, not shame and fear. Sixties protesters' emphasis on rights also provided the ARM with an important strand of its ideology: that adoptees had a right to access their records. The ARM's rights ideology was reinforced by the 1960s Warren Court's emphasis on the expansion of individual rights. Landmark decisions on voting, school prayer, criminal rights, libel law, pornography, and school and housing segregation signaled that "a Rights Revolution was at hand."[6]

Finally, there was an immediate trigger that set off the second adoption rights movement. In 1971 there emerged the movement's most vocal and visible leader, Florence Fisher, a New York City housewife. Fisher had been adopted as an infant, but that fact was kept from her until she became a young adult. During a long and frustrating search for her natural parents, Fisher was denied knowledge about the identity of her family from lawyers, doctors, the clerk of New York's Surrogate Court, and the nuns of St. Anthony's Hospital. She finally located her mother after twenty years of searching.

Important social movements are often ignited by small events. The civil rights movement was galvanized by Rosa Parks's refusal to give up her seat in a crowded bus; the environmental movement was inspired by the publication of Rachel Carson's *Silent Spring*. Fisher's traumatic odyssey prompted her to place a brief notice in the *New*

York Times requesting contact with other adoptees "to exchange views on the adoptive situation and for mutual assistance in search for natural parents." After an overwhelming response, Fisher founded the Adoptees' Liberty Movement Association (ALMA). Along with aiding adult adoptees searching for their natural parents, ALMA's principal goals were "to abolish the existing practice of 'sealed records'" and to secure the "opening of records to any adopted person *over eighteen* who wants, for any reason, to see them."[7]

The connection between the first adoption rights movement and the second was substantial. Many of Fisher's efforts to build and organize an adoptees' rights movement borrowed, without public acknowledgment, one or another of Paton's ideas. These included the placing of an ad in the print media to attract supporters and modeling ALMA, with its mutual-consent, voluntary adoption registry, on Paton's search group, Orphan Voyage. But Fisher added a completely different tone and emphasis to the movement, which clearly differentiated it from the earlier search groups. Perhaps inspired by sixties leaders such as Stokely Carmichael, Bella Abzug, and Jerry Rubin or simply a product of her own commanding personality, Fisher's rhetoric was angry and inflexible. To news reporters, Fisher unabashedly admitted, "Yes, I'm militant," and refused to compromise when advancing the movement's goals. Typically, she was quoted in the press as declaring, "We demand free access to our original birth certificates and the records of our adoption."[8] ALMA's emphasis on adopted adults' "rights" and its demand to repeal sealed adoption records statutes were unprecedented.

In 1971, the torch of leadership was symbolically passed when Paton asked Fisher to take her place at the World Conference on Adoption and Foster Care held in Milan, Italy, and deliver a paper on American orphans.[9] From her headquarters in New York City, Fisher organized local branches of ALMA in Chicago, Los Angeles, and Fort Lauderdale. In 1973 she published a book recounting the dramatic story of her success in reuniting with her natural family entitled *The Search for Anna Fisher.* By 1974, Fisher had become the undisputed leader of the adoption rights movement and the head of the nation's largest and most influential adoption search group.

ALMA's example sparked the creation of hundreds of other adoptee search groups across the United States, Canada, and the United Kingdom with such names as Yesterday's Children (Illinois), Adoptees' Identity Movement (Michigan), Reunite (Ohio), Parent Finders (Canada), and Genealogy Source (U.K.). By 1975, over 3,000 adult adoptees and 1,500 mothers had returned to 155 adoption agencies searching for information about their families and children. The multiplicity of adoptee search groups led in 1978 to the formation of a national umbrella organization, the American Adoption Congress (AAC). Composed of most adoptee search groups, except ALMA, and thousands of individuals, the AAC was dedicated to changing the public's attitudes toward sealed adoption records and determined to lobby legislators to repeal laws that prevented adult adoptees from viewing their records.[10]

Opposition to the ARM emerged immediately. In the wake of the publication of *The Search for Anna Fisher*, the Adoptive Parents Committee, 1,000 members strong, denounced ALMA's goals of opening adoption records as "an invasion of privacy on the part of the child into the lives of the biological parents who may not want to be identified." In 1974, Ralph D. Maxfield, who had been adopted as a child, founded the Association for the Protection of the Adoptive Triangle, a nonprofit informational organization dedicated to preventing open adoption records activists from "gaining their 'rights' at the expense of the 'rights' of everyone else." He and his 3,000 members argued that permitting adoptees access to their adoption records threatened "the very existence of the institution of adoption by destroying the factor of confidentiality." In 1980, these groups were supplanted by the National Committee for Adoption, an informational and advocacy group that opposed open records and promoted the continued confidentiality of adoption records.[11]

The initial reaction to the ARM by most of America's major institutions—from the national media and professional social work organizations to state and federal courts—was also negative. The influential East Coast media greeted the ARM with indifference. Despite the multiplication of adoptee search groups throughout the nation and the publicity surrounding Fisher's book, the national media were not particularly interested in reporting on the ARM. Between 1971 and 1975 the *New York Times* barely noticed the movement, publishing only one article, which appeared not in the news section but in the "Family, Food, Fashions, and Furnishings" section. During the same period, the *Washington Post* did not carry a single piece on the ARM. Similarly, the three major television networks' evening news shows ignored the movement, failing to report on ALMA and the adoptees' search movement until late 1976. Of the two major news magazines, only *Time* carried a single article.[12]

The reasons why the East Coast media overlooked the ARM, a social movement born literally in its own backyard, can be surmised. Florence Fisher was an unknown housewife, unconnected to the nation's circles of power. Moreover, the objects of her anger—adoption agencies and adoptive parents—were, at least in society's eyes, altruistic and admirable. Not surprisingly, given Fisher's low social and political status and her attack on respected social institutions, the East Coast media waited to see which way the wind was blowing. And because that wind initially came howling out of the "loony" West, the media were naturally reluctant to take the ARM seriously. The top TV networks' failure to headline the ARM is easily explained by their predilection to follow the lead of the major East Coast newspapers, which all but ignored the movement.[13]

By 1976, however, the mass media's interest in the ARM had increased significantly. A seismic shift in American's toleration of official claims of secrecy took place as the result of an unrelated media event that dominated the news and deeply affected the national psyche: the political scandal known as Watergate. It began on June 17, 1972, when Republican White House operatives broke into the headquarters of the Democratic National Committee in the Watergate complex in Washington, D.C., and ended two years later on August 9, 1974, with the resignation of President Richard Nixon. In between, Watergate became a national, public event. Millions of Americans were riveted to their televisions or read in their newspapers the latest installment of the unfolding constitutional crisis. At the heart of Watergate was the issue of secrecy. Would President Nixon be able to conceal the evidentiary link between the Watergate burglars and the White House? Again and again—when Nixon fired Special Prosecutor Archibald Cox, for example, or when an eighteen-minute gap in the White House tapes was revealed—the public subliminally experienced what every member of the Adoption Rights Movement had routinely encountered: the shock and anger of being denied information to which they felt entitled. At the same time, another series of events—the revelations of perjury and corruption by high-ranking White House officials during the Senate Select Committee hearings, the Supreme Court's unanimous decision ordering Nixon to turn over the tapes, and ultimately Nixon's resignation from the presidency— reinforced in the public's mind the view that openness, truthfulness, and the free flow of information were essential to a democratic society. At the most basic level the connection was inevitable: what was good for democracy must, by extension, be good for adoptees.[14]

Building on Americans' decade-long distrust of the government's involvement in the Vietnam War, Watergate was the last straw: it thoroughly, if temporarily, discredited the concept of the legitimacy of government secrecy by revealing that those who invoked secrecy or executive privilege did so above all to conceal their abuse of power or participation in illegal or immoral activities. As a result of Watergate, Congress passed a series of laws that reflected the nation's distrust of government and that were designed to make public disclosure of governmental operations easier, including the War Powers Act of 1974, the Privacy Act of 1974, the Federal Elections Campaign Amendments of 1974, and the renewal of the Freedom of Information Act. Watergate thus made official claims of secrecy suspect in the culture at large and created the cultural context for a national presumption in favor of honesty and disclosure in public affairs in general.

Although few made the connection between Watergate and the ARM, the burden of proof shifted ever so slightly from those demanding access to adoption records to those invoking the right to conceal information. By analogy, it followed that those officials who favored keeping adoption records sealed must be covering up adoption agency blunders or were harming adoptees by preventing them from having access to information crucial to their psychological and medical health. Adoption agency officials were put on the defensive; the traditional presumption of doubt about releasing adopted records shifted from adult adoptees and birth mothers to social workers, who in the wake of the adoption rights movement and Watergate had to justify their practice of not opening adoption files.

A second factor crucial to legitimizing the adoption rights movement was the popularization of the psychological argument that knowledge of one's birth parents was crucial to the adopted person's self-identity. In contrast to the red-hot rhetoric of "adoptee *rights*" that militant activists like Florence Fisher demanded, the public was inundated with the cool, objective, pseudoscientific discourse of social science research supporting the idea that searching for one's biological family was of great therapeutic value and of little risk or harm to the participants.

These ideas gained their power from being widely disseminated and amplified by the West Coast print media, especially the *Los Angeles Times*. In the symbiosis that developed, the *LA Times* reported repeatedly on the research of three Los Angeles professionals who, in turn, used the print media to advance the ARM and their careers. The three were a child psychiatrist, Arthur D. Sorosky, Assistant Clinical Professor in the Division of Child Psychiatry at UCLA, and two social workers, Annette Baran, Director of the Adolescent Treatment Program in the Triage Department of Psychiatry at UCLA, and Reuben Pannor, Director of Social Work and Research at the Vista Del Mar Child-Care Service in Los Angeles. Sorosky, Baran, and Pannor quickly became the intellectual patron saints of the adoption rights movement, demonstrating an uncanny knack for using the mass media as a research data base as well as for advocacy and self-promotion. While articles about adoption languished in specialized journals, Sorosky, Baran, and Pannor's method of promoting the cause of opening the adoption records in the news media and mass circulation magazines (in addition to professional journals) exposed their work to an unprecedented degree to the social work community and the public at large. The influence and ubiquity of Sorosky and associates' studies on the ARM cannot be overemphasized. No other body of work would be so universally cited as portraying accurately the psychological dynamics of adult adoptees and natural parents searching for their biological relations.

Sorosky, Baran, and Pannor began their research in late 1972 and by 1973 had formed the Adoption Research Project. From 1974 through 1978, Sorosky, Baran, and Pannor published at least eleven articles and a book. In one year alone, January 1974 to January 1975, they published four articles, three of which appeared in the social work journals *Social Casework,* the *Journal of Youth and Adolescence,* and the *Journal of Jewish Communal Service.* The fourth appeared in the mass-circulation magazine *Psychology Today,* ensuring wide dissemination of their findings. All of the articles contained virtually the same information, often with identical wording. All advocated opening adoption records, either by refuting what they saw as the unfounded fears of natural parents, adult adoptees, and adoptive parents, or by trumpeting the positive results of a policy of openness. Single-handedly Sorosky, Baran, and Pannor provided the ARM and other proponents of open adoption records with language and arguments that bore the incontestable cachet of social science and medical authority.[15]

Sorosky, Baran, and Pannor transformed the language of adoption masterfully. They succeeded in popularizing the term "adoption triangle," though this was soon altered to "adoption triad."[16] By connecting natural parents, adoptees, and adoptive parents under a single rubric, Sorosky and associates forcefully reminded social workers and the public that adoption included natural parents, especially a mother, who had become all but invisible as the profession emphasized finding parents for dependent children and concealing the identity of unwed mothers. They were also influential in popularizing the term "birth parents" and "birth mother" in place of "natural parents" and "natural mother," in order to avoid offense to adoptive parents, who might resent the implication that they were "unnatural" parents. The inclusion of birth mothers in the adoption triangle underscored another radically new idea that challenged the conventional way of conceiving of adoption policy and practice: the notion that adoption is a lifelong experience for all adoption triad members. Although birth mothers relinquished all their legal rights to their children, Sorosky, Baran, and Pannor linked them with the other members of the adoption triad for life because "their feelings of loss, pain, and mourning do not disappear."[17]

In addition to transforming adoption language, Sorosky, Baran, and Pannor addressed the particular worries each member of the adoption triad had about opening the adoption records. This strategy was necessary because, for different reasons, searching was assumed to be inherently perilous for each adoption triad member. The risk to adoptees was thought to be twofold. First, initiating a search invited being labeled an ingrate at best, socially maladjusted at worse. Second, a successful search contained the potential for disappointment and even the possibility of rejection by one's birth mother. For the birth mother, a successful search could lead to the revelation of a past life that she had successfully concealed from her new family. Having sought and received a promise of anonymity, a birth mother had much to lose if suddenly "discovered" by the child she had relinquished for adoption. Consequently, it was believed that birth mothers were opposed to opening sealed adoption records to facilitate searches by adoptees. It was widely assumed that adoptive parents also opposed open records because they envisioned the possibility that they would lose their child's love to the birth mother.

Addressing the motivation of adult adoptees who searched for their birth parents, Sorosky, Baran, and Pannor removed the stigma from searching by revealing that a mere 4 percent of searchers in their sample of 50 adoptees conformed to the "standard psychiatric assumption that the search for the natural parent was a search for love and affection." Instead, their evidence demonstrated that for most adopted persons searching for one's birth parents stemmed from "an innate curiosity about their genealogical past." The desire for background information was "ubiquitous to all adoptees" because adoptive parents either withheld genealogical information from them or revealed the adoption late in the child's life, thereby shocking and confusing them. Those who searched did so "simply because they have bright, curious minds and approach all of life's mysteries in the same manner." These searchers were "preoccupied with existential concerns and a feeling of isolation and alienation due to a break in the continuity of life through the generations that their adoption represents." Searching was triggered by milestones such as marriage, the birth of the adoptee's first child, or the death of an adoptive parent, that produced a feeling of genealogical bewilderment. The three researchers reassured adoptees that searching "may have nothing to do with quality of the adoptive relationship." In fact, it took "a special kind of person to persevere" in searching under current restricted conditions.[18]

Sorosky, Baran, and Pannor qualified their argument by noting two exceptions to their benign theory of universal adoptee search motivation. They admitted the existence of obsessive and neurotic adoptee searchers and identified what they labeled "quasi-searching," the practice of adolescent adoptees who were merely trying out new identities or behaviors. But they gave the distinct impression that these searchers were a small minority who could be safely ignored. According to the authors, what most concerned adopted persons who searched for biological family members—their "uppermost consideration"—was the completely respectable sixties ideal: "the need to establish a clearer self-identity." Not only was searching not a sign of mental instability, Sorosky, Baran, and Pannor reported, the overwhelming majority of adult adopted persons in their study "personally benefitted from the reunion" and felt more "whole and integrated as individuals." Even adoptees who had disappointing reunions felt that they had benefitted from the experience, "no matter what the outcome was."[19]

However, in the articles they published in professional psychiatric journals the three researchers presented a much less benign interpretation of why adoptees searched. These articles are significant not only for what they included but also for what they left out of the pieces they wrote for social work journals and mass-market magazines. Completing a review of the psychoanalytic literature on the incidence of identity conflicts in adopted persons, Sorosky, Baran, and Pannor found that they fell into four categories: "(a) disturbances in early object relations; (b) complications in the resolution of the oedipal complex; (c) prolongation of the 'family romance' fantasy; and (d) 'genealogical bewilderment.' " Missing was any mention of adopted persons' "innate curiosity about their genealogical past" or the notion that they possessed some special power of perseverance. Instead, Sorosky and associates concluded that the existing psychoanalytic literature validated their research findings that adult adoptees were "more vulnerable than the population at large to the development of identity problems in late adolescence and young adulthood because of the greater likelihood of encountering difficulties in the working through of the psychosexual aspects of personality development." Two years later, the researchers expanded on their findings. Adopted adolescents were now held to be more prone than nonadopted adolescents to aggressive, sexual, identity, dependency–independency, and social conflicts. They also were said to be uniquely prone to develop symptoms of an "adoption syndrome," which included genealogical bewilderment, compulsive pregnancy, the roaming phenomenon, and the search for biological relatives. In these articles, Sorosky, Baran, and Pannor provided the ARM with its most persuasive therapeutic rationale: adopted persons searched because there was something psychologically wrong with them.[20]

Assuaging the fears of birth parents, especially birth mothers, at opening adoption records was another matter. How could one convince birth mothers that repealing the sealed adoption records laws was benign when they dreaded that the revelation of bearing an illegitimate child in the past would destroy their present family? Moreover, did the adoptee's need to know take precedence over a birth mother's right to privacy? Rather than tackle these issues head on, Sorosky, Baran, and Pannor presented findings that suggested birth mothers' fears were greatly exaggerated by adoption agencies and adoptive parents. In their sample, Sorosky, Baran, and Pannor discovered that contrary to social workers' beliefs, "two thirds of [birth] parents indicated a strong desire to be available for reunion should the child they relinquished request it." With society's changing attitudes toward illegitimacy, it was now much easier for birth mothers to admit what had occurred in the past. Birth mothers no longer feared, as they did a generation earlier, that revealing the fact that they bore a child out of wedlock would ruin their lives. From the hundreds of the letters they received, the researchers quoted a forty-eight-year-old married mother of five to illustrate this common theme: "I would give anything if she wanted to meet me. I could tell my family. My husband knows, and my children would understand. I don't feel that I have the right to interfere with her life . . . That doesn't mean that I don't continue to love her and to want to know her. If she's out there looking for me, I hope she finds me." Even birth fathers, the most elusive of adoption triad members, were reported to be "delighted to be found" by their birth children. Some were actively searching themselves.[21]

Although society's more liberal attitude toward sex lessened the stigma of illegitimacy that birth mothers felt, it was a psychological imperative that ultimately was responsible for their newfound desire for contact with the children they had relinquished for adoption. According to Sorosky and associates, birth mothers "harbored deep, unresolved feelings" after giving up their children that traumatized them for the rest of their lives. The researchers cited the same forty-eight-year-old married mother's experience as typical:

> My social worker told me I was doing the best thing for the baby by placing her for adoption. She assured me that I would forget the pain,

and that after I married and had a family, I would never think of this baby any more. She was dead wrong. You never put such an experience behind you. No matter how happy I am, or how good I feel about my family, I will always wonder about that first baby, and wish that somehow I could see her and know how she is.

Sorosky, Baran, and Pannor concluded from such letters that "a significant percentage of birth mothers have a life-long unfulfilled need for further information and in some cases for a contact with the relinquished child." Such a claim became the ideological basis for the open adoption movement.[22]

Sorosky, Baran, and Pannor had the least sympathy for adoptive parents' fears of opening adoption files and genealogical searches. They used pejorative language couched in psychological jargon to condemn what they identified as adoptive parents' overprotectiveness and inflexible child-rearing techniques. Adoptive parents' anxieties represented a "resurgence of the old pre-adoption childless feeling of failure, deprivation, separation, and loss" due to "an irreversible scar: infertility and its psychological sequelae." These neurotic anxieties were responsible for their reluctance to liberalize the laws regarding adoption records. The three researchers found adoptive parents' apprehensions groundless. There was no evidence to support the notion that adoptee searches would lead to the loss of their children to the birth parents. Yet despite their negative assessment of adoptive parents, they attempted to assuage their fears too. Sorosky and associates flatly asserted that adoptive parents had nothing to fear from the opening of sealed adoption records, adoptees' genealogical searches, or reunions. In fact, they claimed that many adoptees never sought to contact their birth families but instead wanted complete information "only in such areas as ethnicity, genealogy, and medical background." They concluded optimistically that "adoptive parents are more educable than had been previously thought" and suggested they needed "help in seeing the adoptee's quest for genealogical information or for an encounter with the natural parents as a personal need which cannot be comprehended by a nonadopted person." In professional psychiatric journals, however, Sorosky, Baran, and Pannor described solely in negative terms adoptive parents' responses to their children searching for their biological parents and left out the optimistic prediction.[23]

The three researchers allowed the hostility they felt toward professional social workers and adoption agencies to appear more openly in their psychiatric journal articles. In comments that did not appear in social work journals or popular magazines, they wrote that adoption agencies added to the adoptees' and birth mothers' confusion by playing the role of protector, "in which capacity they have become watchmen and censors of the truth." The results of restricting the truth, they stated, "have often been negative, largely because the information given out by adoption agencies has been recognized as shadowy, unreal, and, therefore unsatisfying to the adoptee." Instead of protecting their clients, censorship conveyed a "feeling that full information would reveal 'awful truths.'"[24]

Given the centrality of the issue of identity to the ideology upon which the adoption rights movement was based, it is necessary to pause and evaluate the empirical and methodological basis for the various assertions made by Sorosky, Baran, and Pannor. Their conclusion that adolescent adoptees were more prone to identity conflicts was based partly on studies that are almost laughable in their empirical naïveté. For example, Sorosky and associates and countless adoption activists following in their wake cited the work of H. J. Sants, who coined the term "genealogical bewilderment" in 1964 as evidence of the existence of a psychological disturbance afflicting adult adoptees. The first paragraph of Sants's piece does not give one confidence in the author's research skills. It begins by attributing the first use of the term "genealogical bewilderment" to a 1952 paper by his erstwhile colleague, British psychiatrist E. Wellisch, but the phrase appears nowhere in the cited work. Sants then describes Wellisch's contribution as "a study of the maladjustment of these adopted children" of which there was a "large number." The study in question, however, was merely a four-paragraph letter to the editor. The bulk of this letter consists of an analogy of the terms "shadow" and "mirror-image" in the fictional works of two German romantic writers, Adalbert van Chamisso and E. T. A. Hoffman, to the deprivation of genealogy in adopted children. Wellisch's letter was not a clinical study in any sense of the term, nor does he reveal how many children he had studied.[25]

Sants's study purports to show that genealogical bewilderment is widespread among adopted persons. But it also is based on fictional literary accounts, ranging from Sophocles' play *Oedipus Rex* to the story of the Ugly Duckling, underpinned by the psychoanalytic theories of Freud and Melanie Klein. The following passage is an example of Sants's methodology:

> A characteristic of the genealogically bewildered, particularly from adolescence onwards, is their relentless pursuit of the facts of their origin. They visit the nursing home where they were born, interview nurses and question adoptive relatives. Oedipus expresses this need when he says 'I ask to be no other man than that I am, and I will know who I am.'

A quotation from a literary work is made to stand for clinical research or a representative sample. One looks through this study in vain for actual flesh-and-blood adult adoptees, genealogically bewildered or otherwise. Nevertheless, the concept of "genealogical bewilderment" would become a tenet of the adoption rights movement.[26]

Although the reader can at least find a number of personal accounts of adult adoptees in the studies of Sorosky, Baran, and Pannor, their research design and methodology were similarly flawed. From a social science methodological perspective, it is a wonder that any of these articles were published. Their sample was so small, self-selected, and unrepresentative of the adoption triad community at large that, statistically speaking, their conclusions were all but worthless. They based their initial articles on interviews with and letters from a total of 22 adoptees, 47 birth mothers, 170 adoptive parents, and 11 reunions between adoptees and birth mothers. Their appeal in the *Los Angeles Times* for adoption triad members to write them produced "thousands of letters," yet this sample too remained vague or self-selected and unrepresentatively small.[27]

The three researchers recognized their methodological shortcomings and confessed them repeatedly. They informed readers forthrightly that "our study, obviously, does not meet all the criteria for a scientific research project." Two years later, they again noted that "unfortunately, this type of research does not lend itself to a careful scientific design with adequate controls." Elsewhere they wrote that "definitive conclusions cannot be drawn from a relatively small number of letters." They justified their lack of scientific rigor by blaming the phenomena they were studying: the secrecy surrounding adoption. But they also expressed a naive faith in the reliability of their unrepresentative sample of letter writers by declaring that "the very fact that they responded indicates a sense of responsibility, maturity, and concern on their part." In spite of these shortcomings, Sorosky, Baran, and Pannor insisted that none of "these obstacles" (i.e., the unscientific nature of their research) should "deter our efforts to clarify issues of great concern to millions of people." Nevertheless, from a scientific point of view, the validity of their work was highly questionable.[28]

Not only was the methodology employed by Sorosky and associates deeply flawed, but their research skills, too, left much to be desired. They failed to uncover a significant body of research that contradicted their sweeping assertion that adolescent adoptees suffer from genealogical bewilderment or identity conflicts. In particular, they ignored a mountain of data indicating that 95 percent of adopted children were never referred to professionals for therapeutic help of any sort. Moreover, in the nearly fifty years since Sophie van Senden Theis's 1924 follow-up study of adoption outcomes, researchers had conducted fourteen additional studies evaluating 2,616 adoption placements. They found that approximately three out of four were "successful." But Sorosky, Baran, and Pannor cited none of these studies.[29]

Although the news media often balanced their accounts of the ARM by presenting opposing viewpoints, usually with adoption agency officials questioning the wisdom of opening the records, they never questioned Sorosky, Baran, and Pannor's methodological shortcomings; they simply reported their conclusions. It is perhaps unfair to single out the news media for this failing, for they were not alone. The three researchers' work was repeatedly cited uncritically by experts in professional journals of education, pediatrics, psychiatry, social work, child welfare, and law. In over a decade, only one child welfare expert, Alfred Kadushin in 1978, devoted two short paragraphs to the methodological flaws of the ARM activists in the course of a 110-page article evaluating 191 adoption studies. Such criticism was not repeated until 1986, when Patrick A. Curtis, research director of the Children's Home and Aid Society of Illinois, noted that Sorosky and associates' book, *The Adoption Triangle,* "depended on bias sampling." Curtis then raised a penetrating criticism. Noting that in Scotland, where birth records had been open for fifty years, only approximately 7 percent of adult adopted persons, or 1.5 adopted adults per 1,000, inquired about their biological parents, Curtis rhetorically asked, "One wonders, when the prohibitions were absent, what happened to the need?" Likewise, in England, where the 1975 Children Act permitted British adult adoptees access to their birth records, one researcher extrapolated from a two-year period that only 21 percent of adult adoptees would apply for their birth records. In the United States, a similarly low percentage of searchers has been recorded. In light of the universalistic claims about the identity problems of adoptees that researchers like Sorosky, Baran, and Pannor and a host of others have promulgated, one is hard pressed to explain why so many adult adoptees felt so little need to search.[30]

Rather than question the methodology of Sorosky and associates, the West Coast news media showcased their research. The symbiosis between the social scientists and the media is well illustrated by the publication of a 1973 page-one story in the *Los Angeles Times* that ran soon after the appearance of *The Search for Anna Fisher* and a full six months before formal publication of Sorosky and associates' research findings. The story centered on the demand by adult adopted persons to have access to their adoption records and retold the story of Florence Fisher's search for her birth mother and the founding of ALMA, and described adoptees' ongoing efforts to secure the opening of all adoption records. The *LA Times* article cast Sorosky, Baran, and Pannor as objective experts who were sorting out these complex emotional issues with "scientific detachment." Although they gave their expert opinion, Sorosky, Baran, and Pannor typically did not shrink from forecasting the future. They predicted optimistically that the courts would soon rule on adoptees' rights and warned adoption agencies that they should be prepared "for the upheaval which is sure to follow." The article concluded with a request by the researchers for triad members to write about their experiences, particularly birth mothers and those who had participated in a reunion. Their request bore fruit: the "large number of letters" they received resulted in a survey questionnaire to letter-writers, the results of which they quickly reported in the professional journal *Social Casework*.[31]

In the next year and a half, the *Los Angeles Times* continued to feature articles about the adoption rights movement, many of which uncritically quoted or cited one or another of the social scientists.

For example, the paper followed up its initial story of the ARM movement with an interview with Sorosky a week after he had delivered a paper on the controversy over sealed adoption records to the Academy of Child Psychiatry. Sorosky stated that the policy of confidentiality had been "the cause of insoluble problems," notably identity problems in adoptees and a "life-long, unfilled need" in many birth parents for information or contact with the children they had relinquished for adoption. Sorosky called on adoption agencies to re-evaluate their disclosure policies and recommended that boards of professionals investigate requests for reunions and act as intermediaries between the parties. Sorosky candidly noted that although his findings were "in the pilot stage" he was prematurely bringing them to the attention of the mental health and social work community in the "hope [that] the publicity will establish our reputation as a center for the scientific research of this phenomenon."[32]

Similarly, the *Los Angeles Times* devoted several columns to *The Stranger That Looks Like Me,* a TV movie about an adoptee who searches for her biological parents. The piece ended by quoting Reuben Pannor's expert opinion that the movie was a "straightforward, honest presentation . . . What I would hope from this film is that people realize that young people should not have to go through this kind of anguish trying to find their parents." A month later it reported on an adoption workshop chaired by Sorosky at the annual meeting of the American Orthopsychiatric Association, where he told the participants that there was evidence that denying an adopted person the right to know his "natural heritage may be detrimental to his psychological health."[33]

The *Los Angeles Times* was also the first paper to feature, as news, what would become a staple of mass-circulation magazines and later TV talk shows: the search and reunion of adopted persons with their birth parent. As early as 1972, the *LA Times* reported on how Peggy Lloyd, the adopted daughter of comedian Harold Lloyd and his wife, Mildred, searched and found her "real mother." In the next two years, similar stories would appear, one of them featured on the paper's front page. By 1974, the *LA Times* combined the two genres—social science "research" and search and reunion stories—so that the one validated the other. For example, in the case of Katrina Maxtone-Graham's successful search for her birth mother, the *LA Times* quoted Sorosky on the benefits of reunions ("over 80% have gained in these cases") and the need to reform "the traditional school of thought." Social science testimony was especially effective in supporting these dramatic true-life soap operas. All of the searchers, whether Florence Fisher or Katrina Maxtone-Graham or Jane Doe, were portrayed as modern-day heroines having to overcome enormous obstacles that were always being thrown in their way. These *LA Times* search and reunion stories, as well as others, all carried the theme of a modern rite of passage that contained "liminal" phases made up of "extraordinary events characterized as 'timeless,' 'out of the ordinary,' and, often, miraculous." As entertainment, adoption search and reunion stories were very emotionally satisfying. From the perspective of mobilizing popular support for opening adoption records, the ARM strategy was brilliant: who could resist a happy ending that was also therapeutically beneficial?[34]

The combination of emotional drama, therapeutic self-help, and demand for individual rights in adoptee autobiographies and search and reunion news stories was in fact tailor-made for mass-circulation magazines, which were quick to exploit the melodrama inherent in adoptee searches. Even before Florence Fisher and ALMA burst on the scene, mass-circulation magazines sensed the potential market and occasionally ran stories about adopted persons searching for their biological parents. In 1971, for example, *Seventeen* dramatically recounted an adopted girl's difficult odyssey in an unsuccessful search for her birth mother. But beginning in 1974 and continuing through and beyond the 1970s, mass-circulation magazines such as *McCall's*, *Parents' Magazine*, *Reader's Digest*, *Seventeen*, and *Good Housekeeping* bombarded its readership with articles entitled "Who Are My Real Parents?" "The Adopted Child Has a Right to Know EVERYTHING," "Search for a Stranger," and "We're a Family Again." The articles dramatized the plight of adopted persons who were initially prevented from discovering their family heritage, championed the right of adopted persons to view their adoption files, and showcased successful search and reunions. *Reader's Digest,* for example, presented the story of a thirty-seven-year-old doctor who had only recently discovered he was adopted. Setting out to search for his birth mother, he overcame the resistance of adoption agencies and was finally reunited with her. The piece ends with his mother asking him for forgiveness and his response: "My throat tightened and the tears stung my eyes. Forgive her? The very idea that I should judge her was outrageous. I stood woodenly, immobilized by my emotions. She made the first move. Slowly, humbly, she held out her arms. For the first time in 37 years, I touched my mother and she touched me."[35]

In addition to courting their readers' emotions, mass-circulation magazines appealed to their intellect by quoting the three researchers as experts who supported adoptee searches. An article in *Parents' Magazine* excitedly noted that now "there's evidence to show that it may be the best thing for adopted children to know who their natural parents were" and introduced its readers to the three social scientists' research results. In this article and others, Sorosky and associates condemned secrecy in the adoption process and described the motives and results of adoptee search and reunions in universalistic terms and optimistic hues. For example, in *McCall's* magazine Sorosky denied that adopted persons were emotionally unstable for searching and instead stressed the "natural genealogical curiosity that even the most successful adoptee feels" to search for his biological parents, while Annette Baran assured readers that "adoptees are very respectful of birth parents' privacy. They always write first." She also noted that "the reunion usually has no effect on the adoptee's relationship with his adoptive parents."[36]

Search and reunion stories carried another message that served unintentionally to undermine the legitimacy of adoptive kinship and reinforce society's preference for biological kinship. For many birth mothers connected with the ARM, relinquishing a child for adoption was a traumatic event from which they never healed. This sharply called into question the 1950s notion that the perfect solution to unwed pregnancy was adoption. Carol Schaefer, for example, described relinquishing her child in terms of amputation and psychic dissociation. According to her account, after giving up her child, she was left with "half of myself. I disconnected my feelings and was left with half a soul." For Schaefer, the system of secrecy in adoption inflicted irreversible psychic wounds. Conversely, accounts of successful reunions conveyed the idea that biological kinship was superior to adoptive kinship and that searching could provide a cure to the "illness" of adoptive kinship. Following many years of searching for her biological mother, Katrina Maxtone-Graham, in her autobiography, *An Adopted Woman,* exulted, "I . . . had been at last an instrument of my own fate . . . The greatest event of my life had been accomplished by me . . . In my moment of truth it was I who had had the power of action. And thus it was that I had become a real human being." In similar terms, Florence Fisher recounted the climax of her search: "We talked for a few minutes and then she began to tell me what I had always wanted to know. That night I met *my mother*—and my past. And the dark veil began to fall away." Repeatedly these autobiographies and mass media accounts portrayed birth mothers and adult adoptees as numbed or maimed by traditional adoption practice and made whole again or reborn by reuniting with their biological relatives.[37]

Many of the protagonists of these autobiographical accounts were also highly critical of adoption agencies. In the 1950s, impatient childless couples had denounced agency policies for qualifying adoptive applicants as just so much red tape, resulting in long waits for a child. At that time adoption was viewed as a legitimate institution that provided solutions to pregnant single women, childless couples, and unwanted children. The unwed mother escaped from the stigma of illegitimacy and began a new life, infertile couples were able to form a family, and the child grew up in a loving, stable, two-parent home. In the 1970s, social workers and adoption agencies were again the targets of criticism, but this time for refusing adopted persons and birth mothers access to their records. Katrina Maxtone-Graham, for example, viewed the agency that prevented her from seeing her file as "my irrational attacker, the Children's Aid Society."[38]

With West Coast newspapers and mass-circulation magazines repeatedly featuring stories about the adoption rights movement, the East Coast news media finally took notice of the phenomenon. On May 11, 1975, the *New York Times* ran its first news piece on the ARM since its initial coverage of Florence Fisher almost two years earlier. Although the story was buried on page 33 of the Sunday edition, interested *Times* readers were finally made aware of Sorosky's research on adoptee search and reunions when the newspaper reported on a paper he delivered at the annual meeting of the American Psychiatric Association. The *Times* dutifully reported Sorosky's usual optimistic message long familiar to West Coast readers: 90 percent of reunion respondents had reported "feelings of satisfaction"; 82 percent of birth parents were "mostly positive about the reunion experience"; and after reunions adoptees felt "even deeper love and appreciation for their adoptive parents." Similarly, Sorosky admitted that adoptive parents were less supportive of reunions but noted that "only in a few cases was there any permanent damage done to the adoptive family relationships."[39]

In the next two years, the *New York Times* carried numerous articles on the adoption rights movement, from a variety of perspectives. There were op-ed pieces debating the ethics of permitting adoptees access to their files, news stories of legal challenges by adoptee search groups like ALMA to open sealed adoption records, reviews of adoption rights activists' books, magazine pieces advocating opening adoption files, and numerous letters to the editor on both sides of the adoption records controversy.[40] Prominent in all of these forums was a newcomer to the adoption rights movement, Betty Jean Lifton. From the point of view of the eastern media elites, Florence Fisher was an unknown person from the lower middle class, while Sorosky and associates were social scientists from the slightly loopy West Coast. Betty Jean Lifton, though, was a home-grown product: born in New York City, a Columbia University graduate, and a professional writer, she was well connected with the East Coast intelligentsia through her husband, the Pulitzer-Prize-winning author and psychiatrist Robert Jay Lifton.

Lifton burst on the adoption rights movement scene in 1975 with the publication of her book *Twice Born: Memoirs of an Adopted Daughter.* Like *The Search for Anna Fisher, Twice Born* was the story of an adopted person's frustrating search for her biological parents. Adopted at age two and a half, Lifton did not learn of her adoption until she was seven, when her adoptive mother told her and then promptly swore her to secrecy. The secret became a "monster," an obsession that Lifton claimed colored all her relationships and activities. The search for her biological mother was a way to exorcise this demon. Like Florence Fisher, Lifton's reunion with her biological mother was not a successful one; she did not find what she was looking for and was unable to form a good relationship with either her adoptive or her biological mother. Nevertheless, Lifton felt strongly that adopted persons were social pariahs who were unable to develop a sense of identity, wholeness, or belonging unless they sought and found their biological parents. Besides Lifton's social connections, the power of *Twice Born* came from her evocation of literary, mythological, and psychiatric concepts on behalf of the adoption rights movement, in stark contrast to the more mundane and prosaic style of *The Search for Anna Fisher.*[41]

Lifton was quoted extensively in the *New York Times* in the next two years as an adoption rights authority. In a 1975 article printed shortly after the publication of *Twice Born,* she sharply disagreed with Child Welfare League of America's executive director Joseph Reid about the need for secrecy in adoption, declaring that "the sealing of records is as repressive for natural parents as it is for adoptive [sic] children, increasing their sense of secrecy and guilt." Shortly thereafter, the paper opened its magazine section to Lifton, who contributed an article that encouraged adoptees to search for their biological parents, denounced adoption agency secrecy, and advocated opening the sealed adoption records. Lifton cited the work of several psychiatrists, including the research of Sorosky and associates, and repeated their mantra that "virtually all adoptees feel a sense of 'genealogical bewilderment' which expresses itself in a need to search" and that "the majority of adoptees felt that they had personally benefited from the reunion," whether successful or not. Whereas Sorosky, Baran, and Pannor downplayed the psychological difficulties caused by adopted persons' inability to access their adoption records, Lifton made them central to her argument. In a letter to the editor of the *Times,* Lifton pointed out that serial killer David Berkowitz was adopted and contended that that fact played an important role in explaining his behavior. Repeating the inaccurate generalization that adoptees were disproportionately represented in psychiatric clinics and residential treatment centers around the country, Lifton declared it was no coincidence "that a man who was not permitted to know whose son he was, signed himself 'Son of Sam.'" Lifton called for the opening of adoption records, "so that future generations of adoptees do not have to vent their rage and frustration inward on themselves, like those in our clinics, or outward, like David Berkowitz on society."[42]

The idea that searching for one's birth family was unnatural or a sign of mental instability was the final impediment to the popular acceptance of the adoption rights movement. That notion was swept away by another media event, one that, like Watergate, had little to do with adoption per se: the January 1977 TV production of *Roots*. Based on Alex Haley's 885-page opus, *Roots: The Saga of an American Family,* the twelve-hour, week-long miniseries recounted the history of an African American family by tracing its ancestry from the capture of a young West African, Kunta Kinte, by American slave traders. Its success far surpassed ABC network executives' expectations. The eight episodes of *Roots* averaged a 44.9 rating and a 66 share of the audience. The final episode attracted a staggering 80 million viewers (a 51.1 rating and a 71 share), making it the highest-rated TV show of its day. Mayors in thirty cities proclaimed the week "Roots Week," and more than 250 colleges and universities offered or proposed to offer courses based on the film and book. *Roots* went on to garner thirty-seven Emmy nominations and received nine Emmys. At the Television Critics Circle Awards *Roots* was named "Program of the Year," while its author received numerous honors, including a National Book Award and a special Pulitzer Prize.[43]

There are many reasons for *Roots*'s extraordinary popularity, ranging from readers' predisposition to view favorably the TV version of Haley's best-selling novel, a cold spell during the gasoline crisis that kept many people at home, and the lack of competition from rival TV networks, to the simple fact that it showcased good acting in an entertaining, informative, optimistic, and dramatic American success story. But there was also the universal appeal of certain themes in *Roots,* the persistence of identity and the importance of family lineage and ancestry. These themes were present throughout the production but were particularly heightened in the last episode, when the camera dissolved to reveal that the narrator was Haley himself, who proceeded to tell of his twelve-year, obsessive search for his family that eventually led to a book called *Roots.* As Leslie Fishbein notes, "Haley had done what blacks had only dreamed to be possible, he has traced his ancestry back to Africa; he has found his roots, and those roots have made him free." *Roots*'s universal appeal transcended racial politics, and by building on the early 1970s ethnic awareness movement the production had touched a nerve in "the average American's yearning for a sense of heritage."[44]

In the aftermath of *Roots,* that yearning became a national mania as Americans discovered genealogy. *Newsweek* devoted its July 4, 1977, cover story to "Everybody's Search for Roots," and printed twenty sources for aiding in genealogical searches including books with the titles *Searching for Your Ancestors* and *Finding Your Roots.* One scholar noted that following *Roots,* "letters to the National Archives, where Haley did genealogical research in census manuscripts, tripled, and applications to use the research facilities increased by 40 percent." At Salt Lake City's huge Mormon Church genealogical library, which contained 60 million names and 918,000 microfilm rolls, requests for information doubled as a result of *Roots.* Mormon spokesman Donald LeFevre reported that the most common reason people gave for coming was "I just want to know who I am." Suddenly, the deepest psychological desires of adoption rights activists and their many followers was being felt at the grassroots level by unadopted Americans and were even being reinforced by big business. Continental Trailways, for example, launched a high-powered advertising campaign, "Take Our Routes to Your Roots," and offered a special $75 fare to any part of the United States. Overnight, *Roots* made searching for one's family members a normal desire rather than deviant behavior. This point was not lost on adopted persons, especially those who had been denied access to their records. As one adopted person, who had been told "quite sternly" that she "would never be allowed to see" her adoption file, noted in a letter to the *New York Times,* "Mr. Haley's book and the television show have dramatized a need that I think most people have: to identify with someone who can give them a sense of continuity and of belonging."[45]

By 1978, the battle to gain the sympathetic attention of the East Coast media had been won. Representative of the ARM's triumph was the glowing review printed in the *New York Times* for Sorosky, Baran, and Pannor's book, *The Adoption Triangle.* After openly sympathizing with adopted persons' desire for access to the "true facts about their birth," the anonymous reviewer rhetorically asked: "Isn't that what 'Roots' was all about?" The reviewer went on to advocate that "in these post-Watergate days of full disclosure" it was time to open adoption records. In closing, the reviewer interjected a personal note: "I hope the authors win their reforms."[46]

The mass media were crucial to the dissemination of the ARM's message and to the eventual changes in adoption practice and the laws governing adoption records. The media's role, however, was complex and changed over time. Indirectly, the coverage of the Watergate political scandal was particularly important to the movement's success. It delegitimatized official claims of secrecy, put advocates of closed adoption records on the defensive, and provided a national context for the acceptance of the idea of opening adoption records. More directly, the mass media, particularly the print news and mass-circulation magazines, uncritically popularized the ARM's social science ideology, which minimized the problems that could result from opening the adoption records and stressed the psychological damage birth mothers and adult adoptees suffered from their inability to view them. It was this psychological focus, with an emphasis on adoptee search and reunions, that the Los Angeles print media, followed later by national consumer magazines and finally the national news media, preferred to feature, rather than the discourse of constitutional rights. A prisoner of its own ideological predilection for expert opinions, the media were predisposed to accept uncritically Sorosky, Baran, and Pannor's social science research findings. Moreover, by emphasizing the sentimental nature of adoptee searches rather than Fisher's claim that adoptees had a constitutional right to view their adoption records, the media avoided directly challenging the adoption agencies, social institutions that generally commanded respect. And in the end, the entertainment value of successful searches and reunions, both real and fictional, with their inherent melodrama, became irresistible. By late 1977, the adoptee search and reunion movement had spawned a new media genre: therapeutic entertainment.

As a result of the mass media, it became more difficult for defenders of sealed adoption records to refute the ARM's logic, emotional power, and cultural appeal to a policy of openness and family reunion. For mostly misguided reasons, the mass media made a critical difference in promoting the ARM.

The Adoption Records Wars

During the 1970s the adoption rights movement (ARM) experienced great success in getting its message out to the public. The shifting cultural change toward increased openness in government affairs generally and the national craze for genealogical searches had predisposed the American public to accept the movement's goals. At the same time, the mainstream mass media portrayed the movement as deserving the public's sympathy and respect. But the ARM's actual accomplishments remained few. If one takes the adoption activists' stated goal of unrestricted access for adult adopted persons and birth parents to adoption records as the measure of success, the movement had failed. The ARM's demand to abrogate unilaterally the promises of secrecy previously made to unwed mothers proved unacceptable to the adoption establishment, the courts, and state legislatures. But if one uses a less absolute measure of success and a longer time frame, roughly the past two decades, beginning in 1976, the picture is quite different: the ARM has had a significant effect on liberalizing both adoption agency disclosure policies and state laws regarding adoption records. Indeed, the relentless activism of adoption search groups paved the way in the 1980s for a progressive revision of the Child Welfare League of America's *Standards for Adoption Service,* changes in state laws governing sealed adoption records, and passage of legislation creating search procedures based on mutual consent and voluntary adoption registries. The resulting compromises worked out among adoption search activists, social work professionals, judges, and state legislators ensured the privacy of all members of the adoption triad, but fell considerably short of the ARM's major goal of unimpeded access to adoption records.

At the beginning of the adoption rights movement, professional adoption circles paid little heed to its message. The 1960s and early 1970s were a time of consolidation and expansion of liberal trends begun in the postwar era. In 1967, the Child Welfare League of America (CWLA) created the Adoption Resource Exchange of North America, an independent national clearinghouse for hard-to-place children, which helped agencies find homes for almost 200 special-needs children annually. By 1969, public and private adoption agencies' concerted efforts to find homes for minority children resulted in more than 19,000 children being placed. Eight percent of the children adopted that year (14,000 of 171,000) were African American. These programs still left tens of thousands of older, minority, and physically and mentally disabled children needing placement. The social work profession responded in a number of ways to increase special-needs adoption. In their vigorous recruitment efforts, agencies were sometimes surprised to discover that now and then a white family would request a black infant for adoption or, when approached by caseworkers, would agree to adopt a black baby. By 1965, transracial adoption had become the "little revolution," as agencies all over the nation increasingly placed black babies with white families. Three years later, the CWLA revised its Standards to reflect the new practice, unequivocally stating that "racial background in itself should not determine the selection of the home for a child" and recommending that "agencies should be ready to help families who wish to adopt children of another race." In 1971, transracial adoptions reached their peak when 468 agencies reported 2,574 such placements.[1]

While professional adoption workers went far in overhauling inflexible practices and liberalizing the definition of adoptability, the tumultuous events and radical attitudes of the 1960s overtook their efforts. Essentially liberal in its political and social beliefs, the social work profession did not anticipate that sixties radicalism would have any substantive effect on adoption policies or practices. Adoption officials and caseworkers were thus caught by surprise when dissidents from within and without the profession began to challenge its basic tenets in the early 1970s. The first manifestation of discontent emerged when black social workers, influenced by the Black Power movement, with its emphasis on racial separatism, revolutionary violence, and black nationalism, began denouncing transracial adoption.[2]

The effect of Black Power on social work was first felt in May 1968, during the National Conference of Social Welfare held in San Francisco, when five hundred black social workers founded the National Association of Black Social Workers (NABSW) and walked out of the meeting when conference officials denied their demands to end white racist social welfare policies. Four years later, at the NABSW's third annual conference, Audrey T. Russell, president of the Alliance of Black Social Workers in Philadelphia, denounced the CWLA as the "white bastion of professional child welfare standards and practices" and attacked transracial adoption as "a diabolical trick." "Black children belong with black folk," Russell stated. Transracial adoption was "a lethal incursion on the black family, just weakening us. It needs to be stopped." The next day, Cennie J. Williams, Jr., president of the NABSW, exacerbated tensions by announcing that black children should remain in foster homes and institutions rather than be placed in the homes of white families. Russell's and Williams' statements, printed in the New York Times, provoked tremendous controversy, and their views were contested by white and more moderate black social workers and by parents who had adopted transracially. Radical black social workers amplified their opposition to transracial adoption in the popular press and professional journals.[3]

The NABSW's case against transracial adoptions was remarkably effective. Few if any social workers justified transracial adoption to promote integration. The most common defense of transracial adoption, put forward by moderate black and white social workers, was summed up by the sentiment that "a white home is better than no home." Nevertheless, the voices of moderation did not heed their own advice. Instead, in practice, they sided with the NABSW's position and began refusing to place black children with white parents. In the following years, transracial adoptions declined steeply. In 1972, transracial adoptions fell 39 percent, to 1,569; by 1975 only 831 transracial adoptions occurred.[4]

The nation's professional social work leaders also failed to anticipate the ARM. But unlike social workers' rapid accommodation to black social workers' demands to stop transracial adoption, adoption leaders' attitude toward the ARM tended to be dismissive, even hostile. The adoption establishment's opposition to the ARM was initially reflected in the dearth of articles published in professional journals about the sealed adoption records controversy. From 1971 through 1975, only one article on the issue appeared in the two most influential social work journals, *Child Welfare,* the house organ of the Child Welfare League of America, and *Social Work,* the journal of professional social workers. Nor did professional social work journals cover overseas events that were encouraging to the movement. For example, Great Britain's passage in 1975 of the Children's Act, giving adult adopted persons the right to copies of their original birth certificates, went virtually unreported. The unfavorable review that *The Search for Anna Fisher* received in the pages of *Child Welfare* also indicated the leadership's unsympathetic attitude toward the ARM. Citing the unrepresentative nature of Florence Fisher's experience, the reviewer noted that it would be "unfortunate if the general public assumes her adoptive experience and frame of mind to be typical of many adult adoptees."[5]

Before 1975, the social work profession's disregard for the ARM reflected accurately its top officials' opposition to the adoptee search movement. In short, they viewed activists like Florence Fisher as emotional cranks. The publicity about the sealed adoption records controversy emanating from the national news media and mass-circulation magazines, however, forced the adoption establishment to confront the issue. When pressed to articulate the CWLA's policy toward the ARM, executive director Joseph H. Reid bluntly stated the organization's position in a private letter: "The league does not favor open records." Reid explained the organization's stand as a matter of principle: "We do not believe that it is in the public interest to violate the contract with the natural parents that their identity will be protected." He also stated his position publicly: "A woman who has put the matter behind her and found a new life is entitled to be free from the fear of a knock on the door." In November 1975, Reid again publicly stated that the League was duty bound to honor the guarantee of anonymity it had made to birth parents who had relinquished their children for adoption and that its official position for the future was to continue to keep birth parents' names confidential.[6]

Reid's public position reaffirmed the CWLA's 1968 revised *Standards for Adoption Service,* which continued to recommend the confidentiality of all proceedings and parties to the adoption, the confidentiality of agency records, and the sealing of court adoption records and original birth certificates. CWLA officials justified secrecy on the grounds that both the child's well-being and the adoptive parent-child relationship would suffer from the intervention of the biological parents. They also assumed that the biological parents, having once relinquished the child, had the right to pursue their own lives without fear of intrusion by either the child or the adoptive parents. But the League's *Standards* also insisted that adoption agencies should collect and preserve information about both the child and the biological parents and that positive nonidentifying information should be given to the adoptive parents. Missing from the *Standards* was any consideration of the question whether an adult adopted person had the right to any or all information in the adoption record, including the identity of his or her biological parents.[7]

Under the drumbeat of Sorosky and associates, the pressure of mass media publicity, and the lacunae in the League's standards, the CWLA leadership privately began to re-examine its position. By March 1975 the League's concern about the sealed adoption records controversy had resulted in its dispatching a high-ranking official, Deborah Shapiro, to the annual meeting of the American Orthopsychiatric Association to report on a panel discussion, entitled "The Right to Know—Adoption," which included papers by Sorosky and Baran and commentary by Betty Jean Lifton. Shapiro turned in a four-and-a-half-page single-spaced typed memo summarizing and commenting on the panel's proceedings. She reported on the unusual qualities of the panel: attendance exceeded expectations; the papers were interesting; no one left early; and discussion afterward was full and lively. Shapiro thought Sorosky, unlike the other speakers, was "rather sharply anti-agency" and "accused social workers of playing the role of God." In contrast to Sorosky, however, Shapiro thought that Annette Baran conveyed "a quality of reasonableness and didn't seem as overcommitted as some of the partisans to the controversy." Not surprisingly, Sorosky, Baran, Lifton, and most of the audience of social workers favored opening the records and denounced secrecy in adoption. Shapiro concluded her report by stating that "altogether, it was a stimulating productive meeting, worth the trip to Washington."

Shapiro's positive assessment of the panel's attack on sealed adoption records was emblematic of the League's changing attitude toward the adoption rights movement.[8]

During the following year, CWLA officials held a series of internal meetings to hammer out a strategy to deal with the press and with search organizations' increasingly outspoken attack on sealed adoption records. The result was a dramatic reversal of the CWLA's earlier attitude. In February 1976 on the editorial pages of its house organ, *Child Welfare*, the CWLA publicly recognized the legitimacy of the ARM. It now viewed the issue of unsealing adoption records as a challenge that "cannot be dismissed as simply the expression of a few vocal dissidents." It urged adoption agencies to be receptive to adoptees' desire for information about their biological families. If adopted persons asked agencies for information or aid in dealing with pain and distress, it was incumbent upon them "to be nonjudgemental, to respond with an open mind, respect, empathy, and the caring that is social work's reason for being." The editorial concluded with a plea for agency officials to consider "the possibility that adult adoptees may be right in demanding the elimination of secrecy."[9]

Recognizing the ARM's legitimacy and calling for open-mindedness did not constitute a policy, however. In fact, for the next several years, partly because of the intrinsic difficulty of the issue and partly because the leadership was baffled at what course of action to pursue, the CWLA failed to take a stand for or against permitting adult adoptees access to identifying information in their adoption records. Instead, League officials consulted with experts and conducted survey research in an effort to amass sufficient data to construct an informed policy. Their initial response was to apply to the federal government for a grant to study the issue. In April 1976, the CWLA sent a thirteen-page proposal to the Office of Child Development at the U.S. Department of Health, Education, and Welfare (HEW) to establish a task force "to examine the implications of the sealed adoption record controversy for adoption agency practice and for the field of adoption in general and to recommend guidelines based on that examination." They candidly confessed that the adoption rights movement had taken the CWLA leadership by surprise. League officials explained that they had not "anticipated that learning of one's adoptive status would lead to a desire to meet one's natural parents." Instead, they assumed that "a loving adoptive home would answer a child's need for identity and security and that involvement with the natural family might jeopardize that identity and security." Moreover, because of the strong social stigma attached to giving birth to an infant born out of wedlock, the leadership assumed that the birth mother wanted to conceal her identity forever. They never "anticipated that the [birth] mother might wish to have contact with the relinquished child at a later point."[10]

Noting that "times have changed," CWLA officials justified the need for their study by citing a host of reasons. These ranged from extensive media attention and recent state legislation to current and anticipated suits claiming that adult adoptees had a legal right to know the full details of their past, including the identity of their birth parents. They cited Sorosky, Baran, and Pannor's conclusions that searching was essential for an adopted person's sense of identity, made adoptees happy, and strengthened their commitment to their adoptive parents. The "most significant factor" necessitating the review, though, was the "substantial and large number of adult adoptees who are returning to agencies to request either information about their biological parents or assistance in locating them."

Although the proposal was comprehensive and lucid, HEW turned down the project. Lacking funding for its ambitious undertaking, CWLA officials scaled back its original proposal, eliminating the portion that called for consulting adoption triad members' views on opening adoption records. Instead, in April 1976 the League conducted a nationwide survey of two hundred public and private adoption agencies.[11]

In July, CWLA research associate Mary Ann Jones compiled the survey results and wrote a report, which the League published as *The Sealed Adoption Record Controversy*. It provided the first comprehensive overview ever written of private and public adoption agencies' policies and practices on a wide variety of issues revolving around the question of whether to disclose information to adoption triad members. The survey revealed that secrecy was far and away the rule: 90 percent of the agencies (a total of 163 had responded) guaranteed adoptive and biological parents anonymity, though only 3 percent put the guarantee in writing. Agencies almost never disclosed identifying information. Only one agency revealed the name of the biological parents upon request.

The agencies were more liberal on the issue of disclosing nonidentifying information, with most of them providing a substantial portion of the case record, except in matters dealing with rape or incest. Most significantly, the survey revealed that the majority of adoption agencies took a hard line toward the ARM. Although sympathetic to their quest for identity, most agencies did "not believe that the laws should be changed to permit the adult adoptee access to the information in court or agency records on request, either now or in the future." The survey clearly revealed that most adoption agencies were content with the status quo of keeping adoption records sealed from triad members.[12]

As Jones was compiling the survey results, the CWLA leadership simultaneously planned a conference for late September 1976 to which were invited eighteen adoption service administrators and specialists "to further inform League staff of the thinking, concerns, and opinions of representatives of adoption services on the sealed adoption record controversy." At the conference, the central question the representatives discussed was whether adult adopted persons should be permitted to obtain the names of their biological parents upon request. Not surprisingly, there was little consensus on this basic issue; conference participants even had difficulty staying focused on the question. Positions ranged along a spectrum from total opposition to total assent. Some representatives believed access to identifying information should be granted only with a court order, while many more voiced concern about violating the promise of secrecy agency officials had made to both the biological and the adoptive parents at the time of the adoption. There was a consensus, however, that in the future such a commitment could not and should not be made.[13]

After the conference, the CWLA leadership sought additional views. In October, League officials circulated a series of questions to prominent people in professions outside of social work and adoption agency practice, including psychiatrists, lawyers, and doctors. In addition, the leadership solicited the views of members of adoptee search groups. All of the data so laboriously amassed—the survey of adoption agencies' policies and practices and the results of talks and questions to experts and specialists inside and outside of social work—was digested by the CWLA staff and presented to the CWLA's Standards Committee in November.[14]

The fruit of that labor appeared in the 1978 revised edition of the CWLA's *Standards for Adoption Services*. In a totally new section, the revised *Standards* recommended that adoption agencies offer post-adoption counseling to returning adult adoptees "to assist them to explore their attitudes toward themselves as adopted persons." In this context, the *Standards* suggested that social workers should generously provide nonidentifying information, such as medical history and information about biological family members. Missing from the revised *Standards* was the earlier recommendation that adverse non-identifying information be withheld from adoptive parents. But the CWLA leadership remained firm when it came to the issue of releasing identifying information. The *Standards* advised adoption workers to disclose identifying information only when ordered to do so by the courts or when legislation permitted. The single concession CWLA leaders made to the ARM was to advise adoption agencies to warn birth and adoptive parents that they "can no longer make firm assurances of confidentiality, in view of possible or future changes in the law or its interpretation." In essence, the *Standards* reflected perfectly the status quo of the majority of adoption agencies, which supported sealed adoption records and opposed violating the pledges of secrecy made to birth parents.[15]

Individual adult adoptees, however, were not waiting for the CWLA to revise its policy on sealed adoption records. Spurred on by adoption search groups and America's newfound genealogical zeal in the wake of *Roots*, thousands of adopted persons went in search of their original families. When thwarted by punctilious vital statistics clerks and adoption agency officials, many decided to sue. In the legal arena, however, state and federal courts resisted the ARM's demands to repeal unilaterally the sealed adoption records statutes, though with fifty different state jurisdictions adoptees won some victories.[16]

Initially, adoptees went to court in states that permitted the inspection of adoption records for "good cause." The results were mixed. Lacking a clear definition of "good cause," judges across the United States interpreted the phrase widely and applied the law unevenly. The arbitrariness of judicial decisions is well illustrated in cases where adoptees sought to view their adoption records for genuine medical reasons. In 1981, for example, a New York court ruled favorably in the case of a female adult adoptee who filed suit to see her adoption records. The judge was convinced that the adoptee had demonstrated good cause because of her fear that she had been exposed to DES, a drug prescribed in the 1950s to prevent miscarriages, but which current medical knowledge had revealed increased the risk of cancer in those women whose mothers had taken the drug while pregnant. In the same year, however, a Missouri appellate judge ruled against opening the adoption records of James George, a thirty-three-year-old adopted adult who was dying of chronic leukemia. George's one chance of survival was to find a suitable bone marrow donor, which in medical terms meant a donor from his immediate biological family. The judge contacted the alleged natural father, who denied paternity and refused to be tested for compatibility. There the matter ended. In turning down George's application to see his adoption records, the judge reaffirmed confidential adoption by upholding the legal severance of relinquishment and the birth parents' right of privacy.[17]

In a number of other cases, courts attempted to balance the conflicting rights of each member of the adoption triad. Judges often took this approach when adult adoptees, reflecting the social science strand of the ARM's ideology, argued that they had a psychological need to reunite with their birth families. Adult adopted persons contended that when the state prevented them from knowing the names of their biological parents, they suffered psychological damage from their inability to form a healthy self-image. In an Illinois case decided in 1977, for example, an adult adoptee presented to a Cook County judge psychiatric evidence claiming that his emotional security would be greatly improved if he gained access to his adoption records. Although the judge found the adult adoptee's brief convincing, he also concluded that both the adoptive and the biological parents had a legitimate right to privacy, which argued for keeping the adoption records closed. The judge held that due process required that the other adoption triad members be given an opportunity to testify. Nevertheless, the judge shifted the burden of proof to the adoptive and birth parents. If they failed to demonstrate they would suffer substantial harm, the judge ruled that the records should be opened. Other judges reaffirmed the Illinois case, which concluded that secrecy could be compromised for good cause involving psychological health, but they also made it clear that even when siding with adult adoptees, they would refuse to run roughshod over birth parents' right to privacy. Although adopted adults won occasional victories in state courts by convincing judges that they had good cause to view their adoption records, no court ruled that they had a constitutional right to the information in their adoption records.[18]

Initially, adoption search organizations neither lobbied state legislatures nor filed rights-based lawsuits to repeal sealed adoption records statutes. Originating as a self-help, consciousness-raising type of social movement, adoption activist groups and their leaders concentrated on organizing at the grassroots level and aiding adoptees in their search for their birth parents. Indeed, before May 1977, as Florence Fisher noted, her group, the Adoptees' Liberty Movement Association (ALMA) had "*never* advocated any legislative change" to state laws because if "we try to change the law State by State the adoptees who are being hurt by the present laws would all be dead and buried before the States would open up unconditionally." Instead, ALMA favored challenging the constitutionality of the sealed adoption law in the U.S. Supreme Court and having that court declare unconstitutional all state laws sealing adoption records. By late 1975, Fisher was contemplating just such a federal lawsuit in anticipation of an appeal to the Supreme Court. But she delayed filing it when she was contacted by the New York State Temporary Commission on Child Welfare. The commission had been appointed by the state assembly to make recommendations on a senate bill to unseal adoption agency and court records. Fisher hoped that the commission would not only endorse the senate bill but would also enlarge it by recommending that adoptee's original birth certificates be unsealed as well.

The commission's report, however, failed to support ALMA's position. It declared the senate bill unacceptable. Although in favor of unsealing adoption records, the commission refused to recommend that the law be made retroactive. Instead, it proposed opening adoption agency and court records only to adopted persons who had attained their eighteenth birthday *after* passage of the law. In practice, such a proviso meant that adoption records would not be opened until 1994 and then would benefit only persons adopted in the future. For adoptees not covered by the bill's provisions—the vast majority of adult adopted persons—the commission recommended that adoption agencies act as confidential intermediaries between them and their biological parents. Once again, the state's concern for preserving intact biological families and shielding the identity of birth parents from social stigma prevailed over the rights of adult adoptees.[19]

Feeling betrayed, Fisher lashed out at the commission's recommendations. She complained that "the *only* adoptees affected positively by this bill are those who have just been conceived!!!" As for the commission's recommendation that adoption agencies act as intermediaries, she called it "absurd and unacceptable to any adult adoptee who considers himself a human being and not an object. The intrusion of a social worker or, indeed, any third person, into a reunion between parent and child is an *obscene violation of the privacy of all parties.*" According to Fisher, the commission had it exactly backwards: there was no one better qualified to handle a reunion than an adult adopted person and "no one *less* qualified than the social worker whose orientation has been toward separation of parent and child—not reunion." Fisher accused the commission and the state legislature of duplicity to conceal their ulterior motive: "to save caseworkers' jobs and keep up the flow of *income!*" Fisher speculated that because of the recent dearth of infants available for adoption, social workers had found a "superb solution" to the problem of impending unemployment by manufacturing a need to counsel adult adoptees who were searching for their biological parents. Fisher would have nothing to do with the "charade" and refused to testify before the Commission and legislative committee. She angrily concluded, "LOBBYING FOR LEGISLATION IS NOT *THE* ANSWER! COURT ACTION *IS!*" Thus, in May 1977, ALMA filed a class-action federal lawsuit against New York's sealed adoption records law. Although not the first or last case to argue the constitutional merits of repealing statutes sealing adoption records, *Alma Society, Inc., v. Mellon* (1979) exemplifies both the ARM's wide-ranging and creative legal arguments based on rights and the court system's reasoning in rejecting those arguments and upholding the state's interest in keeping records sealed.[20]

ALMA challenged the validity of New York's sealed adoption records law on the basis that adoptees were constitutionally entitled to the information contained in the adoption records without showing "good cause." This constitutional right to know one's origins, ALMA claimed, was to be found in the First, Thirteenth, and Fourteenth Amendments. Sealing adoption records, ALMA argued, prevented adoptees from acquiring useful information and ideas (such as knowledge of their birth parents), a penumbral right the Supreme Court had recognized as being within the protection of the First Amendment.

A second constitutional argument was based on a novel interpretation of the Thirteenth Amendment, which prohibited not only slavery and involuntary servitude, but also badges or incidents of slavery. According to ALMA's brief, one of the five badges or incidents of slavery the amendment's framers had in mind was the severing of the parental relationship, depriving the children of slaves of the care and attention of their parents. ALMA drew the analogy that adult adoptees being prevented by the state from communicating with their birth parents were like antebellum slave children being sold before they were old enough to remember their parents. ALMA argued that because New York's sealed adoption records law effectually denied them the opportunity ever to know their "natural origins," it had abolished their relation with their birth parents. Like slave children, adult adoptees were prohibited from communicating with their birth parents and thus were forced to wear a badge of slavery.[21]

A third constitutional argument alleged that sealed adoption records violated the Fourteenth Amendment in two ways: it infringed on the fundamental right of privacy, which included the right to know one's origins; and it violated the Fourteenth Amendment's equal protection clause by making adult adoptees a suspect class, depriving them of a right to information that nonadopted persons possess. ALMA's claim that adoptees were treated as a suspect class rested on earlier Supreme Court decisions recognizing persons born out of wedlock as a quasi-suspect class. Any legislation affecting them was entitled to strict judicial scrutiny, which meant any state legislation interfering with their rights had to be narrowly constructed and justified by a compelling state interest.[22]

The United States District Court for the Southern District of New York dismissed ALMA's suit on the merits. On appeal, Judge James L. Oakes of the United States Court of Appeals for the Second Circuit addressed and rejected each of ALMA's constitutional arguments. In denying ALMA's First Amendment argument, Judge Oakes held that adult adoptees had no "fundamental" right to learn the identities of their birth parents. Instead, Judge Oakes found that the adoptees' right to that knowledge had to be balanced against the birth parents' right of privacy, to be left alone. In such a balancing, the court sided with the adoptive parents, the "family unit already in existence."[23]

It also found no merit in ALMA's invocation of the Thirteenth Amendment badges, or incidents, of slavery position. Judge Oakes reasoned that if it allowed ALMA's "absolutist view," it would render the Fourteenth Amendment's due process and equal protection clauses superfluous, which it could not permit. As the judge dryly put it, "We are appropriately reluctant to reach such a result." Moreover, he pointed out that it was not New York State's sealed adoption statute that deprived adoptees of their birth parents, but the adoption statute itself, which ALMA's brief did not challenge. Judge Oakes ruled that ALMA's Thirteenth Amendment argument was "misdirected."

Finally, Judge Oakes rejected ALMA's Fourteenth Amendment claim that adoptees were denied equal protection because adoptees were like persons born out of wedlock. He stated that the analogy was false: statutes sealing adoption records bore no relationship to illegitimacy. Adoptees shared none of the social stigma or legal liabilities that rendered illegitimacy a quasi-suspect classification and thus were not entitled to strict scrutiny.

Although Judge Oakes rejected ALMA's claim, he subjected the New York adoption records statute to closer inspection and found that the records served compelling state interests. In particular, the law sealing the records was directly related to the important state policy of encouraging the adoption of abandoned and neglected children. Judge Oakes reasoned that because secrecy protected the privacy of both adoptive and birth parents, it encouraged the use of regulated adoption institutions without fear of interference or disclosure, thus promoting the best interests of the children, the principle underlying the adoption laws. Judge Oakes concluded that the encouragement of adoption and the protection of birth parents' privacy were compelling state reasons justifying sealed adoption records and overrode the adult adoptee's right to know. By the mid-1990s, the Second Circuit Court's constitutional refusal to repeal sealed adoption laws still had not been overturned.[24]

If the ARM failed to make much headway in the courts, a small revolution was occurring among social workers, adoption agencies, and state legislatures. It manifested itself in increasingly sympathetic attitudes toward returning clients who were searching for members of their birth families and in more liberal disclosure policies. The Louise Wise Services (LWS), one of the oldest private adoption agencies in the United States, took the lead in changing its adoption records disclosure policy. It took this step because it had noted that, as a result of assistance from adoption search groups, LWS clients were "often successful in locating birth parents within a short time," even after staff caseworkers refused to give them identifying information. Noting the ineffectiveness of the agency's restrictive disclosure policy, LWS executive director Florence Kreech proposed that the agency should cooperate and assist adult adoptees in their search. Given the reality that most adult adoptees who searched found their birth parents, Kreech concluded that it would be better for all members of the adoption triad if the LWS participated in the search by offering professional help to cushion any trauma that might ensue. Beginning in December 1976, the LWS Board of Directors approved just such a policy. LWS caseworkers would now be thoroughly engaged in every stage of the search. They would interview and counsel adult adoptees on the pros and cons of searching for their birth parents. They would then contact the adoptive parents and help them recognize the value of cooperating openly rather than have the adult adoptee operate in secrecy. Moreover, the caseworkers would be involved in finding the birth parents, meeting and counseling them about the effects of a reunion, and ultimately, with their permission, arranging a meeting.[25]

CWLA officials viewed the LWS's pioneering policy favorably. They saw no contradiction between the League's new standards and the agency's acting as an intermediary for adult adoptees searching for their birth parents, especially since the LWS's policy mandated that if the birth parent refused to meet with the adopted adult or if LWS caseworkers were unable to locate the birth parent, the agency would not reveal any identifying information to the adult adoptee. League officials interpreted the LWS's innovative policy as simply providing a method for carrying out their new standards that agencies make their services available to adoption triad members seeking identifying information. As CWLA researcher Mary Ann Jones explained, "the

League has always suggested that agencies experiment and find ways, new and different, of carrying out the standards." Jones indicated that space could be found in the CWLA's journal *Child Welfare* for describing new methods of implementing policies dealing with the sealed adoption records controversy.[26]

Within the field of social work, professional journals had always been the traditional method of keeping adoption workers abreast of new trends, programs, studies, laws, and books. The pages of professional journals were empty about the ARM while the adoption establishment disapproved of it. After 1977, however, social work journals began to publish articles about the ARM, few of which reflected negatively on the issue of unsealing adoption records. Indeed, nearly every article placed the sealed adoption records controversy in a positive light.[27] Social work journals' favorable tilt toward supporting open records was inaugurated in 1977 by *Social Service Review* with the publication of C. Wilson Anderson's article "The Sealed Adoption Record Controversy." Ostensibly a review of the subject, it provided strong support for opening adoption records by endorsing the views of Sorosky and associates as well as the constitutional arguments supporting the rights of adult adoptees to access their records. *Child Welfare* also began to publish supportive pieces. In the immediate years following the publication of the CWLA *Standards*, the journal conferred its imprimatur on the ARM by favorably reviewing books that championed open records and chronicling agencies' new policies that punctured long-held fears about open records. In 1978, for example, *Child Welfare* reprinted an approving review of Sorosky, Baran, and Pannor's book, *The Adoption Triangle*—the ideological backbone of the ARM—by Elizabeth Cole, one of the nation's foremost experts on adoption. Cole pronounced it "a worthwhile addition to the growing literature on the effect of sealed records on adoptees, birth parents, and adoptive parents." The next year, *Child Welfare* described the success of a program initiated by the Children's and Family Service of Youngstown, Ohio, to assuage the fears of adoptive parents that the ARM was a threat to their relationship with their adoptive children. As a result of a group education program in which thirteen adoptive couples participated, staff members reported that participants felt less threatened by the ARM and more positive toward adult adoptees who were searching. Other professional journals, such as

Social Work and *Public Welfare,* also carried studies that presented the ARM in a favorable light.[28]

State legislators also began to react gradually to the groundswell of popular opinion favoring open records. In 1979 alone, dozens of bills to grant adult adoptees access to adoption records were introduced on the floors of state legislatures. Emotions often ran high as proponents and opponents of open records presented their views. Typical was the New Jersey legislature's experience in 1981 when it introduced an open records bill. In public hearings the legislature heard oral testimony from forty-four people, including Florence Fisher, which was supplemented by numerous letters from adoption agency officials, triad members, and others involved with adoption, such as Reuben Pannor. Many of those speaking in favor of the open records law stressed the adult adoptee's psychological "need to know." For example, Betty Allen, a school psychologist and adult adoptee, testified that "the need to know our own history is very strong for most of us. It is not idle curiosity. It may be almost impossible to fully understand the intensity of this need without having experienced, firsthand, the frustration of knowing that information exists, but is denied to those of us it mostly deeply affects." Allen also candidly addressed the fear of uncovering unexpected facts about one's birth family: "To learn the truth is not always a smooth and comfortable process . . . In my own case, I found that my mother was a deaf mute. Not able to fend for herself, let alone a child, she spent many years in the New Jersey Training Home . . . It was, nevertheless, the high point of my life, at age forty-nine, to meet her and to understand more about both of our lives." Others, such as Peggy Stapelton, recently reunited with her birth mother, made emotional pleas to the committee: "Please end our enslavement. Open your minds, your hearts, and open our records." Pam Hasegawa, an adult adoptee and coordinator of the New Jersey chapter of ALMA, impugned the motives of adoptive parents who opposed open records:

> The sealed records laws, while they may have been passed with good intentions, have warped our society into believing that only a person who doesn't care for her child would give it up. The fact that those who oppose open records claim such a burning desire to protect the privacy of women who placed children for adoption makes me wonder how they really feel about natural mothers. I sense in such opponents

not a deep concern for the natural mothers of the children they are parenting, but a fear that adoptive parents may lose the relationships they have poured their lives into.[29]

Testifying in opposition to the bill were representatives from organized groups of adoptive parents and individual birth mothers. For Debra Oliver, legislative liaison for the Adoptive Parents Organization of Trenton, opening the records invaded the privacy of triad members and abrogated the promise of confidentiality made to them. She told the legislators:

> The retroactive nature of this bill would strip away the confidentiality guaranteed to those birth parents and adoptive parents who entered into adoption agreements many years ago . . . The role of the birth parent in the opening of birth records is a controversial one. If she placed the child for adoption in the belief that the record was forever sealed, what now happens to that implied contract? Some say she abdicated her rights at the time of the relinquishment. Others say her rights must be protected because she was promised anonymity. Because we believe that all parties in the adoption triangle maintain their rights throughout their lifetime, we believe the birth parent should be contacted first and indicate a willingness to take part in a reunion.

The legislature also received an anonymous letter sent by a birth mother who conveyed her opposition to the bill. She raised a new issue that would later become a staple of open records opponents and would be politicized by Presidents Ronald Reagan and George Bush: adoption as an alternative to legalized abortion.

> Enactment of open records proposals will introduce great insecurity into the adoption process for birthparents and adoptive parents alike. The pregnant woman contemplating the adoption alternative cannot possibly know today what her life will be like two decades from now. In many instances only the legal assurance of a lifetime of confidentiality can provide a woman the opportunity to choose the difficult, but unselfish option of making an adoption plan for her child. Such a guarantee is imperative if she is to plan for her future, secure in the knowledge that her past will be as private for her as it is for the woman who chooses abortion. Furthermore, without the assurance of confidentiality, pregnant women may more readily be enticed into the growing black market, where records are not kept.

This last point brought the argument for secrecy full circle, harkening back to the late 1930s when unwed mothers threatened not to patronize state-licensed adoption agencies without the assurance of anonymity. Although both proponents and opponents argued long and eloquently, the New Jersey legislature failed to pass an open records bill. In this respect, the New Jersey legislature's action was typical. During 1979, some twenty-eight states defeated or allowed bills to die in committee that would have provided adult adoptees with some sort of access to information in sealed adoption records. Thus, the adoption search group activists rarely got what they wanted from state legislatures: open records on demand.[30]

Despite these setbacks, by the early 1980s state legislatures began to liberalize their adoption records laws. These changes reflected concessions, as both sides of the dispute began giving ground. On the issue of permitting adult adoptees access to adoption records, for example, search group activists began to work with adoption agencies, which favored secrecy. As a result, state legislators began moving toward compromise positions, which took into account the rights and needs of all adoption triad members. As early as 1977, the Minnesota legislature, responsible sixty years earlier for passing the Children's Code, which contained the first law mandating confidentiality in adoption proceedings, moved to a more open system. Initiated by Minnesota adoption search groups and with the cooperation of the state's adoption agencies, the legislators enacted a statute whose "search and consent" procedure allowed adult adopted persons access to their sealed birth certificate with provisos attached to protect the privacy of birth parents. Access to the sealed birth certificate would be filtered through adoption agency personnel, who would act as confidential intermediaries between the adult adoptees and the birth parents. At the adult adoptee's request, agency personnel would be assigned the task of locating and notifying the birth parent(s) in a personal and confidential manner within six months. After notification, the birth parent had four months to either refuse or consent to the release of the information. Both groups considered the Minnesota law a victory. Adoption agencies preserved the privacy of birth parents. Search groups "now had a legal right to an agency search and . . . adoption records could be opened under certain circumstances without a court proceeding."[31]

Child Welfare publicized this confidential intermediary method in a "Special Report" by Ruth C. Weidell, a Minnesota Department of

Public Welfare adoption supervisor, who described the law's successful operation during its first two years of existence. During that period, 332 adult adoptees returned to Minnesota adoption agencies requesting access to their sealed birth certificates. The overwhelming majority were Caucasian; 69 percent were female; 59 percent desired contact with their birth families; and 25 percent made contact with birth relatives. Weidell viewed the law as presenting adoption agencies with an opportunity to expand their services to the adoption triad. By 1980, an additional four state legislatures had enacted court-appointed neutral confidential intermediary systems.[32]

The effects of the nationwide agitation for open adoption records were easily discernible in the Department of Health, Education, and Welfare's (HEW) 1980 proposed Model State Adoption Act and Model State Adoption Procedures.[33] The Model Act originated in Congress's effort to fulfill its mandate authorized in Public Law 95-266, the Child Abuse Prevention and Treatment and Adoption Opportunities Act of 1978, which was the first national statute to define clearly a role for the federal government in the adoption of children in foster care.[34] Congress required HEW Secretary Joseph Califano to appoint a Model Adoption Legislation and Procedures Advisory Panel composed of seventeen members drawn from public and private adoption organizations and agencies and "persons interested and with expertise" in adoption. Among the members Califano appointed were an adoptive parent, an adult adoptee, a birth parent, and representatives from advocacy groups, including Concerned United Birthparents (CUB) president Lee H. Campbell. The advisory panel's guiding principle was disclosure, which was particularly noticeable in the sections on adoption records, where the Model Act repudiated the traditional notion of secrecy. The panel members stated their position candidly: "It is the philosophical position of the Model Act that secrecy is not and has never been an essential or substantive aspect of adoption." Moreover, the Model Act asserted, "modern attitudes and realities of adoption no longer support the cloak of secrecy upon which sealed records laws were based." Consequently, the sections governing adoption records opened them up to adoption triad members. Section 502 opened up original birth certificates, upon request and "as a matter of right," to birth parents and adult adoptees without recourse to a court order. Section 503 retained the prohibition on the public's access to court records, but opened up all court files containing records of judicial proceedings of adoptions to "any party" who was an adult at the time of the application, thus in effect permitting adult adoptees access to their records. Section 504 opened up adoption agency records to any adult who had been a participant in the adoption. It explicitly declared that "it shall not be a violation of the privacy of a parent whose rights were terminated for a record to reveal the identity of such parent to his adult son or daughter," which in effect abrogated the promises of anonymity adoption officials had made to unwed mothers. To clarify this point, Section 507 made the "rights of access to records" established in the Model Act retroactive and not limited by "prior law or assurances of confidentiality." As the authors noted, this section "essentially opens records for all adult adoptees."[35]

As originally proposed, the Model Act can almost be envisioned as a legislative coup d'état, an end run around all opposition to sealed adoption records legislation. Had it been approved without changes and subsequently adopted by the states, the ARM's leadership could have declared unconditional victory. But that was not to be. Standard operating procedure required that the Department of Health, Education, and Welfare solicit commentary from the public. It received more than 3,000 comments, of which 82 percent opposed the Model Act in general; 90 percent of adoptive parents who responded objected to the open records provisions. The CWLA also found fault with the proposed legislation. In February 1980, CWLA officials formed an ad hoc committee that studied in great detail every section of the Model Act and issued a report. The following month, a special CWLA Board of Directors Committee reviewed the report and rejected the Model Act. In the opinion of the CWLA leadership, the proposed model statute went far beyond its mandate and made numerous unsound recommendations, especially concerning opening adoption records. Writing for the CWLA committee, Edwin Watson stated, "We . . . believe that these statutory provisions are attempting to move much too fast." Instead, Watson recommended substituting Minnesota's search and consent procedure, which permitted a meeting only after both parties had agreed to sharing identifying information. By 1981, when HEW promulgated the act, renamed the Model Act for Adoption of Children with Special Needs, the offending open adoption records provisions had been rewritten "to protect the privacy of birth parents." Yet without question the HEW's proposed Model Act of 1980 remains one of the most radical blueprints for cutting the Gordian knot of the sealed adoption records controversy.[36]

The defeat rankled. Several years later, ARM activist Betty Jean Lifton reopened the Model Act issue by giving credence to the "adopted child syndrome," a concept invented by David Kirschner, a clinical child psychologist. Kirschner coined the term in 1986 while testifying for the defense in a criminal court case against Patrick DeGelleke, an adopted teenager accused of setting fire to his home and murdering his parents. Kirschner testified that DeGelleke exhibited all the classic signs of a "syndrome," which included a cluster of traits and behaviors such as theft, pathological lying, learning disabilities, setting fires, defiance of authority, preoccupation with excessive fantasy, lack of impulse control, and running away from home. According to Kirschner, "adopted child syndrome" was a contributing factor to the boy's psychotic rage. Other experts testified that there was no evidence to support such a syndrome and that it was unrecognized in psychiatric textbooks. The jury agreed with the prosecution's experts and DeGelleke was found guilty of second-degree murder and arson. Kirschner later admitted that he had not used a representative sample or a control group of normal children and that in fact he had not conducted any research at all; "the adopted child syndrome" was bogus, a product of his imagination.[37]

Lifton used the DeGelleke case to put the adoption system on trial and advance the cause of the adoption rights movement. She wrote a *New York Times* op-ed piece that claimed that "most adoptees exhibit" some of the traits of the adopted child syndrome "as a result of their confusion about heritage." Denying assertions by adoption professionals that no such syndrome existed, Lifton again mistakenly claimed that there was a disproportionate number of adoptees in psychiatric clinics. As evidence, Lifton updated her earlier accusation that there was a connection between secrecy in adoption and "the most infamous murderers of this century," citing the likes of "David Berkowitz ('Son of Sam'), Kenneth Bianci ('the Hillside Strangler'), Joseph Kalinger ('the Philadelphia Shoemaker') and Gerald Eugene Stano (who killed 32 people in Florida)." According to Lifton, the way to prevent cases like DeGelleke and other murderers was to re-store the open records provision of the 1980 Model Act that HEW had removed.[38]

Revision of the Model Act, however, did not prevent further statutory breakthroughs. In 1982, the Minnesota legislature was again in the vanguard of reform. It radically revised the state's adoption law by extending its search and consent procedure for original birth certificates to sealed adoption records. The innovative feature of the new statute lay in shifting the burden from adoption triad members seeking identifying information in their adoption records to those who desired to keep the records sealed. The law required that a biological parent had to actively assert his or her privacy rights by filing an affidavit expressly denying consent to the release of the information. Any birth parent not filing an affidavit was assumed to have consented to the release of the information in the adoption record. Even more extraordinary, an adult adopted person was provided the opportunity to force a birth parent to appear in court and defend his or her privacy claim even after the birth parent had actively requested confidentiality. In 1988, Nebraska legislators followed Minnesota's example by requiring that adult adoptees be provided with their original birth certificate if there was no "non-consent" form on file. The Minnesota and Nebraska laws made it much easier for adult adoptees to gain access to identifying information, for they would "no longer be hindered by the fact that a biological parent has not consented to the release of information."[39]

By far the most common legislative reform state lawmakers embraced in order to satisfy the privacy rights of all members of the adoption triad was an idea first suggested by Jean Paton in the 1950s: the mutual consent voluntary adoption registry. Private and public adoption registries already existed. In the early 1970s, both ALMA and CUB had established mutual consent adoption registries. And in May 1975, Emma May Vilardi founded a very popular one, the International Soundex Reunion Registry. Two years later, without changing the state's adoption law, New Jersey's Division of Youth and Family Services created an adoption registry to assist adult adoptees and biological parents who wanted to find each other. State legislators built on these precedents. They established central state registry systems whereby adoption triad members could voluntarily register separately their desire to be put into contact with each other. When a match was made, the two sides would be notified, but only after public or adoption officials verified identities and, in some states, provided counseling. Maine and Nevada were the first two states to enact such a system in 1979. By 1985, registries had become the most popular solution to the demand for open records, with sixteen states enacting legislation for their creation.[40]

The successes achieved by proponents of state adoption registries did not come easy. Legislative battles were often fiercely fought. Adoption activists' struggle and eventual failure to pass legislation to establish a national adoption registry illustrates the range of issues and difficulties that they were frequently forced to confront. In 1981 Senator Carl Levin of Michigan introduced the Adoption Identification Act, which provided for a voluntary national computerized data bank—a clearinghouse—through which adult adoptees, after registering, would be matched with their biological relatives. At a Senate hearing on adoption issues, Levin defended the bill's utility by noting that an adoption registry preserved "the delicate balance" between the adoptees who felt a need to know more about their own history and birth parents who chose not to communicate with children they relinquished decades earlier. Levin also emphasized the necessity that both parties consent to the exchange of information, a proviso "designed to avoid intrusion into the life of either party or violation of constitutional privacy rights." Levin repeatedly declared that his "was not a bill which opens files" and also requested that it should not be interpreted as an affront to adoptive parents.

Additional arguments in favor of a national adoption registry were made by representatives from adoption search groups, such as the American Adoption Congress (AAC) and Concerned United Birthparents, and from individual adoption activists, such as Jean Paton. One of their most telling arguments was that a national system was necessary because Americans' high rate of mobility rendered state adoption registries ineffective. As Penny Callan Partridge, president of the AAC, stated: "People can be born in one state, adopted in another, and live in many states during their lives. Likewise people can relinquish children for adoption in a state in which they have never lived and never will." Partridge argued that a national adoption registry would obviate this problem and provide adult adoptees with an important option for searching for their biological family members.[41]

Such arguments were lost on the bill's opponents. Of course the national adoption registry presented unique problems that state registries avoided, namely the intrusion of the federal government into family matters. Even though Senator Levin noted that state participation was voluntary, therefore avoiding any infringement on states' rights, opponents of Levin's bill, such as Warren Master, Acting Commissioner for the Administration for Children, Youth and Families of the Department of Health and Human Services, questioned the necessity and the cost of the federal government's involvement in facilitating adoption triad searches. He suggested that in the current period of fiscal restraint, when there existed more pressing adoption needs, such as funding subsidies for special-needs children, an expensive computerized adoption registry should be left to the private sector. In addition, Master voiced fears that computers were not secure and that registry participants' privacy would be compromised. Another serious objection to a registry, heard at both state and national levels, was that it jeopardized the institution of adoption itself. As Suzanne C. Richardson, president of the Massachusetts Adoptive Family Association, an organization dedicated to "preserving the role of adoption in our society," testified: "The existence of such a registry might cause many individuals who are contemplating adoption to abandon the idea out of fear that some day, someone will come across their names in a computer and use the information to shatter a relationship built after years of love and affection." Richardson also worried that a national registry was the beginning of a slippery slope toward opening adoption records and toward federal involvement in matters traditionally reserved for the states.

William Pierce, president of the National Committee for Adoption, brought up an entirely different issue. He opposed the bill because it did not define a match as the voluntary registration of all *three* members of the biological family, thus insisting that the biological father also register, an impossibly high standard. Pierce explained that without all three parties consenting it was likely that the privacy of one of them would be violated. He envisioned a scene where the birth mother would reveal the identity of the birth father without his consent. In addition, Pierce refused to support the bill because it failed to require the involvement of a qualified social worker as an intermediary once a match was achieved or specify a penalty for any adoption agency that violated the confidentiality of the sealed records. In the end, with influential senators from both parties objecting to Levin's bill as an unwarranted intrusion of the federal government into matters best left to the states, it died in committee.[42]

In addition to search and consent laws and mutual consent adoption registries, a third legislative approach that some adoption search groups advocated was to redefine nonidentifying information, which in many states was statutorily mandated to be given to adult adoptees, to include information that would enable them to identify biological parents—for example, the name of the hospital where the adoptee was born. Although this strategy was not common, the entire cultural shift toward openness and the rights of adoption triad members had unintended consequences when adoptive parents began forcing adoption agencies to reexamine their nonidentifying information disclosure policies by suing for "wrongful adoption."[43]

The first successful suit brought for wrongful adoption occurred in Ohio in 1986 with the case *Burr v. Board of County Commissioners of Stark County.* Twenty-two years earlier, in 1964, Russell and Betty Burr had adopted a seventeen-month-old boy, Patrick, after a county welfare department caseworker assured them that he was a "nice, big, healthy, baby boy." The caseworker explained that Patrick had been born to an eighteen-year-old unwed mother who was living with her parents and working during the day. The grandparents were abusive to Patrick, and the mother had decided to move to Texas for better work; she had voluntarily surrendered her son for adoption. The Burrs legally adopted Patrick soon after the meeting with the caseworker. Over the following years Patrick suffered from numerous physical and mental problems, including learning disabilities, poor motor skills, and hallucinations. In primary school he was classified as "educable mentally retarded" and was later diagnosed as suffering from Huntington's Disease, a fatal genetically transmitted disorder that destroys the central nervous system.

Eighteen years later, in 1982, the Burrs obtained a court order unsealing Patrick's adoption records. The records revealed some unexpected information: Patrick's birth mother was not an eighteen-year-old unwed mother; she was a thirty-one-year-old mental patient institutionalized in Ohio's Massillon State Hospital. The biological father's identity was unknown, but he was presumed to have been a fellow mental patient. The records also disclosed that Patrick's birth mother had a family history of Huntington's Disease and that the county had known at the time of his placement with the Burrs that Patrick was developing slowly. He had previously lived in two foster homes, and a psychologist had recommended that he be monitored for future deviant social and emotional development. The age and mental health of the birth mother, the abusive grandparents, the trip to Texas, and the voluntary relinquishment had all been fabrications created by the caseworker in an effort to facilitate Patrick's adoption. The Burrs testified that they never would have adopted the baby if they had known the truth—that they never even would have gone to see the child.

The case went to trial in 1986. A jury found the adoption agency guilty of fraudulently misleading the Burrs and awarded them $125,000 in compensatory damages. The Ohio Supreme Court, which heard the case on appeal and upheld the lower court's decision, emphasized that its decision was not intended to make adoption agencies guarantors of child placements and that agencies continued to have the right to control how much or how little information to provide to adoptive parents. Rather, the Court held that it was the agency's "deliberate act of misinforming" the adoptive parents, "which deprived them of their right to make a sound parenting decision," that was actionable. Still, *Burr* put adoption agencies on notice that if they were not more forthright in disclosing crucial social and medical information to adoptive parents there could be serious financial consequences.[44]

During the 1980s, the cumulative effect of the nation's changing cultural climate toward secrecy, the sympathetic media attention to the plight of adult adoptees, the shift in position among many adoption professionals, the intense lobbying by adoption search groups, and the liberalization of state laws governing access to identifying and nonidentifying information in adoption files wore down the adoption establishment's resistance. The shift in CWLA officials' attitude toward open records can be charted in a series of positions they took between 1985 and 1988, when the CWLA again revised its adoption *Standards*. In 1985 the CWLA established a National Adoption Task Force to define the underlying principles governing adoption and to promote changes in the practice of adoption that would meet the needs of children. In its published report the CWLA for the first time recommended that "starting with children adopted in 1986, confidentiality shall no longer be in effect once the adopted child reaches 18 or the age of majority." Although CWLA officials did not incorporate this section into the new revised *Standards* in 1988, they did include several others, the most radical of which stated, "Agencies should advocate the development of state and provincial laws that permit adopted adult individuals be given all identifying information, with the birth parent(s) consent, or after an unsuccessful diligent attempt has been made to locate the birth parents as prescribed by law." Under the new *Standards,* adoption agencies were advised to lobby for legislative changes that would shift the burden of proof from those who sought identifying information to those who had been promised confidentiality. The League's new position was still short of the ARM's demand for unequivocal access to the adoption records, but it is indicative of the distance CWLA officials had traveled in a single decade. As late as 1978 they had timidly recommended that adoption agencies simply obey state laws that favored secrecy. It is also indicative of the relative success of the ARM.[45]

Still, none of these compromise positions satisfied open records activists. Their unhappiness with the reforms that were won was due in part to ideological rigidity—there were many leaders, like Florence Fisher, who would accept nothing less than unqualified access to their adoption records—and in part to pragmatic considerations. As state adoption registries and search and consent laws began to operate, it became clear that they simply did not work very well. Part of the problem was the decentralized nature of the adoption registries. Arguing in favor of a national adoption registry, CUB president Lee Campbell informed a Senate committee of the tragedy that occurred because a birth mother registered with CUB and her son with ALMA. They searched fruitlessly for four years. When the son finally located his birth mother, he discovered she had died two months earlier. In addition, the number of matches never exceeded a small percentage of those searching. Even CWLA officials refused to endorse a 1988 congressional bill to establish a "National Voluntary Reunion Registry" because it would set up "a passive system which is likely to be ineffective."

Search and consent laws were also of limited effectiveness. They were based on a crucial unexamined assumption that proved to be fallacious when the law was put into operation: that adoption agency staff were competent to investigate and locate birth relatives. But as adoption researcher H. David Kirk pointed out in analyzing Connecticut's search and consent law, "Social workers are not trained as detectives; such work is alien to the main thrust of the agencies' interests and time commitments." The accuracy of Kirk's remark was underscored after one agency's fruitless seven-month search for a female adoptee's birth mother. The adoptee in question reunited with her birth mother based on information she culled from an hour's research in the public library.[46]

Adoption triad members' dissatisfaction with institutional and legal responses to sealed adoption records had an unintended consequence. From a social reform movement for adopted adults and birth parents to gain access to their adoption records, the adoption rights movement evolved into areas of adoption policy and practice its adherents never contemplated. By the 1980s, adoption activists challenged not only the secrecy of the adoption records, but secrecy in the adoption process itself.

CHAPTER SEVEN

From Open Records
to Open Adoption

Just as the baby boom and the steep rise in illegitimacy during the 1940s and 1950s radically changed adoption, so too innovations in contraceptive technology, cultural values, and constitutional law during the 1960s and 1970s transformed the institution of adoption. The most important consequence of these changes was the drastic fall in the number of infants who were available for adoption. The decline had multiple causes, including the demand for women's reproductive rights and the fact that increasing numbers of unwed mothers were deciding to keep and raise their children. These changes in adoption demographics and attitudes toward illegitimacy in the early 1970s lay the groundwork for open adoption, a major innovation in adoption practice, where the identities of birth and adoptive parents were exchanged and ongoing contact between the parties was encouraged. By the late 1970s and through the 1980s open adoption emerged from within the adoption rights movement (ARM) and moved to center stage. It was spearheaded by a small group of birth mothers who, grieving for the children they had relinquished, organized themselves into self-help groups and advocated open adoption as an alternative to traditional adoption proceedings.

As open adoption advocates gained adherents and the practice spread nationwide, opposition formed. A fierce ideological battle ensued, in which both groups used poorly designed and methodologically flawed social science and psychoanalytic studies to advance their respective positions. As the 1980s came to a close, open adoption activists had gained the upper hand, securing the support of the

Child Welfare League of America (CWLA) and the sympathies of the commercial press. At the same time, however, open adoption activists were raising the ante, demanding that open adoption replace altogether the traditional system of adoption.

Looking back, open adoption activists found few precedents to build on. Before the 1970s, open adoption was an exceptional, even accidental practice, lacking any underlying theoretical rationale. The Home Missionary Society of Philadelphia (HMSP), for example, began as early as 1882 to place a small number of children in families without indentures. HMSP officials simply directed parents who wished to relinquish their children to potential adoptive parents in the countryside; the children's parents and the adoptive parents were expected to make their own agreement. In January 1902, an open adoption agreement initiated by the board of directors of the Washington City (D.C.) Orphan Asylum became the compromise solution between a birth mother who wanted her daughter returned to her and the adoptive parent who refused to give her back. Six months earlier, the board had received the birth mother's request. After much discussion, the directors decided it was in the best interests of the child to remain in the adoptive home, but to let the birth mother know her whereabouts so she could visit her. The adoptive parent initially refused to permit visits, but she later changed her mind and signed a contract permitting the birth mother up to four visits a year at the adoptive parent's discretion. A decade later, in 1912, Washington Children's Home Society director Luther J. Covington signed an agreement stipulating that as a condition for relinquishing his child to the care of the Society, the birth father was "to know the whereabouts of his children and with the consent of the Foster [adoptive] Parents visit them from time to time." Two years later the New York Court of Appeals ruled against an open adoption agreement. The case involved a birth mother who had agreed to the adoption of her infant to the child's aunt on the condition that she be granted visitation rights. When the adoptive parent reneged on the agreement, a trial judge abrogated the adoption. On appeal, the Court reversed the judge's decision, ruling that the adoptive parent's consent to the abrogation, which was required by statute, was missing. The Court of Appeals thus nullified the open adoption agreement, and the birth mother lost any right to visit her child.[1]

Some open adoption advocates have maintained that before World

War II "it was not unusual" for pregnant, unwed women to board with rural couples who then adopted the child born out wedlock. There is no evidence for such a claim, however.[2] Before World War II, the stigma of illegitimacy was so great that the last thing that either birth mothers or potential adoptive parents desired was to attract attention to themselves. Moving a pregnant stranger into a household would attract attention in rural areas where everyone knows everyone else's business. It was to ensure their privacy that so many rural, unmarried, pregnant women traveled to *urban* areas, where they could give birth to their children in anonymity.[3]

If the practice of open adoption was rare, so too was the theoretical discussion of it. The first description of what would be called open adoption was published in 1964 by H. David Kirk, a professor of sociology at the University of Waterloo in Canada, who had read Jean Paton's writings. Kirk originated a theory of adoptive relations that identified numerous problems, imposed by society, that adoptive parents struggled with in raising their children. In this context, Kirk suggested that adoptive parents would increase their empathy with birth mothers if they could meet them before the adoption, and he proposed that the adoption agency arrange the encounter. Kirk also encouraged birth mothers and the adoptive parents to communicate in several ways after the adoption. The birth mother was to write a letter to the child expressing her feelings and motivation about the relinquishment. The adopters were to send brief annual reports of the child's life to adoption agency officials, who would pass them along to the birth mother if she asked for them, a practice reminiscent of the earlier era of disclosure in adoption. In this way, Kirk observed, the birth mother would "be treated as a human being whose relinquishment of her child has not necessarily wiped out her feelings for him."[4]

Despite Kirk's prescience, it was not until March 1975 that the concept of open adoption was invoked for the first time in its modern sense by the adoption rights activists and social science researchers Annette Baran, Reuben Pannor, and Arthur D. Sorosky. A paper Baran read before the annual meeting of the American Orthopsychiatric Association defined an open adoption as "one in which the birth parents meet the adoptive parents, participate in the separation and placement process, relinquish all legal, moral, and nurturing rights to the child, but retain the right to continuing contact and to knowledge of the child's whereabouts and welfare." Baran grounded her advocacy for open adoption in an analysis of traditional adoption patterns of native Hawaiians and Eskimos. In those societies, the family of origin was never concealed from the adoptee and the adoptive family; unlike traditional methods of adoption in the United States the parties did not deny children their "birthright." If those societies accepted adoption without secrecy, why not the rest of America? Baran told the audience that in the not too distant past adoption in America had been open. What had happened? Without any evidence to support her contention, and ignoring or unaware of unwed mothers' role in demanding secrecy, Baran blamed the demise of disclosure in adoption on adoptive parents, those childless couples whose "competition for perfect babies" was rewarded by adoption agencies with "increased guarantees of anonymity and confidentiality." But the times had changed. According to Baran, the era of secrecy—of sealing records, protecting adoptive parents, matching babies, and resolving unwed mothers' psychological conflicts—was over. The problem was that adoption professionals were unwilling to acknowledge these changes. Baran suggested that open adoption was in keeping with the new spirit of openness, a solution to the specific problems of the older child in foster care and the ambivalence of unwed mothers to relinquish their children for adoption. For older children in foster care, the presence of two sets of parents sharing household duties would act as a stabilizing force in the child's life. If birth mothers enjoyed the option of open adoption they would be more willing to choose adoption for their children born out of wedlock.[5]

Baran's blanket condemnation of adoption professionals was unfair. At least among its leaders, the adoption establishment welcomed the idea of open adoption, in contrast to its opposition to unsealing adoption records. CWLA representative Deborah Shapiro, who reported extensively on the conference, singled out for praise Baran's suggestion that open adoption was an appropriate alternative for the unwed mother with an older child, especially when the child was shuffled among multiple foster homes. By keeping the birth parent in the picture, open adoption provided continuity in parenting and reduced the child's confusion about who was the "real" parent. Shapiro was also enthusiastic about a black social worker's comment that "it was unnecessary for Ms. Baran to go as far afield as the Hawaiian and Eskimo cultures for examples of open adoption [because] the black community had always practiced it but had received little recognition for doing so." Shapiro considered this "another powerful point in the case for open adoption," for it represented a partial answer to the problem of recruitment of black adoptive parents. A further indication of the profession's approval was the publication a year later of Baran's paper in *Social Work: The Journal of Social Workers*.[6]

The call by Baran, Pannor, and Sorosky for open adoption coincided with profound sexual, constitutional, and demographic changes in American society that were responsible for creating a crisis in the practice of traditional adoption: the decline in the availability of white, out-of-wedlock infants for adoption. The sexual revolution and the demand for women's reproductive rights played a significant role in precipitating this crisis. The sixties' sexual revolution was a watershed in the history of birth control with the introduction and rapid acceptance by couples of a female oral contraceptive, popularly known as "the pill." By 1970, 58 percent of all married couples relied on the pill, the IUD, or sterilization to control family size. In the following decade, the number of live births in America increased only 11.5 percent, from 3,258,411 to 3,680,537. Important also was the Supreme Court's decision in January 1973 in *Roe v. Wade* to legalize abortion. The Court ruled unconstitutional the prohibition of abortion in the first trimester, thus establishing a constitutional guarantee of a woman's right to abort a pregnancy. In the next decade, thirteen million legal abortions were performed. The result of the contraceptive revolution and the legalization of elective abortion was a steep decline in fertility, most of it stemming from a drop in unwanted pregnancies.[7]

Another important cause for the sharp decline in the size of the potential pool of adoptive children in the 1970s was the extraordinary increase in the willingness of unwed mothers to keep and raise their babies. Whereas earlier some 80 percent of infants born out of wedlock were relinquished for adoption, during the 1970s only around 12 percent of such children were released. By 1981, 96 percent of unmarried teenage mothers were keeping their infants. Moreover, unwed mothers were rarely seeking professional advice about adoption. A 1978 study found that of 500 pregnant single women, only 5 percent ever considered relinquishing their child for adoption.[8]

How does one explain unwed mothers' decision to keep and raise their children? By the mid-1960s, most social scientists and social workers had rejected the postwar psychoanalytic determinism that viewed illegitimacy as a symptom of individual disturbance or family pathology. A number of careful studies of personality that compared pregnant, single women to their unpregnant, single counterparts demonstrated hardly any dissimilarity. Instead, experts discovered environmental, economic, and nonpathological psychological explanations for understanding unmarried motherhood. Similarly, social scientists uncovered complex causes behind the unwed mother's decision not to relinquish a child for adoption. Already undermined by the sixties' sexual revolution, the stigma surrounding out-of-wedlock childbearing was further weakened by the increase in divorce that made single-parent families commonplace. In addition, by the 1970s unwed mothers were able to avail themselves of financial and social assistance in the form of Aid for Families of Dependent Children and Medicaid benefits. In the case of teenagers, the motivations for becoming pregnant ran the gamut from "catching" a particular male, competing with one's mother, or escaping an unhappy family life. For a minority of adolescent girls, bearing a child out of wedlock became a source of self-esteem, especially for those who aspired to motherhood as the pinnacle of achievement. Adolescent unwed mothers also disdained adoption as escapist. After choosing not to have an abortion, adolescent unwed mothers believed they should care for the child. As one teenage mother stated: "I just disagree with adoption. I don't believe a woman should have to go through such pain and have to let her baby go."[9]

A few statistics resulting from these profound changes in American society graphically illustrate the substantial decline in the number of adoptions. Nonrelative adoptions in the United States fell from a record high of 89,200 in 1970 to 47,700 in 1975 and then rose slightly, to 50,720 in 1982. They remained at about this level for the rest of the decade. Exemplifying the downward trend were the statistics and policies of individual adoption agencies. In 1973, the Los Angeles County Department of Adoptions, the largest agency of its kind in the United States, placed only 1,100 children, in contrast to the 2,500 children it placed in a typical year in the late 1960s. Similarly, New York City's Spence-Chapin Adoption Service, one of the country's largest private adoption agencies, decreased its placements from 476 in 1967 to 110 in 1972. By 1975, adoption agencies across the nation began to stop taking requests for healthy, white infants. Social workers often informed prospective adoptive parents that they would likely wait three to five years for such a child.[10]

The result of this crisis in the availability of white infants was the empowerment of unwed mothers who chose adoption for their unborn babies. Social workers began to listen more carefully to birth mothers' requests to be included in the decision of who would parent their children. As early as 1971, the staff at the Los Angeles County Department of Adoptions was breaking down the barriers separating birth and adoptive parents by permitting birth mothers to choose an adoptive couple from among several applicants. By 1974, adoption agencies in the rest of California, as well as in Minnesota and Nebraska, also began to experiment with offering birth parents alternatives to the traditional system of adoption.[11]

The result of these innovative responses by adoption professionals to the scarcity of white infants was the introduction of a continuum of open adoption possibilities into social work practice. The open adoption policies that social workers experimented with at the Child Saving Institute (CSI), a private, nonprofit child-placing agency in Omaha, Nebraska, affiliated with the Disciples of Christ, illustrate this process. In 1976, the agency established a policy that adoptive parents provide pictures and general information about the adopted child to the birth parent for a specific period of time following the child's placement. For example, when a birth parent requested pictures of and information about a relinquished child for five years, CSI selected a couple willing to comply with such a request and had them sign a written agreement. CSI personnel served as intermediaries: the adoptive family sent the agency the material at the agreed-upon time, and the social worker forwarded it to the birth parents. The policy was a great success. Adoptive parents expressed satisfaction in choosing an adoption plan that reassured the birth parent of the child's health and happiness, and birth parents appreciated hearing news of the child while feeling they were more a part of the adoption process. One birth mother commented, "I will always cherish these pictures. They in a special way fill an emptiness I feel inside every once in a while. Whenever I feel this emptiness, I can always look at the pictures."

A year later, CSI social workers embarked on what they called a "semi-open" adoption: the birth parent met the prospective adoptive parents, but they did not exchange identifying information. At these meetings, facilitated by a CSI social worker, both parties exchanged personal information and asked general questions of each other. Again, the response from participants was very positive. One birth mother wrote CSI, "I bet if there [were] more people like Ann and Joe, there would be a lot more happier unwed mothers, knowing their baby is all right. I'm so glad you found them for me. I really don't worry that much knowing that they are taking care of her." Similarly, the adoptive parents of another semi-open adoption expressed their gratitude: "We see that this type of adoption was extremely helpful in that we know a little about the mother and father's background that we can tell Jennifer when she is old enough to understand. We can also explain how hard it was for her mother to give her up. By meeting her it has answered many of the questions we would always have."

CSI adoption workers began to experiment with what they called a "full open" adoption, in which adoptive and birth parents met each other and shared identifying information. These open adoptions were modeled after older-child adoptions, where the child already knew the identity of both sets of parents, and foster parent adoptions, where the birth parents had been in direct contact with the foster parents. Again, the response by adoptive parents was positive. One couple summed up their feelings: "It seems only natural that we would welcome our adopted child's birth parents into our home and family. He exists because they gave him life and nurtured him until his birth. We think of them as relatives."[12] By the late 1970s, a dozen adoption agencies across the nation were experimenting with a variety of open adoption practices. All evolved slowly and originated as a measured response to requests by their clients, especially birth mothers.[13]

Reinforcing unwed mothers' demands on social workers to experiment with open adoption was an ideological campaign waged by activist birth mothers. It was the ARM that first inspired many birth mothers to become involved in organized protest and demand that adoption records be opened. As one birth mother told Betty Jean Lifton, "We're tired of being considered incubators or baby machines. And we're grateful to you Adoptees for waking us up. If you hadn't come out of the closet, we birth mothers would be in pain forever." These were the words of Lee H. Campbell, a young, energetic Massachusetts housewife who founded in 1976 a birth parents' support group called Concerned United Birthparents (CUB), composed mostly of women who had relinquished children for adoption. Within a few years, CUB's agenda evolved from members' consoling each other and engaging in "consciousness raising" to actively searching for their children and advocating the opening of adoption records. CUB activists contended that most birth mothers would be overjoyed "to know the fate of their birthchildren" and vowed that "adoptees have the absolute right to full and accurate information about their origins, including identification of, and meeting with, the birth parents." By 1981 CUB, like the Adoptees' Liberty Movement Association (ALMA), was a nationwide organization with a membership of 2,500 persons in thirty-eight branches spread across the United States.[14]

CUB's major ideological contention was that most birth mothers desired information about children they had relinquished or wanted to meet them. This assertion, like most of the sweeping claims that ARM activists made about the universality of triad members' feelings, was exaggerated. Based neither on clinical data, nor on survey sampling, nor on well-designed research projects, the claim represented little more than the heartfelt emotion of a small minority of birth mothers. That of course does not mean that CUB members' pain and grief were any less real or genuine, only that the leadership made no concerted effort to discover if CUB members' experience was typical of birth mothers in general.

Certainly it would be difficult to conduct such research. Those birth mothers who felt differently about relinquishment and who opposed opening adoption records preferred to remain silent to preserve their anonymity. Evidence of the diversity of birth mothers' views, however, appeared on the op-ed page of the *New York Times* in 1978. That was a peak year for the ARM, when "television programs, magazine articles, and angry young people [were] demanding that old files be opened, old trusts violated so that adopted children [could] discover the identities of their 'real' mothers and stage an emotional grand reunion." With open records legislation pending in the Connecticut legislature, Ann Murphy, identified only as an employee of a Connecticut advertising firm, said she had interviewed 212 unwed birth mothers who had relinquished children decades earlier. According to Murphy, "more than 90 percent said they dreaded the thought of a confrontation with their past." Most of these women had started new lives and viewed with horror the prospect of revealing their past to husbands; a small number had been victims of rape or had had affairs with married men. Repeatedly, these women emphasized that the adoptive parents were the real parents. One woman stated, "I'm just a woman who gave birth. I'm not a mother. I contributed the months of pregnancy and the hours of delivery. The woman who raised my child contributed her whole life. She's the real mother—not me." Whether these birth mothers' attitudes were typical was also difficult to ascertain. Murphy divulged little about her methodology, but her description of using newspaper ads and public notices to attract interviewees, reminiscent of Sorosky, Baran, and Pannor's self-selected sampling techniques, does not inspire confidence in the study's representativeness or accuracy.[15]

Whether representative or not, activist birth mothers' initial demand to open adoption records evolved into the advocacy of open adoption. In 1979, Lorraine Dusky, a journalist, echoed these sentiments in *Birthmark*, a book-length autobiography that was the first to present a birth mother's perspective on giving up a child for adoption. In so doing, she inadvertently demonstrated how support for open adoption records led logically to open adoption. Dusky's involvement in and support for the ARM derived from the guilt and pain she had suffered as a result of not knowing the fate of her daughter. As she wrote, "That will always be the hardest part, never knowing what you are like or who you are, what you have become." Dusky repeatedly proclaimed her love for the child, asked her forgiveness, and vowed she would never forget her. Although Dusky asserted she had no regrets about relinquishing her child for adoption, her anger at the system belied her equanimity: "They call me biological mother. I hate those words. They make me sound like a baby machine, a conduit, without emotions, as if this thing just happened and now it is over and they are going to tell me that I must put it behind me and go out and make a new life."

Dusky's emotional odyssey prompted her to join ALMA, where she became an activist in the ARM. It also made her a firm advocate of open adoption. When asked what advice she would give an unwed mother, Dusky replied, "If the child had to be adopted, I would tell her to insist on meeting those parents"; it was her child, and "she had every right in the world to meet the people who will raise her child, and, yes, pass judgement and decide for herself if they are good enough." And if social workers refused to cooperate, Dusky advised the unwed mother to tell them, "Too bad; I will find parents to adopt my child another way. I know it can be done." Open adoption was becoming not only the logical way to prevent the pain of relinquishment, but also a new method to solve the problem of closed adoption records. If both birth and adoptive parents exchanged identities, there would never be any need in the future to deny adoption triad members access to their records.[16]

Dusky was unusual in presenting birth mothers' desire for open adoption as a right. Most birth mothers advocated open adoption based on a deep-seated psychological need to know. Unsupported by any theoretical perspective, ARM activists were prepared to follow emotion and ideology in arguing that relinquishing a child for adoption was traumatic and that it affected birth mothers for their entire lives. In 1977, Betty Jean Lifton's campaign to open adoption records noted that birth mothers found adoption to be "like an amputation, for the child was part of her psychologically. Signing those papers must be like a death ritual. And the pain traumatizes her whole life, a life she is expected to build upon a secret." The following year, Sorosky, Baran, and Pannor wrote that "although birth mothers relinquish all of their rights and responsibilities to the child and have no physical contact, their loss, pain, and mourning do not disappear." In 1979 Campbell, who had relinquished her son for adoption when she was eighteen and successfully reunited with him sixteen years later, marshaled these views to argue for the opening of adoption records. Maintaining the medical metaphor, she argued that birth mothers needed to know what had happened to their offspring because this vital information was "critical to the healing process." Using her own experience, Campbell noted that meeting her son had dissipated the "pain and the fantasy. The secret had been banished and replaced by healing." Campbell said that as a result she felt whole, empowered, and free to develop her full potential. Again CUB ideology validated the biological construction of parenthood. CUB brochures denounced the cause of birth mothers' suffering, the traditional adoption system, calling it "inhumane." If a woman was unable to support a child and had to choose between abortion and adoption, CUB recommended abortion as "the least painful choice for her." CUB naturally favored open adoption.[17]

In the same year Dusky wrote *Birthmark,* activist birth mothers found "scientific" support and an explanation for their feelings of guilt and pain. Two researchers, Pam Lamperelli, a psychiatric social worker, and Jane M. Smith, a nurse and human sexuality counselor, studied an unrepresentative sample of nineteen unwed mothers and speculated that relinquishing a child for adoption produced a "parallel grief" reaction akin to that experienced by a person who lost a loved one by death or separation. They concluded that unwed mothers were suffering from separation anxiety and were grieving for the infant they had relinquished. Lamperelli and Smith argued that Elizabeth Kübler-Ross's morphology of mourning and grief after the death of a loved one was analogous to the experience of an unwed mother who relinquished her child for adoption. Both go through a process of denial, anger, guilt, depression, preoccupation with the lost person, bargaining, and, finally, acceptance. Lamperelli and Smith believed that unwed mothers accepted the relinquishment of the child fairly quickly and with counseling could move on with their lives. Advocates of open adoption, however, seized on the concept of the grief and mourning process and, without any evidence, denied that birth mothers could ever overcome the psychological damage inflicted by relinquishing a child for adoption. Only if birth mothers had the opportunity to view their child's adoption records, participate in an open adoption, or engage in a successful reunion would they be able to overcome the trauma inflicted by relinquishing their child.[18]

As a member of its Advisory Panel, CUB founder Lee H. Campbell was able to introduce the concept of open adoption in 1980 to a wider audience by getting it incorporated into the Department of Health, Education, and Welfare's Model State Adoption Act and

Model State Adoption Procedures. In section 104(c), the Model Act stated, "nothing in this Act shall be construed to prevent the adoptive parents, the birth parents, and the child from entering into a written agreement, approved by the court, to permit continuing contact of the birth relatives with the child or his adoptive parents." The Model Act broadened the traditional notion of the family in adoption law by defining birth relatives to include birth parents, grandparents, siblings, and other members of the child's birth family. In its commentary, the Model Act justified open adoption as a matter of choice by declaring that the traditional practice of secrecy in adoption "should not necessarily be imposed upon parties to an adoption if they prefer a different approach and if continued contact between birth and adoptive families would not be detrimental to the adoptee." The CWLA leadership reiterated its approval of open adoption by commending the move toward openness. Nevertheless, concerted opposition to the sections providing for open records doomed the Model Act's emphasis on openness in adoption. The sections recommending open adoption, like those recommending open records, were omitted in the final version.[19]

A small but vocal opposition was responsible for eliminating the Model Act's open adoption sections. When the idea was first broached, even Betty Jean Lifton expressed some doubts about open adoption: "I think I'm much more conservative than a lot of my social worker friends who are all for open adoption. But as an adoptee, I have all kinds of questions about how it will work. When you're on one side with your adoptive family, you have a certain security. If you have this other known family, I don't know what that does to your identity with your adoptive family. It's such a delicate balance—how much they talk about it, how much or how often they tell you. It's very hard for people to be wise psychologically when they're emotionally involved. Yet it seems to me a healthy child would want to see those other parents." Another critic, Austin Foster, clinical director of Duncan Residential Center and consulting psychologist of the Edna Gladney Home, an adoption agency in Fort Worth, Texas, that provided open adoption, doubted that the Hawaiian adoption mode was transferable to mainstream American culture. It was too remote from most Americans' experience and the tradition of individual responsibility and achievement. In addition, Foster asked, were social agencies competent to administer open adoptions? In light of their track record with foster care, he thought not. Moreover, Foster argued, open adoption introduced too much confusion and complexity in the child's life through multiple parental figures. Yet despite this public debate, until the mid-1980s the practice of open adoption spread slowly and quietly across the nation and attracted hardly any public comment, positive or negative, from adoption officials or the mass media. The attention of adoption activists and their critics was focused on the legal and legislative battles over unsealing adoption records.[20]

Beginning in 1983 and accelerating throughout the 1980s, however, open adoption became the central contested issue within the adoption rights movement. The seminal event in the promotion of open adoption was the publication in 1983 of *Dear Birthmother: Thank You for Our Baby,* written by Kathleen Silber, director of the San Antonio office of Lutheran Social Service of Texas, and Phyllis Speedlin, an adoptive parent and founder of the Adoption Awareness Center, also in San Antonio. According to its publisher, *Dear Birthmother* is still in print and has gone through six printings, selling more than 80,000 copies. Reflecting the growing popularity of open adoption, sales of the book have increased year after year, instead of leveling off as do most books. Scores of adoption agencies and intermediaries use it and sometimes require it as part of their educational program with clients.[21]

Dear Birthmother grew out of Silber and Speedlin's experience with open adoption. They desired to share with a larger public the resulting "warmth, trust, and love" that the exchange of letters between birth mothers and adoptive parents engendered. When word got out about their experiment in permitting communication between birth and adoptive parents, they received numerous letters opposing the practice. Analyzing the letters, they reduced the objections to open adoption to four basic myths, or fictions. Silber and Speedlin organized their book around these four points, quoting liberally from letters they had received from open adoption participants that contradicted these myths.

One myth that Silber and Speedlin identified was the idea that birth mothers felt no emotion for the children they relinquished for adoption. If they did, mythmakers asked, why would they have given their children away? This perspective portrayed birth mothers as unnatural for relinquishing their children for adoption. Inhuman monsters capable of suppressing their innate yearnings to nurture their children, they dismissed their dreams for the child's future, ignoring the pain of knowing they would never see the child again. To counter this myth, Silber and Speedlin produced letters demonstrating that birth mothers loved their children throughout the pregnancy, felt conflicting emotions about adoption, experienced joy at the child's birth, and struggled for months to come to terms with the relinquishment. Above all, birth mothers were motivated to relinquish their children for adoption by love and the hope for a better life.

A second myth was that secrecy was needed in every phase of adoption to protect all triad members. According to Silber and Speedlin, just the opposite was true: secrecy harmed all triad members. In closed adoptions, adoptive parents were handicapped in carrying out their role as parents. The insistence by social workers that adoptive parents be just like biological parents sent the message that adoptive parenthood was inferior. In addition, because adoption caseworkers never gave them information about the birth parents, adoptive parents imagined the child's parents in shadowy, threatening stereotypes, such as sluts or potential kidnappers. Secrecy also damaged birth parents by denying them knowledge about the adoptive parents and how they were treating the child. Quoting a CUB brochure approvingly, Silber and Speedlin declared that birth parents were condemned to "a lifelong sense of psychological amputation" wondering whether they had made the right decision. Moreover, birth parents translated the advice of adoption caseworkers to forget the decision to relinquish the child into the belief that relinquishment was a shameful mistake or unpardonable sin. Finally, secrecy sapped the adopted person's ability to reach his or her full potential. Instead of developing normally, the adopted person wasted psychological energy pursuing answers to the question "Who are my birth parents?" As a "solution" to these problems, Silber and Speedwell advocated open adoption. With open adoption, they contended, all triad members benefitted. With the information gained about birth parents, adoptive parents abandoned negative stereotypes, empathized with the dilemma of relinquishment, and consequently were better able to perform their role as adoptive parents. Birth parents lost their sense of guilt and shame and felt better about themselves, secure in the knowledge that their children were safe and secure. Adult adoptees no longer wasted psychic energy on genealogical questions because they were all easily and accurately answered.

The third myth that Silber and Speedlin described was that birth parents forgot the existence of the unwanted child they gave birth to. Despite all the evidence to the contrary, this myth refused to die. This was no accident. Silber and Speedlin blamed its persistence on social workers, birth parents' families, friends, and adoptive parents. All needed to believe that birth parents forgot about their children. Social workers saved time and money by not having to develop a program of therapy and counseling for grieving birth parents. Relatives such as grandparents believed in the myth to protect themselves from their own pain and feelings of guilt for their inability to "save" the child. Friends also believed in the myth in order not to remind birth parents of their decision and awaken their grief and anguish. Adoptive parents needed to believe in the myth in order to quell their fears that the birth parents would return to reclaim the child. Open adoption destroyed this myth by providing intensive counseling for birth parents, family members, friends, and adoptive parents.

The last myth Silber and Speedlin identified was one they claimed was perpetrated by social workers, who contended that searching for one's birth parents was wrong, an act of betrayal to the adoptive parents. If the adopted person really loved his adoptive parents, searching would be unnecessary. According to Silber and Speedlin, the reality was far different. Adopted persons were curious about their past and had unanswered questions about their biological families that were typical of healthy, inquisitive minds. In support of this statement, the authors cited Americans' enthusiasm for Alex Haley's *Roots* as proof of the nation's unqualified passion for finding one's heritage. But they also noted, somewhat contradictorily, that the identity crisis of adolescence affected adopted persons in unique ways, which caused them to search for their biological parents. The authors cited research that showed that searching for one's biological parents was not a rejection of adoptive parents (adopted persons continued to love their adoptive parents) and that searching did not result in adoptive parents losing their child. Silber and Speedlin insisted that society could acknowledge the different roles the two sets of parents played in the lives of adoptees as equally important. The biological parents gave the children life and a heritage; the adoptive parents raised and nurtured them. One set of parents could never replace the other. "Each parent is real in a unique way," wrote Silber and Speedlin; "no parent is better or worse. The adoptee has a connection to all his parents which is as real as his life, given or nurtured."

In the process of identifying and refuting these myths, Silber and Speedlin took the offensive. They proclaimed the worth of birth mothers as human beings and denounced the societal stereotypes that condemned them for relinquishing their children for adoption. They strongly advocated open adoption as a viable option to the insensitivity of social workers and the harmful effects of the traditional system of adoption. In their opinion open adoption was the ideal method to ensure that adopted persons received all the information they needed to function as normal human beings. Silber and Speedlin were careful to admit that open adoption was not for everyone. But their intent was "not to become rigid in openness or to create a fifth myth that open adoption [was] the only form of adoption." Rather, they presented open adoption as another choice for individuals, though one that they firmly believed was more humane and appropriate than traditional adoption practice.[22]

Other activists, like Baran and Pannor, envisioned a more hegemonic role for open adoption, though as late as 1978, they had stated that "open adoption could never be expected to replace traditional adoption." By 1984, they had changed their minds. Open adoption, they believed, was no longer simply an option for a birth mother who was unwilling to relinquish her parental rights. Instead, they advocated that the traditional system of adoption should be abolished and be replaced by open adoption. This radical proposal first appeared in an article that Pannor and Baran published in *Child Welfare*. The practice of "secrecy, anonymity, and mystique surrounding the traditional adoption of the past," they proclaimed, "must not be perpetrated but must be replaced by a form of adoption that practices openness and honesty, and thereby permits a healthier and psychologically sounder adoption practice." It was now their firm belief that "all adoptions should fall within the open adoption framework."[23]

Baran and Pannor's demand for abolishing traditional adoption practices was more far-reaching than Silber and Speedlin's, but their arguments, though more complex, were very similar to those of the two San Antonio proponents of open adoption. Pannor and Baran based their argument on the notion that secrecy in traditional adoption inflicted a variety of psychological traumas on each adoption triad member. Their arguments in support of open adoption represented the triumph of a long series of pseudoscientific psychoanalytic studies, usually confined to academic journals, that stigmatized adoption and portrayed triad members as pathological victims. According to Baran and Pannor, closed adoption caused adopted persons to develop genealogical bewilderment, a state of confusion and uncertainty that interfered with the formation of one's identity. Citing H. David Kirk's theory of adoptive relations, Baran and Pannor claimed that adoptive parents also suffered under closed adoption. With its insistence that there was no difference between adoptive and biological parenthood, closed adoption forced adoptive parents into "unnecessary inequities, felt injustices, and serious social tensions."[24] The closed system of adoption injured birth parents, too. In the traditional system, social work professionals had uncritically accepted psychoanalytic studies that labeled unwed mothers as "disturbed" for not agreeing to relinquish children. Because they viewed adoptive parents as their primary clients, social workers armed with these psychoanalytic "truths" forced birth mothers to give up their children. But the lies and myths had come back to haunt social work. Instead of adoption representing the resolution of unwed motherhood, birth mothers had been unable to forget their experience and instead harbored lifelong pain and grief.[25]

Like Silber and Speedlin, Pannor and Baran viewed open adoption as the solution to the psychological problems of each member of the adoption triad. An open adoption, with its ongoing correspondence, pictures, and personal contacts, greatly diminished an adopted person's feelings of rejection by the birth parents. In addition, Baran and Pannor argued, open adoption provided adopted persons with an accurate account of the circumstances of their adoption rather than "the romantic stories, untruths, and distortions they have been told or have imagined." Adoptive parents also stood to gain by an open adoption. By providing adoptive parents with personal knowledge of the birth parents, open adoption diminished their fears and fantasies, which often had a negative effect on their relationship with their children. It also permitted adoptive parents to provide their children with authentic information about their birth parents. Birth parents, too, benefited by open adoption. By meeting the adoptive parents and exchanging information, birth parents became full partners in the adoption placement, permitting them "to cope with feelings of loss, mourning, and grief."[26]

The unexpected popularity of *Dear Birthmother* coupled with the appearance of Pannor and Baran's manifesto on open adoption in the influential journal *Child Welfare* set off alarms among groups opposed to open adoption records. William Pierce, president of the National Committee for Adoption and a formidable critic of the adoption rights movement, denounced openness in adoption in no uncertain terms as a practice that was "very dangerous, tragic, and disastrous." In 1983, Pierce produced a video enumerating the risks that all members of the adoption triad assumed by entering into an open adoption. According to Pierce, open adoption exposed the adopted child to the danger of feelings of rejection if the information imparted was misinterpreted. Moreover, the child might doubt the truthfulness of a sympathetic report about his or her birth parents or resent a negative one. The adopted child might also question why the birth father was not present at the meetings between the two sets of parents.[27]

Pierce also pointed out that the risks assumed by the birth parents in an open adoption included the possibility that they would feel uncomfortable meeting or rejecting adoptive parents in a face-to-face encounter. Furthermore, Pierce noted that in California during unsupervised meetings, birth parents were sometimes pressured by potential adoptive parents who offered them gratuities to agree to relinquish their child for adoption. Complications could also arise if birth parents did not agree to an open adoption. What if one birth parent did not want to participate? Pierce suggested that if an open adoption took place under such circumstances, the rights of the recalcitrant birth parent would be violated.

In addition, Pierce described several risks to the adoptive parents in an open adoption. Adoptive parents were at a decided disadvantage in negotiating for a child, and they might agree to an open adoption even if they felt uncomfortable with one. Moreover, it was possible that couples more qualified to be adoptive parents would be passed over because they refused to enter into an open adoption. Open adoption caused potential adoptive parents great stress as they feared being rejected for what they might say or how they appeared to birth parents. Pierce also noted that birth parents could contact the adoptive family at inconvenient times.

Pierce's criticisms of open adoption do not stand up to close scrutiny, particularly those regarding adopted children and birth parents. There was no inherent quality in a traditional adoption that prevented a child, when told of the adoption, from feeling rejected or from doubting the accuracy or resenting the truthfulness of the story. Similarly, Pierce ignored the point that birth parents freely chose an open adoption; nobody forced them. If they felt uncomfortable with the potential adopters, they could reject them. In the same vein, Pierce ignored the well-known fact that the plural "birth parents" was misleading, since fathers rarely were involved in adoption decisions. Finally, although unauthorized payments by adoptive parents were a potentially dangerous occurrence, strong agency leadership could prevent unsupervised meetings before the open adoption agreement was concluded.

The dangers that Pierce contended open adoption posed to adoptive parents were more realistic and were probably the real reason for the National Committee for Adoption's objections. In the new world of adoption, with its dearth of white infants and with open adoption gaining popularity, adoptive parents were powerless to disagree with birth parents' demands for openness. If these trends continued and they refused to participate in an open adoption, it was likely they would never receive the child they preferred—a healthy, white infant. Pierce assumed that adoptive parents lied to birth mothers about liking open adoption in order to receive a child. Under those conditions, for adoptive parents who felt coerced into participating in an open adoption, all birth parent visits would be at an inconvenient time. Even when all participants freely agreed to an open adoption, there was always the possibility that birth parents would not abide by the schedule for visits or would break the agreement not to interfere in the raising of the child.

Pierce and adoptive parents found allies in the religious wing of the New Right, which supported the traditional system of adoption as an alternative to abortion. Steeped in a traditional religious culture, these groups deplored the sexual revolution and the increase in illegitimacy, viewing the latter as the consequences of sin. In their view, the biggest problem facing unwed mothers was the stigma of illegitimacy, which they assumed had the same deleterious effect on young, unwed women in the 1980s as it had in the 1950s. Given these assumptions, leaders of antiabortion groups, such as Mary Ann Kuharski, co-chair of the Human Life Alliance of Minnesota, denounced open adoption because they believed that the loss of secrecy would inevitably cause unwed mothers to chose abortion over adoption. Moreover, open adoption would "destroy the adoptive family unit" by placing the adoptive parents in fear that the birth parent might one day abrogate the agreement. Open adoption would also injure the child psychologically, since having two sets of parents meant "the child would constantly be threatened with loss of security, permanent roots, and even heritage."[28]

Criticism of open adoptions also arose from an unexpected source when in 1985 five psychoanalytically oriented researchers—Adrienne Kraft, executive director of St. Mary's Services in Chicago, a ninety-year-old child welfare agency that handled many adoptions, and her four associates—published a series of articles defending various aspects of traditional, confidential adoption and identifying numerous detrimental effects that open adoption had on the adoption triad. Their first article dealt with adolescent birth mothers. The researchers agreed with open adoption advocates that grief and mourning were "central to the working through of the placement of the child." But they then made the commonsense observation that as long as some sort of contact persisted through letters, gifts, or actual visits, "the adoption cannot be really experienced as a loss." Consequently, the mourning process was circumvented and the birth mother remained emotionally attached to the child, who in fact had been given up. This complex emotional situation caused the birth mother to feel envious, jealous, and competitive with the adoptive parents. These emotions, the researchers believed, complicated the ongoing psychodynamic problems that the pregnancy represented. The researchers stated that there was a distinct possibility that in an open adoption the birth mother would act on this "pathology" with the adoptive parents and the child, to the detriment of all.[29] In short, the birth parents would interfere with the adoptive family and impede their own grieving process. In contrast, confidential adoptions enabled birth mothers to mourn their losses by allowing the normal process of grieving to run its course. Having achieved closure of the relinquishment, confidential adoption permitted birth mothers "to go on with their lives without guilt and without organizing their lives around adoption."[30]

In another article, Kraft and associates examined the effects that open adoption had on adoptive parents and discovered only unfavorable consequences. In an open adoption, the researchers stated, adoptive parents' "conscious or unconscious separation fears" could be stimulated and reinforced, threatening their sense of security. Indeed, the more contact that took place between birth and adoptive parents, the more likely that a secure and close bond with the infant would be impaired. From these premises the researchers concluded that "contact with the birth parent or birth parents can act as an impediment to the bonding required for healthy infant development." Adoptive parents' reluctance to remain in contact with birth parents was not necessarily an act of selfishness or hostility, but might simply be "an attempt to protect the intense parent-child bond from disruptions." In addition, adoptive parents' feelings of guilt might interfere with effective parenting as they attempted to atone for having benefited at the birth mother's expense. From the perspective of the best interests of the child, Kraft and associates were even more emphatic about the deleterious effect of open adoption on adoptive parents. They felt that "for optimal growth and development of the infant to occur, the ability of the adoptive parent to form and maintain a positive attachment to the child should in no way be undermined." For these reasons the researchers recommended that social workers continue the practice of confidential adoption because, unlike open adoption, it facilitated mother-child bonding and gave the adoptive parents freedom to raise the child without threat of or actual interference from birth parents.[31]

In a third article, Kraft and associates examined the adverse effect open adoption could have on an adopted child's social-sexual development. They suggested that in an open adoption the child faced added risks at almost every stage of development. During infancy an open adoption weakened the attachment between the adoptive parents and the child. During latency and adolescence, open adoption interfered with the child's need to internalize one set of parents and resolve normal adolescent conflicts. Open adoption intensified the adoptive child's identity conflicts and made them unresolvable. In contrast, confidential adoptions permitted the child to internalize one set of parents, which provided the adolescent with a secure psychological basis during the struggle to develop a cohesive identity and sense of self.

Summing up their research, Kraft and associates noted that no system of adoption provided a perfect solution satisfactory to all parties. Nevertheless, it was obvious that they favored confidential adoptions. While striving for impartiality, they urged caution before changing adoption policy and believed it was premature to restructure the traditional system of adoption "without a solid and scientific theoretical basis."[32]

Kraft and associates might have heeded their own advice. The scientific basis of these articles was questionable. Like almost all of the psychoanalytic research concerning adoption, confidential or open, theirs was methodologically flawed. As suggested by the title of their articles, they were theoretical pieces, not clinical ones. However, Kraft and her associates seemed totally oblivious to a quarter of a century of devastating attacks casting doubt on the scientific validity of psychoanalytic psychiatry. Their work rested on questionable Freudian theory concerning adolescent unwed mothers' "unconscious needs," the dubious Kohutian concept of narcissistic injury, and the discredited extension of John Bowlby's maternal attachment theory to the concept of mother-infant bonding.[33] Also troubling was the researchers' frequent use of problematic language. At many critical junctures, the articles were laced with the phrases "seems to," "may be," "distinct possibility," "one can only speculate," and "could have." The tentativeness of their language undermined the authority of their conclusions.[34]

These articles strikingly illustrated the unscientific nature of psychoanalytic theory, which can "prove" one thing or its opposite with the same set of data. Until these articles appeared, psychoanalysts, such as H. J. Sants, Lilli Peller, Herbert Wieder, and Marshall D. Schechter, had repeatedly used Freudian theory to describe traditional adoption in pathological terms and adopted persons as psychologically damaged by the process. Kraft and her associates used the same theory to come to opposite conclusions—"proving" that confidential adoption was a psychologically sound practice that had emotional benefits for all adoption triad members. Like Humpty Dumpty in *Through the Looking-Glass,* who told Alice that words meant anything he said they did, those who used psychoanalytic concepts for interpreting adoption practice were able to make their theories prove anything they wanted.

While open and closed adoption advocates marshaled pseudoscience to advance their positions, they did so mostly outside the public's notice. Their disagreements were buried in reports of professional conferences, obscure social work journals, or unread government publications such as the *Federal Register.* In 1986, however, open adoption became a major topic in the social work community and was finally brought to the attention of the public by the mass media. Suddenly discussion about open adoption seemed to be everywhere. Prestigious social work journals such as *Child Welfare, Public Welfare,* and the National Association of Social Workers' newsletter published articles summarizing and evaluating open adoption theory and practice. Popular magazines like *Newsweek,* which hitherto had ignored open adoption, ran its first story describing the practice.[35]

All of these articles, professional and popular, presented open adoption as a new and controversial practice and carefully presented both sides of the issue. Writing in *Child Welfare,* for example, Patrick A. Curtis, research director of the Children's Home and Aid Society of Illinois, summarized the arguments of Pannor and Baran, Silber and Speedlin, and Kraft and her colleagues, and dismissed all of them as "abstract and value laden," caught up in "theoretical dialectics and supported by anecdotal evidence." Curtis called for empirical studies concentrating on the consequences of closed and open adoption for the child. He went on to suggest that researchers explore the possibility that "over time and between groups of children placed through open versus closed adoption procedures, there may be no substantive differences in the eventual adjustments of the children." Similarly, *Newsweek* quoted Richard Zeilinger, executive director of the Children's Bureau of New Orleans, as saying that open adoption caused emotional conflicts and confused children about who their mother was. In the long run, Zeilinger predicted, the practice would destroy the institution of adoption. Kathleen Silber spoke for the growing popularity of open adoption among birth mothers and denied that it interfered with adoptive parenting. Other open adoption advocates emphasized that it was simply an option for birth mothers, that there was no one right way for everyone, and that it worked well with older children who had memories of their birth parents.[36]

The critical perspective toward open adoption found in professional and popular publications was buried, however, by developments in the mid-1980s. In 1986, the Child Welfare League of America, at its biennial meeting in San Francisco, passed a resolution endorsing open adoption as long as a consensus existed among all members of the triad. Two years later, in its 1988 revision of adoption *Standards* the CWLA added a totally new section recommending to its member agencies that open adoption "be an integral part of all adoption services." The League further advised agencies that "adopted individuals, birth families, and adoptive families are best served by a process that is open and honest; one that supports the concept that all information, including identifying information, may be shared between birth and adoptive parents." The degree of openness was left to individual triad members to be mutually agreed upon. In principle, this was a tremendous victory for the advocates of open adoption. How many and how quickly adoption professionals embraced the practice of open adoption, however, is impossible to calculate, given the lack of accurate statistics on adoption in America.[37]

Criticism of open adoption virtually disappeared from the public realm, smothered by the growth of a viable commercial publishing industry that marketed openness and disclosure in adoption in general and open adoption in particular. The most noticeable product sold was information about how to conduct an open adoption, search for birth family members, and raise an adopted child. Before the mid-1980s, adoptee or birth mother autobiographies, like those of Florence Fisher, Lorraine Dusky, and Betty Jean Lifton dominated the book market. But with the beginning of Silber and Speedlin's *Dear Birthmother* in 1983, there was an outpouring of advice and self-help literature catering to proponents of openness and disclosure in adoption.

Openness in adoption became big business. Books poured from the presses with titles such as *Children of Open Adoption and Their Families; Adoption Encounter: Hurt, Transition, Healing; BirthBond: Reunions between Birthparents and Adoptees—What Happens After;* and *Whose Child Am I? Adults' Recollections of Being Adopted.* Persons interested in participating in an open adoption got detailed advice from Mary Jo Rillera and Sharon Kaplan's *Cooperative Adoption: A Handbook* or Jeanne Warren Lindsay's *Open Adoption: A Caring Option*. Rillera and Kaplan's book walked the birth mother through every step of the process from mentally preparing for an open adoption, to what to say at the first meeting, to answering questions such as "Who gives the baby a name?" and "What about bonding?" and provided guidelines for documenting the legal agreement. Lindsay's book was more general, advocating open adoption by providing a historical overview of traditional and open adoption and contrasting the consequent traumatic psychological effects of the former with case histories and testimony of the positive effects of the latter.[38]

Even telling the child of the adoption became the subject of book-length treatment. Miriam Komar's *Communicating with the Adopted Child* and Mary Watkins and Susan Fisher's *Talking with Young Children about Adoption* brought to the public's attention a school of thought about adoption revelation that emphasized openness.[39] As described earlier, by the early 1970s, there was disagreement in professional and popular literature about whether to tell or not. Professional social workers recommended telling early and often, while psychoanalysts advised adoptive parents either to refrain totally from the practice or to delay the telling until after the latency stage of the child's development. This impasse was broken in the mid-1980s by the empirical research of David Brodzinsky and his colleagues conducted at the Rutgers Adoption Project on the cognitive abilities of children. Combining Jean Piaget's theory of children's cognitive development with carefully designed, controlled experiments with adopted and nonadopted children, Brodzinsky's research demonstrated that before six years of age, children, adopted or not, were simply incapable of comprehending the meaning of adoption. It emphasized the difference between the method of telling preferred by adoption professionals, which assumed that knowledge in children was the product of a slow, incremental accumulation of information about adoption, and Brodzinsky's own adaptation of Piagetian theory, which postulated that "children of different ages are characterized by qualitatively different cognitive structures, or rule systems, which allow them to conceptualize the world, including the world of adoption, in qualitatively different ways." Brodzinsky and his colleagues then devised guidelines outlining what they identified as six levels of understanding of the meaning of adoption that corresponded with the child's growth. At each age, adoptive parents were advised to be prepared to answer their child's evolving questions about adoption. The issue of adoption revelation was no longer whether to tell but when and what to tell. Brodzinsky and his colleagues had provided a detailed map of this heretofore confused landscape.[40]

The steady progress that openness and disclosure in adoption had made by the close of the 1980s, however, failed to satisfy open adoption leaders such as Baran and Pannor. Impatient with what they viewed as the reactionary attitudes of adoption professionals who felt threatened by change and uneasy at some of the trends they perceived in their followers, Pannor and Baran in 1990 reiterated before the annual meeting of the American Adoption Congress their call for the end to adoption as it had been practiced for almost a century and a half. Baran and Pannor accused themselves and all social workers of being complicit in propping up "a system that causes pain and life-long suffering to all the parties involved." Noting that open adoption advocates had "embarked on a world of 'How to' books, video tapes, and seminars to teach couples methods and ruses of locating and convincing pregnant women to give up their babies," Baran and Pannor exhorted adoption reformers to end such practices. In their place, they should turn their efforts to teaching young women about contraception and how to prevent unwanted pregnancy. Sounding very much like Progressive era adoption professionals, Baran and Pannor counseled their followers to find ways to "make it possible for babies to remain with their birth or extended families." If such reforms were enacted there would be little need for traditional adoption. Meanwhile, it was time to strike out in a totally new direction. Adoption laws that severed all rights of the birth parents upon relinquishment had to be repealed. Instead, Baran and Pannor would make open adoption, what they now renamed "guardianship adoption," the law of the land and prohibit couples who were contemplating adoption from pursuing any other alternative.

Baran and Pannor's call for the end of traditional adoption was the inevitable outgrowth of the movement's reliance on an ideology that labeled adoption triad members psychologically damaged as a result of secrecy in adoption. Ironically, as had occurred so often in the history of adoption, biological kinship was seen as superior to the artificial one of adoption.[41]

The Prospects for Adoption

For advocates of openness and disclosure in adoption it is the best of times and the worst of times. Throughout the 1990s adoption rights movement (ARM) activists and search and reunion groups have maintained the momentum generated in the previous decade. The mass media have continued to provide the American public with an almost uniformly sympathetic view of the ARM and its goals. Daytime TV talk shows, popular magazines, and newspapers have reported innumerable successful adoption reunions between adult adoptees and birth parents. The *New York Times,* for example, ran a story on the successful reunion between an African American woman who searched and found her mother, a white woman who had been raped thirty-three years earlier. The *Times* also published an account by an adoptive parent of a Native American who described her son's happy reunion with his tribal family. In her opinion, so important was the biological tie her adopted son had reestablished that she argued against recent efforts to weaken the Indian Child Welfare Act of 1978, efforts that would have barred the adoption from occurring had it been in force at the time she adopted her son. In the mid-1990s, search and reunion accounts became the story line of Hollywood films such as *Mighty Aphrodite* and *Flirting with Disaster.* Their box-office success suggests that searching for biological kin is now widely accepted in American culture.[1]

With such widespread publicity, adoptee and birth parent search and reunion groups multiplied and prospered. Although there are no official statistics, in 1986 the magazine *People Searching News* reported contact with more than 800 search and support groups. The number has undoubtedly increased since. With the growth of search and reunion groups have come many innovations to assist adoption triad members in locating family members. Comprehensive search manuals, such as Jayne Askin's *Search: A Handbook for Adoptees and Birthparents,* are available, and triad members can get initial guidance from Mary Jo Rillera's PURE, Inc., Triadoption Services, a 900-number telephone referral service for organizations in their local area. They can also join public and private adoption registries, hire private investigators, and subscribe to newsletters to aid them in searching for family members. In addition, with the increasing popularity of the Internet, there has been an explosion of adoptee and birth parent bulletin boards, news groups, and World Wide Web sites where triad members can discuss search techniques, advocate legislative changes, stay abreast of current legal developments, and get advice on everything from which adoption agencies practice open adoption to explaining adoption to a child.[2]

Publishers were happy to supply new converts to the ARM with books. Increasingly aware of the profit potential in items related to the ARM, commercial publishers sought out ever more specialized audiences. In addition to autobiographies and search manuals, publishers targeted female adoption triad members, who could read about themselves in *The Adoption Reader: Birth Mothers, Adoptive Mothers, and Adopted Daughters Tell Their Stories.* Publishers also detected a mystical strain that ran through many accounts of adoption triad reunions and targeted that audience with books like *Synchronicity and Reunion: The Genetic Connection of Adoptees and Birthparents,* which purported to find an interrelationship between "psychopathy (separation and loss), psychophysiology (longing and pain) and the anomalistic psychological phenomena of intuition, telepathy, and synchronicity."[3]

Most of the social science research published in the 1990s continued to support opening adoption records. Paul Sachdev, professor of social work at Memorial University of Newfoundland, conducted a survey questionnaire in Ontario, Canada, of the experiences of 123 adoptees who had reunited with their biological mothers and other relatives. Sachdev found that an overwhelming majority of adoptees

(86.9 percent) were pleased or moderately pleased with meeting their birth parents; three-fourths of the biological mothers reacted with moderate to strong enthusiasm when contacted by the adoptees; and a majority of adoptive parents supported their child's search efforts. The vast majority of adoptees reported that their relationship with their adoptive parents either improved or remained the same; only five adoptees experienced a deterioration of the adoptive relationship as a result of the reunion. Following the initial contact, half of the adoptees saw their biological mothers regularly, while almost another fifth saw them occasionally. A huge majority of adoptees (85.4 percent) reported feeling a sense of relief that the search was over and no longer had to "dwell on fantasies and bewilderment about their genealogy." Sachdev believes that he has refuted adoption professionals' claims that secrecy is necessary to provide safeguards against unwanted intrusion by triad members and that contact would disrupt families. His study also demonstrated that adoptive parents did not lose the love of their children after contact was made with birth parents. Sachdev exhorted legislatures and adoption agencies to stop promoting an adoption system that causes "needless grief, pain, and fears among members of the adoption triangle" and to join with reformers "to restructure the adoption process" on the principles of openness and disclosure.[4]

The publicity, advocacy, and positive research praising the opening of adoption records resulted in continued gains in state legislatures. By the mid-1990s, seventeen states permitted a court-appointed, neutral confidential intermediary to inquire whether birth family members were interested in meeting each other. The spectacular growth in state intermediary systems represented a 300 percent increase from the previous decade. Moreover, nineteen states had established formal mutual consent adoption registries, and another six states had authorized releasing identifying information upon mutual consent without a formal registry, a 64 percent increase. Copying a successful open adoption records law in New South Wales, Australia, Tennessee's legislature broke new ground in the United States in March 1996 by permitting persons adopted before 1951 to view their adoption records. The novelty of the law lay in a proviso that protected the privacy of birth parents by allowing them to file a "veto contract" prohibiting the release of information unless the children agreed not to contact them. The legislature mandated civil and criminal penalties for violating the veto. Without a veto contract on file, however, the adoption records would be open to all adult adoptees. In addition to this wide spectrum of procedures allowing triad members access to their records, four states—Alaska, Kansas, Tennessee, and Washington—permitted them direct access to original birth certificates.[5]

During the 1990s laws favoring the disclosure of family information to adoptive parents multiplied. In the wake of *Burr,* the legal definition of wrongful adoption expanded. Court decisions in five states upheld wrongful adoption suits against child-placing institutions, not only for intentional misrepresentation or deliberate concealment but also for negligence, defined as failing to inform adoptive parents of a child's medical or social history or providing inaccurate information about a child's health or background. A Massachusetts jury in 1991, for example, awarded an adoptive couple $3.8 million because the state's Department of Social Services withheld the information that the adopted child was retarded and his biological mother schizophrenic.[6]

Thanks to the wrongful adoption suits, adoptive parents are much more likely to receive all of the nonidentifying information—favorable and adverse—about the child's developmental, medical, and genetic history as well as nonidentifying information about the biological parents. This has come about not only from the revision of the CWLA *Standards* concerning nonidentifying information, but also as a consequence of state legislation. By 1990, at least twenty-one states had enacted mandatory disclosure statutes requiring adoption agencies or intermediaries to provide adoptive parents with information about the child's medical history; eleven states required disclosure of the child's social history; and almost every state ordered the disclosure of the biological parent's medical history.[7]

Open adoption also fared well in the 1990s at the hands of authors, researchers, and advocates. In 1990, the *New Yorker* serialized Lincoln Caplan's book *An Open Adoption.* Caplan, an adoptive parent and staff writer for the magazine, deftly combined a history of adoption with the story of how a childless couple in their thirties, Dan and Lee Stone, met and interacted with birth parents Peggy Bass and Tom Spaeth. Peggy, seven months pregnant, had chosen the Stones for an open adoption of her soon-to-be-born child, Rebecca. Although the

two couples experienced some rough patches before Peggy relinquished Rebecca to the Stones, all was eventually resolved happily;
the value of open adoption was affirmed. The book was reviewed
favorably on the front page of the *New York Times Book Review.*[8] Research by social work professionals also supported the practice of
open adoption. A review of five studies representing 121 adoptions
with some degree of openness concluded that a preponderance of
both sets of parents viewed their experience favorably. Mainstream
commercial publishers like Macmillan and HarperCollins helped
popularize these favorable views with the publication of self-help
books like *The Open Adoption Book* and *The Open Adoption Experience.*[9]

As openness in adoption flourished, the reputation of traditional
adoption repeatedly came under attack. In stark contrast to the aura
of confidence and vigor surrounding the cause of openness and disclosure in adoption, traditional adoption was increasingly stigmatized as an unfeeling and abusive institution. It was repeatedly involved in incidents that cast it in an unfavorable light, beginning as
early as the 1986 landmark Baby M custody case, which the media
depicted as heartless, upper-class adoptive parents, the Sterns, forcing
a working-class birth mother, Mary Beth Whitehead, to abide by the
surrogate contract she signed and give up her child to them; and the
1987 killing of six-year-old Lisa Steinberg by her abusive "adoptive"
father.[10]

Negative images of traditional adoption practices continued to
come before the public's attention throughout the 1990s—witness
the highly publicized marital woes of director-actor Woody Allen,
who was charged with sexual molestation of his adopted daughter,
Dylan, and who admitted involvement in an amorous relationship
with another of Mia Farrow's adopted daughters, twenty-one-year-
old Soon-Yi Previn. In addition, the bogus concept "adopted child
syndrome" resurfaced in the trial of serial killer Joel Rifkin, who
claimed to be insane as a result of the "trauma" of adoption. And
there was widespread criticism of the discrimination against white
families who wished to adopt black children. Intercountry adoption
also contributed to traditional adoption's image problems, as critics
repeatedly charged that infertile American couples have purchased
infants in overseas "markets" such as Romania, Paraguay, and

China. In addition to "baby buying," rumors falsely accused inter-country adoption officials of running organ transplant rings for world customers under the auspices of adopting children from overseas.[11]

The negative image of traditional adoption was reinforced in ARM therapeutic advice and self-help adoption publications. One of the most popular in this vein, Nancy Newton Verrier's *The Primal Wound: Understanding the Adopted Child,* used pseudoscientific psychoanalytic theories to support the premise that adoption was a traumatic experience for the adoptee. According to Verrier, the trauma began with the child's separation from the birth mother and ended "with his living with strangers." As a result, "the primal experience for the adopted child [was] abandonment," a form of post-traumatic stress disorder characterized by depression, anxiety, helplessness, numbing, and loss of control. Although Verrier suggested some ways of healing this "wound," she pessimistically concluded that adoptees would live out the rest of their lives with "a perpetual feeling of being a victim, of being powerless, of being helpless to help oneself." The idea that traditional adoption was by definition dysfunctional was also the basic assumption behind the launching in 1990 of the journal *Adoption Therapist,* containing such articles as "The Adult Adoptee: The Biological Alien" and "The Orphaned Element of the Adoptive Experience."[12]

The image of traditional adoption suffered from a resurgence in the cultural belief that blood ties have primacy, a trend that caused adoptive parents to feel second-rate. A series of court decisions in the 1990s reaffirmed America's traditional conviction of the superiority of biological families. In 1993, a Federal appellate court dismissed charges against a woman accused of taking her children at gunpoint from their foster parents in South Carolina. The judge based his ruling on the premise that federal kidnapping laws did not apply to biological parents. Upon hearing the decision, an advocate for adoptive parents declared, "They're saying adoption means nothing."[13]

Courts repeatedly sided with biological parents in highly publicized contested custody cases. The most celebrated example was the 1993 Baby Jessica case, where a judge ruled that four-and-a-half-year-old Jessica should be separated from her adoptive parents and returned to CUB member and birth mother Cara Clausen and her ex-boyfriend and birth father, Dan Schmidt. The case, which made newspaper headlines for months, was *Time*'s cover story and the subject of a searching *New Yorker* profile. The next year, the nation was treated to a replay of the importance of blood ties when the Illinois Supreme Court revoked the adoption of three-year-old "Baby Richard" and returned him to Otakar Kirchner, his biological father. The case revealed that Baby Richard's biological mother had lied to Kirchner about the boy's existence and on discovering the truth Kirchner successfully argued that he had never surrendered his parental rights. As the nation watched the tearful boy being taken away from his adoptive parents, neighbors and onlookers shouted "Monster!" at the biological father. Nevertheless, the decision was later upheld by the U.S. Supreme Court.[14]

But in other respects, it was the worst of times for the advocates of openness in adoption. Despite long years of agitation, the ARM still had not achieved its primary objective of gaining unlimited access to original birth certificates and identifying information in adoption case records and court proceedings. Birth mothers' right to privacy proved an insuperable obstacle. The irony of this fact has been lost on most ARM activists. Though one of the central tenets of the ARM's ideology rests on the superiority of blood ties and the denigration of adoptive kinship, judges and lawmakers, sharing with adoption activists a bias toward biological kinship, have been unwilling to abrogate the promise of secrecy that adoption agencies had explicitly made to birth mothers. By the mid-1990s, the Second Circuit Court's 1979 refusal to repeal sealed adoption laws in *ALMA Society, Inc., v. Mellon* on constitutional grounds had still not been superseded. Similarly, at the state level, few legislators had been persuaded to permit members of the adoption triad unimpeded access. In some states, like New Jersey, time seemed to stand still. In 1981, Pam Hasegawa, coordinator of the New Jersey Chapter of ALMA, testified before the state legislature in favor of open records. Sixteen years later, Hasegawa, now a leader of the New Jersey Coalition for Openness in Adoption, was still trying to convince the Garden State's legislators of the need to enact a law permitting adult adoptees access to their original birth certificates.[15]

In 1994, adoption activists were stymied in their efforts to reform the newly drafted Uniform Adoption Act (UAA) developed by the National Conference of Commissioners on Uniform Laws. After five years of intense debate between adoption activists and their opponents on the issue of opening sealed adoption records, the commissioners concluded that adoption records should be sealed for ninety-nine years. The best method for the release of identifying information, they stated, was a voluntary, mutual consent registry. That decision maintained the status quo on open records in most states. ARM groups, such as the American Adoption Congress and Concerned United Birthparents, immediately denounced the UAA. Along with a number of mainstream organizations, such as the Child Welfare League of America and the National Association of Social Workers (NASW), they opposed the entire UAA, but ultimately failed to convince the commissioners that adoption records should be opened. The NASW's commentary on the Act was noticeable for its hostility to adoption in general. Sounding very much like Progressive Era adoption professionals and present-day advocates of open adoption, NASW stated that it opposed the Act because "NASW believes that the objective of child placement should be to provide a safe, nurturing, and secure alternative home only when it is not possible for the child to remain with his or her own family." As usual, proponents of openness in adoption viewed blood ties as far superior to artificial ones.[16]

By the mid-1990s, even the compromise position of the "search and consent" intermediary system came under attack. Criticism of overzealous intermediaries harassing persons who refused to meet with an adoption triad member surfaced in the press. The problem resulted when judges appointed volunteers, many of whom were active in the ARM, to read adoption records and conduct searches for birth family relatives. In one case, after successfully searching for and contacting an adult adoptee, an activist intermediary did not hang up the phone after being told that the adoptee did not want to meet family members. Instead, the intermediary read from the adoption case record a litany of childhood abuse that was unknown to the adoptee. Shocked and angered at receiving this unwanted information, the adoptee has since hired an attorney and filed a civil suit against the intermediary. Although some states, such as Washington, have a training program for intermediaries, public criticism of even the compromise position for opening adoption records does not bode well for the ARM's ultimate goal.[17]

The adoption rights movement was also tainted in the 1990s by criminal wrongdoing. The charge centered around the activity of Sandra Musser, a birth mother who in 1977 reunited with the daughter she had relinquished for adoption twenty-three years earlier. After that experience Musser had become an outspoken advocate of opening adoption records and the founder of the Musser Foundation, a search and reunification business for adult adoptees seeking to find their birth parents. In 1993, Musser was convicted in federal court of conspiring with Barbara Moskowitz to use various ruses to obtain identifying information about birth parents from confidential Social Security and medical records. In her defense, Musser declared that her conduct was a form of civil disobedience against the immorality of laws that seal adoption records. She was sentenced to four months in federal prison for fraud, conspiracy, and theft of government property. The case received extensive publicity when Musser appeared on a segment of the television series *60 Minutes*.[18]

Support for traditional adoption also surfaced in the 1990s. In the wake of the Baby Jessica case, polls revealed overwhelming sympathy for the adoptive parents and disapproval of returning the child to her biological parents. A well-received book by Harvard law professor and adoptive parent Elizabeth Bartholet eloquently defended intercountry adoption. Congress passed legislation giving a $5,000 tax credit to families adopting a child, and President Clinton announced in his radio address that he wanted the government to ensure that 54,000 foster children a year be adopted by the year 2002. A study comparing teenage mothers who chose to rear their children with those who placed their children for adoption revealed no significant differences in depression or personal efficacy among the placers. Indeed, over a two-year period, the birth mothers who placed their children for adoption completed more schooling, were more likely to be employed, and were less likely to be receiving welfare than those who chose to keep their babies. Research on adopted adolescents tended to undermine criticism of adoption as a system that psychologically damaged its clients. A national, representative study of 715 adoptive families and their biological counterparts conducted by the Search Institute, a nonprofit Minnesota-based organization, found that adopted teenagers were no more likely than nonadopted teenagers to suffer from mental health or identity problems. A majority of adolescents surveyed said adoption had always been easy for them and that they did not think about adoption very much. If anything, traditional adoption seemed to have been an advantage for the children studied. A majority of the adopted teenagers scored high on measurements of self-esteem and scored better on sixteen indicators of well-being, including friendship and academic achievement, than did nonadopted adolescents in the national sample. Adopted adolescents also reported slightly fewer signs of high-risk behavior, such as binge drinking and theft, compared to nonadopted teenagers.[19]

After twenty-five years the ARM still actively lobbies to unseal adoption records. Will the standoff between the advocates of openness in adoption and their opponents ever be resolved? Will triad members ever be permitted unlimited access to their adoption records? Will open adoption replace traditional adoption? The history of adoption suggests that such complex issues will not be settled easily or soon. For every trend toward openness and disclosure, there are countercurrents favoring the survival of secrecy. Take, for example, the prediction that secrecy will naturally disappear because of the changing demographic profile of adopted children. One prominent trend today is the increase in the adoption of older children, children from other countries, and children with special needs (many of whom are also older); together such cases make up more than one-quarter of all nonrelative adoptions. Because older children retain memories of their biological parents and children from overseas are rarely adopted by parents whose ethnic heritage matches their own, the argument goes, it will be impossible to maintain secrecy about the existence of a second set of parents; hence there will be no rationale for sealing the records. Yet as strong as these trends are, many children are still adopted by parents who want secrecy. Witness the increasing number of both birth and adoptive parents who adopt independently to avoid agency adoptions, which increasingly follow the CWLA's recommendation to practice open adoption and make no promises of confidentiality to birth mothers. It is estimated that one-third to one-half of all nonrelative adoptions today are independent adoptions. It is hard not to conclude that there will always be some adoptive triad members with a claim to privacy.[20]

Or consider the possibility that the ARM will achieve its goal to unseal the adoption records by legislative enactment. Some lawmakers may come to look more kindly on the ARM agenda. With the passing of the post–World War II generation of birth mothers who insisted that adoption professionals safeguard their privacy, state legislators may feel little pressure to keep records sealed. Demands that legislators open adoption records will be reinforced by an alliance with the new search and reunion movement led by adult donor-insemination offspring, since these people are already protesting the secrecy and deception surrounding assisted reproduction. But again, offsetting tendencies exist. Increasing numbers of birth and adoptive parents engaging in independent adoptions may lobby legislators to hold the line against "extremist" ARM activists and reject bills that would unilaterally unseal adoption records. In all likelihood, we will see legislators support compromise solutions like search and consent systems and voluntary adoption registries, where the privacy of all members of the triad is protected.[21]

Compromise solutions on issues of secrecy and disclosure should not be summarily dismissed. If the history of secrecy and disclosure in adoption demonstrates anything, it is that extreme positions rarely work in a situation with as many diverse motivations, interests, and rights as those occasioned by adoption. Opponents of openness and disclosure in adoption must recognize that birth mothers and adult adoptees who wish to meet their blood kin have genuine needs and rights. ARM activists should recognize that birth and adoptive parents have a legitimate desire for privacy, whether because they want to start life anew in an imperfect world that still stigmatizes unwed motherhood or because they wish to raise a family without interference. If either extreme wins, real people lose. What needs to be established is a unified, easily accessible, effective system of disclosure that operates with the voluntary consent of triad members. Whether such a system takes the form of a national computer adoption registry or a national "search and consent" intermediary system could be worked out by enlightened lawmakers. The way to a solution to the difficult issue of sealed adoption records must begin with an acceptance that both sides have legitimate rights and needs.

The middle ground is also desirable in open adoption. For some birth mothers and adoptive parents, open adoption is a fine alternative, and it should be encouraged for those who truly wish to participate. But it should not be the only choice for couples seeking to adopt a child. Its principal rationale—that traditional adoption is inherently harmful to all members of the adoption triad—is based on deeply flawed social science studies, pseudoscientific psychoanalytic studies, and bogus "adoption syndromes" and is demonstrably false: there are too many psychologically healthy birth mothers and adopted persons to allow one to entertain seriously the idea that traditional adoption is inherently harmful to those involved. And the jury is still out on the benefits of open adoption; it is simply too new an innovation. Most likely it will neither be as beneficial as its proponents claim nor as harmful as critics contend. Children thrive under remarkably diverse types of parental upbringing. Both open and traditional adoption should continue to be available so that the best interests of the child may be served.

Whether adoption triad members like it or not, shifting values and circumstances outside the adoption process will continue to shape the ensuing debate in ways no one can predict. Should the "new Puritanism" sweep the nation, it is possible that abortion will again become illegal, unwed motherhood will be restigmatized, infants will again become more available for adoption, and secrecy will reestablish itself. Barring such a drastic turn of events, adoption will continue to be characterized by both secrecy and disclosure, with all the attendant hopes and anxieties the two entail.

. . . .

Notes / Acknowledgments / Index

Notes

Abbreviations

ALP	Joan H. Hollinger et al., eds., *Adoption Law and Practice* (New York: Matthew Bender, 1989)
Annals	*Annals of the American Academy of Political and Social Science*
CAS	*Annual Reports of the Children's Aid Society, Nos. 1–10, February 1854–February 1863,* reprinted in David J. Rothman, ed., *Poverty, U.S.A.: The Historical Record* (New York: Arno Press and the New York Times, 1971)
CBR	Children's Bureau Records, Record Group 102, National Archives, Washington D.C.
CHSW	Children's Home Society of Washington
CHSW CR	Children's Home Society of Washington Case Record, Children's Home Society of Washington, Records Department, Seattle, Washington
CHSW Recs.	Children's Home Society of Washington, Records Department, Seattle, Washington
CW	*Child Welfare*
CWLA	Child Welfare League of America
CWLA, *Bull.*	Child Welfare League of America, *Bulletin*

CWLA Recs.	Child Welfare League of America Records, Social Welfare History Archives, University of Minnesota, Minneapolis, Minn.
CWS	Alfred Kadushin and Judith A. Martin, *Child Welfare Services,* 4th ed. (New York: Macmillan, 1988)
EA	Christine Adamec and William L. Pierce, eds., *The Encyclopedia of Adoption* (New York: Facts On File, 1991)
ICH&AS	Illinois Children's Home and Aid Society
MH	*Mental Hygiene*
NCFA	National Committee for Adoption
NYT	*New York Times*
NYTM	*New York Times Magazine*
PM	*Parents' Magazine*
PNCCC	*Proceedings, National Conference of Charities and Correction*
PNCSW	*Proceedings of the National Conference of Social Work*
SC	*Social Casework*
SSR	*Social Service Review*
SW	*Social Work*

Preface

1. The CHSW was originally called the Washington Children's Home Society. In 1959, the name was changed to the Children's Home Society of Washington to make clear to the public it was a not a state-run or state-supported child welfare institution ("Children's Home Society of Washington, History," n.p., 1970, mimeographed, CHSW Recs.). Except for the description of the Society's founding, the current name will be used throughout the book.

1. The Rise of Adoption

1. From 1951 to 1975, the Department of Health, Education, and Welfare's National Center for Social Statistics collected annual national statistics on adoption. Today most adoption statistics are the result of the efforts of private organizations. For adoption statistics, see *Adoption Factbook*

II 1989 (Washington, D.C.: NCFA, 1989), pp. 3–5; Victor Eugene Falango and Carol R. Falango, "Adoption Statistics by State," *CW* 72 (May–June 1993): 317. According to NCFA estimates, unrelated adoptions have remained stable at about 50,000 annually since 1974, a significant decline from the 80,000–90,000 annual figure of the late 1960s and 1970s. Of 51,167 unrelated domestic adoptions in 1986, the NCFA estimates that 35,127 were arranged by adoption agencies and 16,040 by private individuals. There were also 10,019 foreign adoptions. Unless otherwise indicated, the term "adoption" in this book refers to unrelated adoptions.

2. Joan H. Hollinger, "Introduction to Adoption Law and Practice," in *ALP,* pp. 1, 8–12. The inferior nature of adoptive kinship is part of a larger problem that adoptive parents must overcome, what sociologist H. David Kirk has identified as "role handicap," the idea that the majority of adopters deny the cultural distinction between adoptive parenthood and consanguine families. H. David Kirk, *Shared Fate: A Theory and Method of Adoptive Relationships,* 2d rev. ed. (Port Angeles, Wash.: Ben-Simon, 1984; orig. pub. 1964), chs. 1–4.

3. Hollinger, "Introduction," in *ALP,* pp. 13–14.

4. John F. Brosnan, "The Law of Adoption," *Columbia Law Review* 22 (1922): 333. These purposes included "preventing the extinction of a bloodline, preserving a sacred descent group, facilitating the generational transfer of a patrimony, providing for ancestral worship, or mending the ties between factious clans or tribes." Jamil S. Zainaldin, "The Emergence of a Modern American Family Law: Child Custody, Adoption, and the Courts," *Northwestern University School of Law* 73 (1979): 1041.

5. Robert I. Levy, "Tahitian Adoption as a Psychological Message," in Vern Carroll, ed., *Adoption in Eastern Oceania* (Honolulu: University Press of Hawaii, 1970); Keith L. Morton, "Tongan Adoption," in Ivan Brady, ed., *Transactions in Kinship: Adoption and Fosterage in Oceania* (Honolulu: University Press of Hawaii, 1976); David Schneider, *American Kinship: A Cultural Account,* 2d rev. ed. (Chicago: University of Chicago Press, 1980): pp. 23–29, quotation on p. 25.

6. Jack Goody, *The Development of the Family and Marriage in Europe* (Cambridge, Eng.: Cambridge University Press, 1983), pp. 71–75. Goody attributes the Church's animus toward adoption to financial advantage. Kristin Elizabeth Gager, *Blood Ties and Fictive Ties: Adoption and Family Life in Early Modern France* (Princeton, N.J.: Princeton University Press, 1996), pp. 3–7.

7. Michael Grossberg, *Governing the Hearth: Law and the Family in*

Nineteenth-Century America (Chapel Hill: University of North Carolina Press, 1985), pp. 268–269.

8. Lawrence A. Cremin, *American Education: The Colonial Experience, 1607–1783* (New York: Harper & Row, 1970), p. 113.

9. Geraldine Youcha, *Minding the Children: Child Care in America from Colonial Times to the Present* (New York: Scribner, 1995), p. 18; Robert Francis Seybolt, *Apprenticeship and Apprenticeship Education in Colonial New England and New York* (New York: Columbia University Press, 1917). Quotation from Edmund S. Morgan, *The Puritan Family* (New York: Harper & Row, 1943), p. 77.

10. O. Jocelyn Dunlop and Richard D. Denman, *English Apprenticeship and Child Labour* (New York: Macmillan, 1912), pp. 68–71.

11. Seybolt, *Apprenticeship,* p. 34; Homer Folks, *The Care of Destitute, Neglected, and Delinquent Children* (New York: Macmillan, 1902), pp. 10–11. The 7.3 percent represented approximately 173 out of a possible pool of 3,123 children per year. See Holly Brewer, "Constructing Consent: How Children's Status in Political Theory Shaped Public Policy in Virginia, Pennsylvania, and Massachusetts before and after the Revolution" (Ph.D. diss., University of California, Los Angeles, 1994), p. 385.

12. John Demos, *A Little Commonwealth: Family Life in Plymouth Colony* (New York: Oxford University Press, 1970): p. 89; Joseph Ben-Or, "The Law of Adoption in the United States: Its Massachusetts Origins and the Statute of 1851," *New England Historical and Genealogical Register* 130 (1976): 260, 265; Yasuhide Kawashima, "Adoption in Early America," *Journal of Family Law* 20 (1981–1982); Zainaldin, "Modern American Family Law," pp. 1084–1085.

13. Quoted in Helen L. Witmer et al., *Independent Adoptions: A Follow-Up Study* (New York: Russell Sage Foundation, 1963), p. 29, n. 1. Zainaldin, "Modern American Family Law," p. 1043, n. 12, correctly identifies the name as "Blair," not "Bair," as Witmer has it.

14. David M. Rothman, *The Discovery of the Asylum: Social Order and Disorder in the New Republic* (Boston: Little, Brown, 1971); William I. Trattner, *From Poor Law to Welfare State: A History of Social Welfare in America,* 5th ed. (New York: Free Press, 1994), ch. 4.

15. Susan Lynne Porter, "The Benevolent Asylum—Image and Reality: The Care and Training of Female Orphans in Boston, 1800–1840" (Ph.D. diss., Boston University, 1984), p. 198. Statistics on orphanages from Timothy Andrew Hacsi, " 'A Plain and Solemn Duty': A History of Orphan Asylums in America" (Ph.D. diss., University of Pennsylvania, 1993), Appendix A1.

16. New York State Senate, "Report of the Select Committee Appointed to

Visit Charitable Institutions Supported by the State, 1857," in Robert H. Bremner, ed., *Children and Youth in America: A Documentary History* (Cambridge: Harvard University Press, 1971), vol. 1, p. 648; Bernard Wishy, *The Child and the Republic: The Dawn of Modern American Child Nurture* (Philadelphia: University of Pennsylvania Press, 1968), chs. 2–3; Susan Tiffin, *In Whose Best Interest? Child Welfare Reform in the Progressive Era* (Westport, Conn.: Greenwood Press, 1982), chs. 3–4.

17. Marilyn Irvin Holt, *The Orphan Trains: Placing Out in America* (Lincoln: University of Nebraska Press, 1992), chs. 2–3; R. Richard Wohl, "The Country Boy Myth and Its Place in American Urban Culture: The Nineteenth-Century Contribution," *Perspectives In American History* 3 (1969); Joseph M. Hawes, *Children in Urban Society: Juvenile Delinquency in Nineteenth-Century America* (New York: Oxford University Press, 1971), p. 107; "Fifth Annual Report" (1858), *CAS*, p. 55; "Third Annual Report" (1856), ibid., p. 9; Henry Thurston, *The Dependent Child: A Story of Changing Aims and Methods in the Care of Dependent Children* (New York: Columbia University Press, 1930), pp. 102, 104; Tiffin, *In Whose Best Interest*, p. 89.

18. Bruce Bellingham, "Institution and Family: An Alternative View of Nineteenth-Century Child Saving," *Social Problems* 33 (December 1986): 543; "Third Annual Report" (1856), *CAS*, p. 7; "First Annual Report" (1854), ibid., p. 9. The 47 percent figure comes from Holt, *Orphan Trains*, pp. 128–129, who cites the 1893 CAS Annual Report statement that 39,406 of the 84,318 children the CAS placed out had one or both parents living.

19. Quoted in Holt, *Orphan Trains*, pp. 129–130.

20. Ibid., p. 62; quotation from "Third Annual Report" (1856), *CAS*, p. 10.

21. "Third Annual Report" (1856), *CAS*, p. 9; Charles L. Brace, "The 'Placing Out' Plan for Homeless and Vagrant Children," *Proceedings of the Conference of Charities and Corrections* (Albany, N.Y.: Joel Munsell, 1876), p. 140. In 1861, Brace recorded the first account of a formal adoption: "Mr. F., who has A. W., told me he was glad that I brought him the papers of adoption, so that no one can now, at any time, claim the object of [his] soul . . . In such an event, he thought he would take the child and run if he could not save it otherwise." "Eighth Annual Report" (1861), *CAS*, p. 71.

22. Stephen B. Presser, "The Historical Background of the American Law of Adoption," *Journal of Family Law* 11 (1971–1972): 474; Grossberg, *Governing the Hearth*, p. 271. As early as 1808, Louisiana's legal code contained an adoption statute, but in 1825 it was abolished. Ibid., p. 270.

23. Zainaldin, "Modern American Family Law," pp. 1084–1085.

24. *Acts and Resolves Passed by the General Court of Massachusetts*, 1851, ch. 324 (Boston, 1851), p. 816; Zainaldin, "Modern American Family Law," pp. 1042–1043, 1085; Witmer et al., *Independent Adoptions*, pp. 30–31.

25. Martin Wolins and Irving Piliavin, *Institution or Foster Family: A Century of Debate* (New York: CWLA, 1964), pp. 10–21; Holt, *Orphan Trains*, pp. 121, 134–136. Western delegates to the National Convention of Charities and Correction did not take Easterners' criticism seriously. See Miriam Z. Langsam, *Children West: A History of the Placing-Out System of the New York Children's Aid Society, 1853–1890* (Madison: State Historical Society of Wisconsin, 1964), p. 58.

26. "Fourth Annual Report" (1857), *CAS*, p. 9; Langsam, *Children West*, pp. 58–59; *PNCCC* (Cincinnati, 1882), pp. 147–148.

27. Thurston, *Dependent Child*, pp. 124–125, quotation on p. 125; LeRoy Ashby, *Saving the Waifs: Reformers and Dependent Children, 1890–1917* (Philadelphia: Temple University Press, 1984), pp. 39–41.

28. George Harrison Durand, "The Study of the Child from the Standpoint of the Home-Finding Agency," *PNCCC* (Indianapolis: William P. Burford, 1907), pp. 259–260, quotation on p. 259.

29. John Whiteclay Chambers II, *The Tyranny of Change: America in the Progressive Era, 1890–1920*, 2d ed. (New York: St. Martin's Press, 1992), pp. 140–150, quotation on p. 140.

30. "Letter to the President of the United States Embodying the Conclusions of the Conference on the Care of Dependent Children," *Proceedings of the [1909] Conference on the Care of Dependent Children* in Robert H. Bremner, ed., *Children and Youth: A Documentary History* (Cambridge: Harvard University Press, 1971), vol. 2, p. 365; Theda Skocpol, *Protecting Soldiers and Mothers: The Political Origins of Social Policy in the United States* (Cambridge: Harvard University Press, 1992), ch. 9; Robyn Muncy, *Creating a Female Dominion in American Reform, 1890–1935* (New York: Oxford University Press, 1991), chs. 2, 4.

31. E. Wayne Carp, "Orphanages vs. Adoption: The Triumph of Biological Kinship, 1800–1933," in Donald T. Critchlow and Hal H. Parker, eds., *With Us Always: A History of Private Charity and Public Welfare* (Lanham, Md.: Rowman and Littlefield, 1998), pp. 125–147; E. Wayne Carp, "Professional Social Workers, Adoption, and the Problem of Illegitimacy, 1915–1945," *Journal of Policy History* 6, no. 3 (1994); Galen A. Merrill, "Some Recent Developments in Child-Saving," *PNCCC* (Boston: Geo. H. Ellis, 1900), p. 226.

32. Other historians have noticed this radical change in child-savers' strategies, but none has attributed it to Brace's child-placing practices. See,

for example, Michael B. Katz, *In the Shadow of the Poorhouse: A Social History of Welfare in America* (New York: Basic Books, 1986), ch. 5; Molly Ladd-Taylor, *Mother-Work: Women, Child Welfare, and the State, 1890–1930* (Urbana: University of Illinois Press, 1994), p. 137. This does not mean that other factors were not at work. Katz attributes the change to "psychology, sentiment, anxiety, and male backlash" (*In the Shadow of the Poorhouse*, ch. 5, esp. p. 124).

33. "Letter to the President of the United States," *Proceedings of the* [1909] *Conference on the Care of Dependent Children*, in Bremner, *Children and Youth in America*, vol. 2, p. 365; Skocpol, *Protecting Soldiers and Mothers*, ch. 8, quotation on p. 472; Mark Leff, "Consensus for Reform: The Mothers'-Pensions Movement in the Progressive Era," *SSR* 47 (September 1973), Roosevelt quoted on p. 399.

34. A. H. Stoneman, "Social Problems Related to Illegitimacy," *Proceedings of the Fifty-First National Conference on Social Work* (Chicago: University of Chicago Press, 1924), p. 148; Katharine P. Hewins and L. Josephine Webster, *The Work of Child-Placing Agencies*, Children's Bureau pub. 171 (Washington, D.C.: Government Printing Office, 1927), p. 80; W. H. Slingerland, *Child-Placing in Families: A Manual for Students and Social Workers* (New York: Russell Sage Foundation, 1919), p. 87; Carp, "Problem of Illegitimacy," pp. 169–173; Julie Berebitsky, " 'To Raise as Your Own': The Growth of Legal Adoption in Washington," *Washington History* 6 (Spring–Summer 1994): 19.

35. R. L. Jenkins, "On Adopting a Baby," *Hygeia* 13 (December 1935): 106; "The Epidemic of Adoption," *Living Age* 294 (Sept. 8, 1917): 632; Peter Romanofsky, "The Early History of Adoption Practices, 1870–1930" (Ph.D. diss., University of Missouri, Columbia, 1969), pp. 67–69.

36. Henry H. Goddard, *The Kallikak Family: A Study in the Heredity of Feeblemindedness* (New York: Macmillan, 1912); Hamilton Cravens, *The Triumph of Evolution: American Scientists and the Hereditary-Environment Controversy, 1900–1941* (Philadelphia: University of Pennsylvania Press, 1978), pp. 47–48. For psychometric testing, see Michael M. Sokal, ed., *Psychological Testing and American Society, 1890–1930* (New Brunswick, N.J.: Rutgers University Press, 1987). The belief that unwed mothers were feebleminded was widespread. See Carp, "Problem of Illegitimacy," p. 172 and n. 77; Ada Elliot Sheffield, "Program of the Committee on Illegitimacy—Committee Report," *PNCSW* (Chicago: University of Chicago Press, 1921), p. 78; "Our Adopted Baby," *Woman's Home Companion* 43 (April 1916): 5.

37. Hastings H. Hart, "The Child-Saving Movement," *Bibliotheca Sacra* 58 (July 1901): 521; Albert H. Stoneman, "Adoption of Illegitimate Chil-

244 · Notes to Pages 20–24

dren: The Peril of Ignorance," CWLA, *Bull.* 5 (Feb. 15, 1926): 8; Carp, "Problem of Illegitimacy," p. 172; Edwin D. Solenberger, "Record of Child-Placing Agencies," *PNCCC* (Fort Wayne, Ind.: Archer Printing Co., 1910), p. 125.

38. Romanofsky, "Early History of Adoption Practices," pp. 117–123; quotation on p. 119.

39. Carp, "Problem of Illegitimacy," p. 170.

40. Ibid.; Slingerland, *Child-Placing in Families,* pp. 168–169.

41. Carp, "Problem of Illegitimacy," pp. 167–171; Emma O. Lundberg, *State Commissions for the Study and Revision of Child Welfare Laws,* U.S. Children's Bureau pub. 131 (Washington, D.C.: Government Printing Office, 1931), pp. 4–5.

42. *General Laws of Minnesota* (1917), ch. 222, sect. 7152, 7159, pp. 335–337; Gioh-Fang Dju Ma, *One Hundred Years of Public Services for Children in Minnesota* (Chicago: University of Chicago Press, 1948).

43. Kriste A. Lindenmeyer, *"A Right to Childhood": The U.S. Children's Bureau and Child Welfare, 1912–1946* (Urbana: University of Illinois Press, 1997), pp. 26–34; quotation on p. 26.

44. Nancy Pottishman Weiss, "Save the Child: A History of the Children's Bureau, 1903–1918" (Ph.D. diss., University of California, Los Angeles, 1974), pp. 174, 175, 197; Muncy, *Creating a Female Dominion,* ch. 2, esp. pp. 56–57. For a sampling of the letters, see Molly Ladd-Taylor, *Raising a Baby the Government Way: Mother's Letters to the Children's Bureau, 1915–1932* (New Brunswick, N.J.: Rutgers University Press, 1986).

45. Emelyn Foster Peck, *Adoption Laws in the United States,* U.S. Children's Bureau pub. 148 (Washington, D.C.: Government Printing Office, 1925); Katharine P. Hewins and L. Josephine Webster, *The Work of Child-Placing Agencies,* U.S. Children's Bureau pub. 171 (Washington, D.C.: Government Printing Office, 1927); Grace Abbott, *The ABC of Foster-Family Care for Children,* U.S. Children's Bureau pub. 216 (Washington, D.C.: Government Printing Office, 1933); Mary Ruth Colby, *Problems and Procedures in Adoption,* U.S. Children's Bureau pub. 262 (Washington, D.C.: Government Printing Office, 1941).

46. Miss Shepperson to Mrs. Hopkins, "Memorandum," Nov. 23, 1943, CBR, File 7-3-3-4, Central File 1941–1944, Box 169. I am indebted to Barbara Melosh, who alerted me to the existence of the adoption material in the Children's Bureau Records, and who generously shared with me her knowledge of the manuscript collection.

47. Agnes K. Hanna to Miss Rosetta Young, attorney at law, Mar. 4, 1936, CBR, File 7-3-3-3, Central File 1933–1936, Box 549; ibid., File 7-3-3-4-1, Central File 1941–1944, Box 171; Mary Ruth Colby to Florence

Clothier, Dec. 4, 1940, CBR, File 7-3-3-4, Central File 1941–1944, Box 169; Mary Ruth Colby to Sophie van Senden Theis, June 30, 1942, ibid., Box 170. Scripts for *The Guiding Light* are enclosed with letters from Freda S. Kehm to Mary Taylor, Feb. 16, 1945, Mar. 17, 1945, Apr. 2, 1945, CBR, File 7-3-3-4, Central File 1945–1948, Box 159.

48. Katherine F. Lenroot to Elizabeth M. Owens, Nov. 11, 1932, CBR, File 7-3-3-4, Central File 1929–1932, Box 418; Katherine F. Lenroot to Geraldine E. Rhoads, Mar. 27, 1941, CBR, File 7-3-3-4, Central File 1941–1944, Box 171.

49. Mary Ruth Colby, "Field Trip to Maine," Nov. 4–8, 1938, CBR, File 7-3-3-4, Central File 1937–1940, Box 822; Mary Ruth Colby to Sophie Van Senden Theis, June 30, 1942, CBR, File 7-3-3-4, Central File 1941–1944, Box 170.

50. "Child Welfare League of America," in Peter Romanofsky, ed., *Social Service Organizations* (Westport, Conn.: Greenwood Press, 1978), pp. 224–230; CWLA, *Standards for Children's Organizations Providing Foster Family Care* (New York: CWLA, 1933).

51. Katz, *In the Shadow of the Poorhouse*, p. 213; Linda Gordon, *Pitied but Not Entitled: Single Mothers and the History of Welfare, 1890–1935* (New York: Free Press, 1994), pp. 185–190; Carl A. Heisterman, "A Summary of Legislation on Adoption," *SSR* 9 (June 1935): 269–277. A typical state social investigation determined the reasons why the natural parents (if living) desired to relinquish the child, whether the adoptive parents were financially able and morally fit to raise the child, and the physical and mental condition of the child. Ibid., p. 272.

52. C. C. Carstens to Members, June 22, 1936, CWLA Recs., Box 15, Folder 5; CWLA Executive Committee, "Adoptions," Nov. 5, 1937, ibid.; Agnes K. Hanna to Elizabeth H. Webster, Oct. 5, 1940, CBR, File 7-3-3-4, Central File 1937–1940, Box 821; Miss Shepperson to Martha Eliot, memorandum "The Cradle Society of Evanston, Illinois," Feb. 24, 1944, ibid., File 7-3-3-4, Central File 1941–1944, Box 169.

53. Colby, *Problems and Procedures in Adoption*, p. 21; "Regarding Adoptions," CWLA *Special Bulletin* (March 1937), CWLA Recs., Suppl., Box 41, "Special Bulletins" folder.

54. CWLA, "Minimum Safeguards in Adoption," Nov. 5, 1938, CWLA Recs., Box 15, Folder 5; Zitha R. Turitz, "Development and Use of National Standards for Child Welfare Services," *CW* 46 (May 1967): 246–248. In 1941, for example, the CWLA suspended the Tennessee Children's Home Society from membership for its failure to adhere to League adoption standards. Linda Tollett Austin, *Babies for Sale: The Tennessee Children's Home Adoption Scandal* (Westport, Conn.: Praeger, 1993), p. 50.

55. Sophie van Senden Theis, *How Foster Children Turn Out* (New York:

State Charities Aid Association, 1924), p. 122. Theis defined "capable" as "subjects who are law abiding, who manage their affairs with good sense and are living in accordance with good moral standards of their communities" (p. 22). James W. Trent, *Inventing the Feeble Mind: A History of Mental Retardation in the United States* (Berkeley: University of California Press, 1994), pp. 181–182; Helen D. Sargent, "Is It Safe to Adopt a Child?" *PM* 10 (October 1935): 26; "Adopting a Baby," *Woman's Journal* 14 (July 1929): 10.

56. Clark Vincent, "Illegitimacy in the Next Decade: Trends and Implications," *CW* 43 (December 1964): 515.

57. Catherine MacKenzie, "A Boom in Adoptions," *NYTM*, Nov. 10, 1940, pp. 6–7, 29; Elaine Tyler May, *Barren in the Promised Land: Childless Americans and the Pursuit of Happiness* (New York: Basic Books, 1995), pp. 127–140, 156, quotation on p. 129; Richard Frank, "What the Adoption Worker Should Know about Infertility," *CW* 35 (February 1956): 1–5; Harvey Uhlenhopp, "Adoption in Iowa," *Iowa Law Review* 40 (Winter 1955): 228, n. 4. Media perception of the percentage of childless couples—15 to 17 percent—was inaccurate. As two scholars have recently noted: "The 1950s had an actual childlessness rate among married couples of less than 10 percent, the lowest proportion of childless Americans for nearly a century." See Margaret Marsh and Wanda Ronner, *The Empty Cradle: Infertility in America from Colonial Times to the Present* (Baltimore: John Hopkins University Press, 1996), pp. 186–187.

58. Sophie van Senden Theis, "Adoption," *Social Work Year Book* 4 (New York: Russell Sage Foundation, 1937), p. 23; I. Evelyn Smith, "Adoption," ibid. 9 (1947), p. 24.

59. Michael Schapiro, *A Study of Adoption Practice* (New York: CWLA, 1956), vol. 1, p. 10. Such statistics were reported in popular magazines. See Alice Lake, "Babies for the Brave," *Saturday Evening Post,* July 31, 1954, p. 27; Reid quoted in Dorothy Barclay, "Adoption Agencies: Pro and Con" *NYTM,* Feb. 17, 1957, p. 42.

60. Frederick G. Brownell, "Why You Can't Adopt a Baby," *Reader's Digest* 53 (September 1948): 55–56; quotation in Dorothy Barclay, "Adoption Problems," *NYTM,* Apr. 2, 1950, p. 48; Austin, *Babies for Sale,* ch. 6.

61. Barclay, "Adoption Problems," p. 48; Sophie van Senden Theis, "Interpreting Adoption," *CW* 27 (November 1948): 10–11; Elsie Stougaad, "Unsound Talk about Adoption," ibid., pp. 17–18.

62. "Regarding Adoptions," CWLA, *Special Bulletin* (March 1937): 8.

63. Schapiro, *Study of Adoption Practice,* vol. 1, p. 20; Trattner, *From Poor Law to Welfare State,* pp. 308–310; Neil A. Wynn, "The Impact of the Second World War on the American Negro," *Journal of Contemporary*

History 6 (May 1971): 42–54; quotation in *Report on Adoption Practices, Policies, and Problems: Report of Workshop, May 1948* (New York: CWLA, 1949), p. 21. The CWLA's president, Joseph H. Reid, later qualified this open-ended premise by noting that "this does not mean that any child who is legally available for adoption should be placed for adoption." Reid urged agencies to be cautious and not "rush blindly into placing every older child who is legally available for adoption." Joseph P. Reid, "Ensuring Adoption for Hard-to-Place Children," *CW* 35 (March 1956): 6. Individual agencies paid these sentiments little heed.

64. Belle Wolkomir, "The Unadoptable Baby *Achieves* Adoption," CWLA, *Bull.* 26 (February 1947): 1; CWLA, *Adoption of Children with Pathology in Their Backgrounds: Report of Workshop Held April 12, 1949* (New York: CWLA, 1949); CWLA, *Adoption Practices, Procedures, and Problems: A Report of the Second Workshop Held May 10–12, 1951* (New York: CWLA, 1952), p. 3; CWLA, "Press Release," CWLA Recs., Box 16, Folder 8.

65. CWLA, *Child Care Facilities for Dependent and Neglected Negro Children in Three Cities: New York City, Philadelphia, Cleveland* (New York: CWLA, 1945), p. 155; Andrew Billingsly and Jeanne M. Giovannoni, *Children of the Storm: Black Children and American Child Welfare* (New York: Harcourt Brace Jovanovich, 1972), pp. 27–38, 72–73; Harvard Sitkoff, *A New Deal for Blacks: The Emergence of Civil Rights as a National Issue*, rev. ed. (New York: Hill and Wang, 1993), pp. 11–18; "Special Problem of the Negro Child," *CW* 27 (May 1948): 5; Lois Wildly, "Reader's Forum," ibid. 28 (January 1949): 10–11. For a brief description of twenty of the programs and projects, see Annie Lee Sandusky et al., *Families for Black Children: The Search for Adoptive Parents II, Programs and Projects* (Washington, D.C.: Government Printing Office, 1972).

66. Howard Altstein and Rita J. Simon, "Introduction," in Altstein and Simon, *Intercountry Adoption: A Multinational Perspective* (New York: Praeger, 1990), p. 3; Notes and Comment, "International Placement of Children," *SSR* 22 (December 1948): 510; "Adoption," in Margaret B. Hodges, ed., *Social Work Year Book, 1949* (New York: Russell Sage Foundation, 1949), p. 25; Norman Cousins, "Hiroshima—Four Years Later," *Saturday Review of Literature* 32 (Sept. 17, 1949): 8–10, 30–31; Kathleen Sproul, "Genus: Parent—Species: Moral," ibid. (Dec. 23, 1959): 26.

67. Susan T. Pettiss, "Effect of Adoption of Foreign Children on U.S. Adoption Standards and Practices," *CW* 37 (July 1958): 31, 32.

68. *Standards for Adoption Service*, rev. ed. (Washington, D.C.: CWLA, 1988), pp. 1–4. The five attributes of modern adoption in this and the next paragraph borrow heavily from Hollinger, "Introduction," in *ALP*, pp. 8–14.

2. The Origins of Adoption Records

1. Susan K. Goodman, "Information for What? Information Policy for Records of Adoption (of People) in the U.S.," *Records Management Quarterly* 27 (April 1993): 3–4.
2. Elton B. Klibanoff, "Genealogical Information in Adoption: The Adoptee's Quest and the Law," *Family Law Quarterly* 11 (Summer 1977): 186–187.
3. Leo Albert Huard, "The Law of Adoption: Ancient and Modern," *Vanderbilt Law Review* 9 (June 1956): 743–763; *ALP,* p. 30.
4. Ida R. Parker, *"Fit and Proper"? A Study of Legal Adoption in Massachusetts* (Boston: Church Home Society, 1927), pp. 48, 68; Elinor Nims, *The Illinois Adoption Law and Its Administration* (Chicago: University of Chicago Press, 1928), pp. 29–30; Elizabeth Jones, "The Administration of the Adoption Law in Cook County, Illinois," *SSR* 11 (December 1937): 670–671.
5. Emelyn Foster Peck, *Adoption Laws in the United States,* U.S. Children's Bureau pub. 148 (Washington, D.C.: Government Printing Office, 1925), p. 11.
6. Joseph W. Newbold, "Jurisdictional and Social Aspects of Adoption," *Minnesota Law Review* 11 (1927): 606, 607, 622; Nims, *Illinois Adoption Law,* pp. 27–28; Jones, "Adoption Law in Cook County, Illinois," p. 668.
7. Richard A. Meckel, *Save the Babies: American Public Health Reform and the Prevention of Infant Mortality, 1850–1929* (Baltimore: Johns Hopkins University Press, 1990), ch. 4; Susan Tiffin, *In Whose Best Interest? Child Welfare Reform in the Progressive Era* (Westport, Conn.: Greenwood Press, 1982), pp. 173–174.
8. Tiffin, *In Whose Best Interest,* pp. 167–168. In a 1915 survey, the Children's Bureau estimated the number of white children born out of wedlock in the United States at 32,400, or about 1.8 percent of all live births. Emma O. Lundberg and Katharine F. Lenroot, *Illegitimacy as a Child-Welfare Problem,* part I, Children's Bureau pub. 66 (Washington, D.C.: Government Printing Office, 1920), pp. 24–26. In 1928, the Bureau of the Census reported 63,942 white children born out of wedlock, or about 2.8 percent of all live births. A. Madorah Donahue, "Children Born Out of Wedlock," *Annals* 151 (September 1930); Emma O. Lundberg and Katharine F. Lenroot, *Illegitimacy as a Child Welfare Problem,* part II, Children's Bureau pub. 75 (Washington, D.C.: Government Printing Office, 1921), pp. 88–93, 139–143; Emma O. Lundberg, "General Introduction," in ibid., part III, Children's Bureau pub. 128 (Washington, D.C.: Government Printing Office, 1924), p. 3.

9. *Statutes of Minnesota,* chap. 73, sect. 7152, 7159; Gioh-Fang Dju Ma, *One Hundred Years of Public Services for Children in Minnesota* (Chicago: University of Chicago Press, 1948), ch. 4; Edward N. Clopper, "The Development of the Children's Code," *Annals* 98 (November 1921): 154–159; Mary Ruth Colby, *Problems and Procedures in Adoption,* U.S. Children's Bureau pub. 262 (Washington, D.C.: Government Printing Office, 1941), p. 118.

10. The other five states were Alabama, Oregon, California, North Dakota, and Wisconsin. Colby, *Problems and Procedures,* p. 119.

11. *Laws of Wisconsin* 1929, chap. 439; Carl A. Heisterman, "A Summary of Legislation on Adoption," *SSR* 9 (June 1935): 289; *Sacramento Bee,* Jan. 22, 1935, p. 6. See also ibid., Jan. 14, 1935, p. 6.

12. Mary Ruth Colby, "Modern Safeguards in Adoption Legislation," CWLA, *Bull.* 20 (December 1941): 5; Joseph T. Alves, *Confidentiality in Social Work* (Westport, Conn.: Greenwood Press, 1984), pp. 79, 80; Mary Ruth Colby, "Progress in Adoption Legislation," *SSR* 16 (1942): 71. Colby notes that three other states provided partial protection of adoption proceedings. In North Carolina only the social investigation was considered confidential, and in Pennsylvania and Tennessee the court protected the social records of children born out of wedlock.

13. Colby, *Problems and Procedures* p. 118.

14. Mary Ruth Colby to Idamae Maturen, Feb. 24, 1939, CBR, File 7-3-3-4, Central File 1937–1940, Box 822; Ruthena Hill Kittson [Jean Paton], *Orphan Voyage* (New York: Vantage Press, 1968), pp. 51–52; Idamae Maturen to Mary Ruth Colby, Feb. 18, 1939, CBR, File 7-3-3-4, Central File 1937–1940, Box 822; Colby, *Problems and Procedures,* p. 120; Children's Home Society of California, "Separate Adoption Index," *California Magazine* 43 (September-October-November 1934), pp. 13–15, Bancroft Library, University of California, Berkeley.

15. Klibanoff, "Genealogical Information in Adoption," p. 187; Wisconsin *Statutes* (1929), chap. 322.06; Missouri *Revised Statutes,* chap. 453.120; Pennsylvania *Adoption Law* (1972), chap. 347, sect. 505.

16. Lawrence C. Cole, "A Study of Adoptions in Cuyahoga County," *The Family* 6 (January 1926): 260; Jones, "Adoption Law in Cook County, Illinois," p. 671; Mary Ruth Colby to Idamae Maturen, Nov. 30, 1938, CBR, File 7-3-3-4, Central File 1937–1940, Box 822.

17. Peter Laslett, *Family Life and Illicit Love in Earlier Generations* (London: Cambridge University Press, 1977), pp. 54–55; James H. Cassedy, *Demography in Early America: Beginnings of the Statistical Mind, 1600–1800* (Cambridge: Harvard University Press, 1969), pp. 18–19; Robert René Kuczynski, "The Registration Laws of the Colonies of Massachusetts

Bay and New Plymouth," *American Statistical Association,* new ser., 51 (September 1900): 1–9; S. Shapiro, "Development of Birth Registration and Birth Statistics in the United States," *Population Studies* 4 (June 1950): 86–87; Meckel, *Save the Babies,* pp. 33–34.

18. Cressy L. Wilbur, *The Federal Registration Service of the United States: Its Development, Problems, and Defects* (Washington, D.C.: Government Printing Office, 1916), p. 44; Meckel, *Save the Babies,* pp. 33–34.

19. John S. Billings, "The Registration of Vital Statistics," *American Journal of Medical Science* (January 1883): 105–106; Children's Bureau, U.S. Department of Labor, *Birth Registration,* pub. 2 (Washington, D.C.: Government Printing Office, 1913), p. 5; Wilbur, *Federal Registration,* p. 34.

20. Children's Bureau, *Birth Registration,* pp. 5–11.

21. Wilbur, *Federal Registration,* pp. 19–22, 79; Children's Bureau, *Birth Registration,* pp. 5–11; U.S. Library of Congress, *General Censuses and Vital Statistics in the Americas* (Washington, D.C.: Government Printing Office, 1943), p. 75. Model statutes, which do not have the force of law, are usually proposed by the National Conference of Commissioners on Uniform State Laws. The commissioners are a group of law school deans, professors, judges, and practicing lawyers appointed by state governors. The finished product is then presented to the states as a prototype, which each state is then free to adopt in whole, in part, or not at all as their particular needs and interests dictate. *EA,* s.v. "Model State Adoption Act."

22. Children's Bureau, U.S. Department of Labor, *Standards of Legal Protection for Children Born Out of Wedlock: A Report of Regional Conferences Held under the Auspices of the U.S. Children's Bureau,* pub. 77 (Washington, D.C.: Government Printing Office, 1921), p. 91; Philip Van Ingen, "Infant Mortality in Institutions," *PNCCC* (Chicago: Hildmann Printing Co., 1915), pp. 126–128; J. H. Mason Knox, Discussion: "Infant Mortality," ibid., pp. 133–134; Amos G. Warner, *American Charities: A Study in Philanthropy and Economics* (New York: Thomas Y. Crowell & Co., 1894), pp. 204–205. Warner noted that "a death rate of 97 per cent per annum for children under three years of age is not uncommon."

23. Ernst Freund, "A Uniform Illegitimacy Law," *Survey* 49 (Oct. 15, 1922): 104, 127, 129. Uniform Laws and Model Acts (or Laws) are identical; see n. 21 above. Ruth-Arlene W. Howe, "Adoption Practice, Issues, and Laws, 1958–1983," *Family Law Quarterly* 17 (Summer 1983): 194, n. 80; Hastings H. Hart, *The Registration of Illegitimate Births: A Preventive of Infant Mortality* (New York: Russell Sage Foundation, 1916), pp. 15–19, quotations on p. 15.

24. Hart, *Registration,* pp. 6–7, 13. By sealed records, child welfare reformers meant literally securing the birth record with sealing wax. For a de-

scription of the process, see Margaret Emery to Orville H. Grays, Dec. 8, 1947, CBR, File 7-3-3-4, Central File 1944–1948, Box 157.

25. Hart, *Registration,* p. 7; Louise de Koven Bowen, "Birth Registration and Establishment of Paternity Determination and Recording of Parentage," in U.S. Children's Bureau, *Standards of Legal Protection,* p. 56.

26. Robert F. Keegan, Discussion: "What Is the Practical Ideal of Protection and Care for Children Born Out of Wedlock," in U.S. Children's Bureau, *Standards of Legal Protection,* p. 104; Freund, "The Present Law Concerning Children Born Out of Wedlock and Possible Changes in Legislation," in ibid., p. 33; Emma O. Lundberg, "Foreword," in ibid., p. 9.

27. Michael Grossberg, *Governing the Hearth: Law and the Family in Nineteenth-Century America* (Chapel Hill: University of North Carolina Press, 1985), ch. 6, quotation on p. 202.

28. Elizabeth Feder, "The Elite of the Fallen: The Origins of a Social Policy for Unwed Mothers, 1880–1930" (Ph.D. diss., Johns Hopkins University, 1991), pp. 223–235; Lillian Grace Topping, "The North Dakota Law of 1919" in U.S. Children's Bureau, *Standards of Legal Protection,* p. 49; "The Illegitimate Child," *Survey* 43 (Feb. 28, 1920): 654; Katharine F. Lenroot, "Social Responsibility for the Protection of Children Handicapped by Illegitimate Birth," *Annals* 98 (November 1921): 126.

29. Lundberg and Lenroot, *Illegitimacy as a Child Welfare Problem,* part I, p. 20. Both regional conferences held in Chicago and New York on illegitimacy adopted resolutions recommending this path. See "Legislation for Children Born Out of Wedlock," *Survey* 43 (Mar. 13, 1920): 747.

30. Lundberg and Lenroot, *Illegitimacy as a Child Welfare Problem,* part I, p. 20; Freund, "The Present Law Concerning Children Born Out of Wedlock," in U.S. Children's Bureau, *Standards of Legal Protection,* pp. 33–34; Agnes K. Hanna, "Guarding Illegitimate Status," CWLA, *Bull.* 13 (May 1934): 3.

31. Hanna, "Illegitimate Status," p. 5; Helen C. Huffman, "The Importance of Birth Records," *PNCSW* (1948), p. 352; Maud Morlock, "Wanted: A Square Deal for the Baby Born Out of Wedlock," *The Child* 10 (May 1946): 169.

32. *General Statutes of Minnesota, Supplement* 1917, chap. 73, sect. 7156, quoted in Peck, *Adoption Laws,* p. 28.

33. Carl A. Heisterman to E. Francis O'Neil, Nov. 19, 1929, CBR, File 10-12-5, Central File 1929–1932, Box 418.

34. Sheldon L. Howard and Henry B. Hemenway, "Birth Records of Illegitimates and of Adopted Children," *American Journal of Public Health* 21 (June 1931): 645, 644, 643.

35. Ibid., pp. 646–647.

36. Agnes K. Hanna to Clarissa Lehman, Oct. 18, 1941, CBR, File 4-2-1-2-4, Central File 1941–1944, Box 85. For adult adoptees' requests for birth certificates, see Maud Morelock to Mrs. Grace L. Knox, May 29, 1942, ibid.; Lee M. Brooks and Evelyn C. Brooks, *Adventuring in Adoption* (Chapel Hill: University of North Carolina Press, 1939), pp. 144, 152, 142; Children's Bureau, U.S. Department of Labor, *The Confidential Nature of Birth Records*, pub. 332 (Washington, D.C.: Government Printing Office, 1949); Helen C. Huffman, "A First Protection for the Child Born Out of Wedlock," *The Child* 11 (August 1946): 34–37; Huffman, "Importance of Birth Records," p. 357.

37. Huffman, "Importance of Birth Records," p. 356; U.S. Children's Bureau, *Confidential Nature of Birth Records*, pp. iii, 7, quotation on p. 7.

38. Huffman, "Importance of Birth Records," pp. 356, 353.

39. Ibid., p. 352.

40. Elaine Tyler May, *Homeward Bound: American Families in the Cold War Era* (New York: Basic Books, 1988); William H. Chafe, *The Unfinished Journey: America since World War II*, 2nd ed. (New York: Oxford University Press, 1991), pp. 123–124; U.S. Children's Bureau, *Confidential Nature of Birth Records*, p. 7.

41. Earl H. Davis, *Birth Certificates: A Digest of the Laws and Regulations of the Various States* (New York: H. W. Wilson, 1942), pp. 7–8; Michigan Work Projects Administration, *Procedures for Obtaining Birth Records: United States and Territories* (Detroit: Michigan Work Projects Administration, Service Division Fact-Finding Unit, 1942), p. xi; Lundberg and Lenroot, *Illegitimacy as a Child-Welfare Problem*, part I, p. 19; William H. Guilfoy, "Birth Registration and Establishment of Paternity," in U.S. Children's Bureau, *Standards of Legal Protection*, p. 114; J. Prentice Murphy, "What Can Be Accomplished through Good Social Work in the Field of Illegitimacy?" *Annals* 98 (November 1921): 130.

42. Suanna J. Wilson, *Confidentiality in Social Work: Issues and Principles* (New York: Free Press, 1978), p. 31. Wilson adds that modern technology has expanded the definition of a case record to include "tape-recorded interviews, microfilms, videotapes, and computerized data" (ibid.).

43. "Third Annual Report" (1856), *CAS*, p. 55; "Fourth Annual Report" (1857), *CAS*, p. 33.

44. Geraldine Youcha, *Minding the Children: Child Care in America from Colonial Times to the Present* (New York: Scribner, 1994), p. 199; Miriam Z. Langsam, *Children West: A History of the Placing-Out System of the New York Children's Aid Society, 1853–1890* (Madison: State Historical Society of Wisconsin, 1964), ch. 2, which also provides variations on the CAS's child-placement procedure.

45. "Third Annual Report" (1856), *CAS,* p. 34; "Tenth Annual Report" (1863), *CAS,* p. 50; "Third Annual Report" (1856), *CAS,* p. 50; "Fifth Annual Report" (1858), *CAS,* p. 12; Henry Thurston, *The Dependent Child: A Story of Changing Aims and Methods in the Care of Dependent Children* (New York: Columbia University Press, 1930), pp. 129, 132–133. A study of the CAS placement of children in Kansas by Francis White, a former CAS placing-out agent, asked rhetorically whether letter writing was a reliable method of keeping informed of the child's condition. White answered, "Emphatically, No!" and noted that "because letter writing was the only dependence" the CAS "lost track" of the entire 1867 party. Francis H. White, "The Placing Out System in Light of Its Results," *PNCCC* (Boston, 1893), p. 89.

46. Robert H. Bremner, *From the Depths: The Discovery of Poverty in the United States* (New York: New York University Press, 1956), pp. 55–56; Walter I. Trattner, *From Poor Law to Welfare State: A History of Social Welfare in America,* 5th ed. (New York: Free Press, 1994), pp. 94–105, esp. p. 102; Ada Eliot Sheffield, *The Social Case History: Its Construction and Content* (New York: Russell Sage Foundation, 1920), pp. 8–9, F. M. Gregg, "Placing Out Children," *PNCCC* (Boston, 1892), p. 418; *Proceedings of the Conference on the Care of Dependent Children,* Senate Document no. 721 (Washington, D.C.: Government Printing Office, 1909), p. 12; W. H. Slingerland, *Child Placing in Families: A Manual for Students and Social Workers* (New York: Russell Sage Foundation, 1919), p. 88.

47. Mary E. Richmond, *Social Diagnosis* (New York: Russell Sage Foundation, 1917), pp. 25, 96–100. For the extraordinary influence of Richmond's work on the social work profession, see Muriel W. Pumphrey's sketch and accompanying bibliographical references in Walter I. Trattner, ed., *Biographical Dictionary of Social Welfare in America* (Westport, Conn.: Greenwood Press, 1986), pp. 622–625.

48. Richmond, *Social Diagnosis,* pp. 357, 43; Roy Lubove, *The Professional Altruist: The Emergence of Social Work as a Career, 1880–1930* (Cambridge: Harvard University Press, 1965), p. 47.

49. *Session Laws of Minnesota* (1917), ch. 212, sec. 11; Georgia G. Ralph, *Elements of Record Keeping for Child-Helping Organizations* (New York: Survey Associates, 1915); Katherine F. Lenroot to W. J. Torrence, Jan. 2, 1920, CBR, File 7-3-4-2, Central File 1914–1920, Box 67.

50. CHSW CR 244. All names of CHSW clients used in this book are fictitious. Gordon Hamilton, *Social Case Recording* (New York: Columbia University Press, 1936), pp. 10–12, quotation on p. 11.

51. CHSW CR 2492. Other child-placing institutions might request in addition the child's race and the parents' income and prison record. See Ralph, *Elements of Record Keeping,* pp. 33–34.

52. Ralph, *Elements of Record Keeping,* p. 120; Jill Doner Kagle, "Recording," *Encyclopedia of Social Work,* 19th ed. (Washington, D.C.: National Association of Social Workers, 1995), vol. 3, p. 2028; Mary E. Richmond, *What Is Social Case Work?* (New York: Russell Sage Foundation, 1922), p. 28. For examples of twenty-five-page story sheets, see CHSW CRs 5823, 6342.

53. "Children's Home Society of Washington, History" (n.p., 1970), mimeographed, CHSW Recs.; CHSW CR 2552.

54. "Whereabouts of Placed-Out Children," *Charities Review* 10 (1900): 9; CHSW CR 6 (emphasis added).

55. CHSW CR 2. Almost every CHSW case record contained an application form. Ralph, *Elements of Record Keeping,* pp. 89, 90.

56. Ruth W. Lawton and J. Prentice Murphy, "A Study of Results of a Child-Placing Society," *PNCCC* (Chicago: Hildmann Printing Co., 1915), p. 172; Ralph, *Elements of Record Keeping,* pp. 91–92.

57. Charles R. King, *Children's Health in America: A History* (New York: Twayne, 1993), ch. 6, quotation on p. 131; *Washington Children's Home Finder* 17 (June 1913): 6.

58. Edwin D. Solenberger, "Record of Child-Placing Agencies," *PNCCC* (Fort Wayne, Ind.: Archer Printing Co., 1910), p. 125; Lawton and Murphy, "Study of Results of a Child-Placing Society," p. 167; *Washington Children's Home Finder* 22 (July 1919): 4. The states were Alabama, California, Colorado, Florida, Georgia, Hawaii, Indiana, Iowa, Louisiana, Mississippi, Missouri, Texas, Utah, Virginia, and Wisconsin. See Margaret Emery to Patricia Morse, July 18, 1947, CBR, File 7-3-3-4, Central File 1945–1948, Box 158. Quotation from Helen D. Sargent, "Is It Safe to Adopt a Child?" *PM* 10 (October 1935): 26.

59. Horace Bridges, "Safeguarding Adoption," *Welfare Magazine* 18 (February 1927): 169.

60. E. Wayne Carp, "The Sealed Adoption Records Controversy in Historical Perspective: The Case of the Children's Home Society of Washington, 1895–1988," *Journal of Sociology and Social Welfare* 19 (June 1992): 37–38; Mary E. Richmond, "Why Case Records?" *The Family* 6 (November 1925): 214–216.

61. ICH&AS, "Where the Society Keeps the Family Records of Over 22,000 Children," *Homelife for Children* 16 (June 1929): 6, 5; "Principles on Adoption," CWLA Recs., Box 15, folder 5; [New York] State Charities Aid Association, *News* 11 (February 1923): 6; CWLA, *Bull.* 2 (Jan. 15, 1923), 3.

62. Grace Abbott, *The ABC of Foster-Family Care,* U.S. Children's Bureau pub. 216 (Washington, D.C.: Government Printing Office, 1933), p. 40.

Before the 1940s, the terms "foster parent" and "adoptive parent" were synonyms, used interchangeably. Thus, for example, the clause of the 1915 New York statute defining adoption stated "the person adopting is designated the 'foster' parent." Clarence F. Birdseye, Robert C. Cumming, and Frank B. Gilbert, *Annotated Consolidated Laws of the State of New York,* Supplement, 1915, ch. 352, clause 110 (New York: Banks Law, 1915), p. 159. For additional examples, see ICH&AS, *Home Life for Childhood,* n.s. 5 (November–December 1916): 4, 5; Cleveland Protestant Orphan Asylum, *Annual Report* (Cleveland, Ohio, 1925), p. 10; Children's Home Finder of Florida, *Annual Report* (1926), p. 1; [New York] Spence Alumnae Society, "Report of the Adoption Committee," *Annual Report* (1940), p. 7. The confusing interchangeability of the terms is nicely captured in the 1944 title of the article "The Adoptive Foster Parent." See CWLA, *Bull.* 23 (1944): 5–14. As late as 1979, one adoption expert was still lamenting the confusion over the meaning of the two terms. See Marietta E. Spencer, "The Terminology of Adoption," *CW* 58 (July–August 1979): 459.

63. Ora Pendleton, "A Decade of Experience In Adoption," *Annals* 212 (October 1940): 193; "Identity of Foster Children Protected," [New York] State Charities Aid Association *News* 35 (May 1946): 2.

64. Peter Romanofsky, "Early History of Adoption Practices, 1870–1930" (Ph.D. diss., University of Missouri, Columbia, 1969), pp. 81–104, 117–39; Sophie van Senden Theis, "One-Sided Picture," review of *The Adopted Child* by Eleanor G. Gallagher, *Survey* 72 (October 1936): 320; CWLA, *Standards for Institutions Caring for Dependent Children* (New York: CWLA, 1932), p. 23, CWLA Recs., Box 13, Folder 1.

3. When Adoption Was No Secret

1. CHSW CRs. I have examined one out of every ten of the CHSW's 21,500 adoption case records, encompassing the years 1895 to 1988. The 2,150-case sample yielded a total of 505 post-adoption contact (PAC) cases, comprising 521 individuals who returned to the Society 641 times in quest of information about themselves, siblings, birth parents, or their adopted child's history. Thus, almost a quarter of all cases in this sample included PACs.

2. CHSW CRs (N = 237); CHSW CRs 1152, 2722, 3052, 4442; CHSW, "Manual of Adoptive Family Services" (n.p., 1969), p. 11, hereafter cited as "Adoption Manual." The "Adoption Manual" is located in the CHSW Recs.

3. The CHSW findings are consistent with similar studies. As Alfred Kadushin and Judith A. Martin note, "In general, female adoptees are more likely to engage in search behavior than are males. Fully two-thirds of searchers are women." *CWS*, p. 587.

4. CHSW CRs 5182, 762, 3182, 5282, 2472. The motivations of CHSW adoptees are congruent with other studies. See the conclusions reached in *CWS*, p. 587.

5. This is a very conservative estimate because it counts only those adult adoptees who specifically stated that they wanted family information to search for their natural parents. What other adult adoptees who failed to state they wanted to search for their natural parents did with family information once they received it cannot be answered with certainty. In several cases, adult adopted persons requested family information from the Society without specifying why and later reported to case workers their joyous reunion with their natural mothers or siblings. See, for example, CHSW CR 2382.

6. CHSW CRs 2, 172.

7. CHSW CR 1682; Child Welfare Committee of America, "Resolutions Unanimously Adopted by the Child Welfare Conference," pub. 59 (New York, 1928), p. 7, Russell Sage Collection, City College of New York, New York; Martha Heineman Field, "Social Casework Practice during the 'Psychiatric Deluge,'" *SSR* 54 (December 1980): 491; Children's Home Society of Florida, *Annual Report*, 1925, p. 11; Alla C. Hood, "Placement for Adoption of Brother and Sister," CWLA, *Bull.* 24 (April 1945): 1, 18; Elizabeth Bannister to Area Supervisors, Memorandum, September 19, 1957, CHSW Recs.

8. CHSW CR 3362. The disparity in birth mothers' responses before and after World War II was due to the changing nature of adoption in twentieth-century America and the demographic makeup of CHSW birth mothers. See Chapter 4.

9. CHSW CRs ($N = 79$).

10. CHSW CR 2462.

11. Quotations from CHSW CRs 1842, 1202, 5012. This paragraph is based on the following CHSW CRs: 16652, 2462, 3512, 4302, 4842, 4942, 5802, 8242, 3432, 3512.

12. For birth certificates, see CHSW CRs 1732, 2462, 2542, 2672, 2842. For parents' attitudes, see CHSW CRs 1732, 2053, 4442.

13. Quotations from CHSW CRs 3032, 3862. For a sample of parents' requests for medical and social information, see CHSW CRs 322, 1372, 1662, 2202, 2462; for nationality, see CHSW CRs 2462, 2772, 3862, 4542, 7082, 9082, 2202, 3542; for religion, CHSW CRs 4742, 4592.

14. For Covington, see CHSW CR 1622. Even on this issue, there were

exceptions. For a 1903 case where a mother pleaded successfully for the return of the child she had given up for adoption, see CHSW CR 452. For similar respect for the primacy of biological kinship, see Julie Berebitsky, " 'To Raise as Your Own': The Growth of Legal Adoption in Washington," *Washington History* 6 (Spring–Summer 1994): 20.

15. See, for example, CHSW CR 4672.
16. CHSW CR 122.
17. CHSW CR 1282. See also CHSW CRs 1162, 6312, 572, 5342, 4272. As late as 1952 Society caseworkers were telling mothers who had relinquished their children for adoption that they would keep their names on file to give to their offspring if they should ever inquire at the Society for their parents. See, for example, CHSW CRs 6632, 4262.
18. CHSW CR 4922. For examples of adoptive parents refusing contact with the child's original parents, see CHSW CRs 2592, 3502, 4632. For a case where the adoptive parents wanted to contact the child's original parents, see CHSW CR 5062.
19. CHSW CR 1302.
20. Quotations from CHSW CRs 3073, 3412; CHSW, "A Survey to Determine Agency Policies and Practices Related to the Release of Adoption Information," January 27, 1978, Folder: CHSW Papers: Questionnaire Requests-Reports, 1974–1979, CHSW Recs. As late as 1978, CHSW Associate Director Joseph T. Chambers frankly admitted that the Society's "practice is to give non-identifying [information] in violation of the law" (ibid.).
21. Quotations from CHSW CRs 1832, 1602. See also CHSW CRs 614, 132, 1022, 1322, 1692, 1872, 1902, 2242, 2382, 2520, 3022, 3792, 4622. For Robert O., see CHSW CR 7062.
22. See, for example, CHSW CRs 212, 2431, 3352, 8082.
23. CHSW CR 1283. See also CHSW CRs 2832, 3552, 6052.
24. For examples of the Society contacting adoptive parents on behalf of siblings searching for their brothers or sisters, see CHSW CRs 1393, 2154, 2914, 4142, 6852, 7672, 7942.
25. CHSW CR 5432. Adoptive parents did not always thwart sibling reunions. See, for example, CHSW CR 8702. The Children's Home Society of Minnesota had an identical policy. See, for example, Case Record 3660, Children's Home Society of Minnesota, St. Paul, Minn.
26. Grace Abbott, *The ABC of Foster-Family Care for Children,* U.S. Children's Bureau pub. 216 (Washington, D.C.: Government Printing Office, 1933), p. 40.
27. CHSW CR 2834. See also CHSW CRs 3356, 882, 2630, 6322, 8512, 8662, 9842.
28. CHSW CR 2472; data can be found in CHSW CR 2473.

29. CHSW CR 7242. For additional examples of caseworkers withholding family information, see CHSW CR 2232, 2630, 3102, 3782.

30. E. Wayne Carp, "Adoption and Disclosure of Family Information: A Historical Perspective," in Eve P. Smith and Lisa A. Merkel-Holguín, eds., *A History of Child Welfare* (New Brunswick, N.J.: Transaction, 1995), pp. 223–224; quotations from CHSW CRs 12, 4942.

31. Ibid., p. 224.

32. Honore Willsie, "When Is a Child Adoptable?" *Delineator* 95 (1919): 35; Catherine MacKenzie, "A Boom in Adoptions," *NYTM* (Nov. 10, 1940), p. 7.

33. Hyman S. Lippman, "Suitability of Children for Adoption," *American Journal of Orthopsychiatry* 7 (April 1937): 273; CWLA, *Report on Adoption Practices, Policies and Procedures* (New York: CWLA, 1947), p. 48.

34. Maud Morlock to Mrs. Margaret Mink, Sept. 25, 1945, CBR, Central File 1945–1948, File 7-3-3-4, Box 159; Amy E. Watson, "The Illegitimate Family," *Annals* 77 (May 1918): 113; CWLA, *Standards for Institutions Caring for Dependent Children* (New York: CWLA, 1932), p. 23, CWLA Recs., Box 13, folder 1.

35. Eleanor Garrigue Gallagher, *The Adopted Child* (New York: Reynal and Hitchcock, 1936), p. 117.

36. Sophie van Senden Theis, review of *The Adopted Child* by Eleanor Garrigue Gallagher, *Survey* 72 (October 1936): 320. George J. Mohr, "Adoption," *CWLA, Bull.* 16 (1937): 5; Florence Clothier, "Placing the Child for Adoption," *MH* 26 (April 1942): 271; Maud Morlock to Mrs. Margaret Mink, Sept. 25, 1945, CBR, Central File 1945–1948, File 7-3-3-4, Box 159.

37. C. V. Williams, "Safeguarding Adoptions" ICH&AS, *Homelife for Children* 14 (December 1927): 11; MacKenzie, "Boom in Adoptions," p. 29; Katharine P. Hewins and L. Josephine Webster, *The Work of Child Placing Agencies*, U.S. Children's Bureau pub. 171 (Washington, D.C.: Government Printing Office, 1927), p. 82; Michael Schapiro, *A Study of Adoption Practice* (New York: CWLA, 1956), vol. 1, p. 87.

38. CHSW CR 16433.

39. Annie Hamilton Donnell, "The Adopted," *Harper's Monthly Magazine* 113 (November 1906): 929.

40. Ida R. Parker, *"Fit and Proper": A Study of Legal Adoption in Massachusetts* (Boston: Church Home Society, 1927), p. 118; Ora Pendleton, "New Aims in Adoption," *Annals* 151 (September 1930): 160; C. C. Carstens, "The Pitfalls of Adoption," CWLA, *Bull.* 15 (October 1936): 4.

41. Minnie Gilbert, "Why the Baby Smiled," *California Homeless Children's Friend* (1911), p. 7; "Homeless Children for Childless Homes," [New

York] State Charities Aid Association *News* 11 (October 1922): 8; ICH&AS, *The Children's Home Finder,* New Series, 4 (March–April 1915), p. 12.

42. ICH&AS, "The Chosen Child," *Home Life for Childhood,* New Series, 5 (July–August 1916), p. 15; Honore Willsie, "Not a Boy, Please!" *Delineator* 95 (June 1919): 33; Hewins and Webster, *The Work of Child Placing Agencies,* p. 82; Grace Abbott to Mrs. George Baldwin, Sept. 11, 1929, CBR, Central File 1929–1932, File 7-3-3-4, Box 406.

43. The dating of the "Freudian deluge" has been the subject of much scholarly debate. Ray Lubove's pathbreaking study, *The Professional Altruist: The Emergence of Social Work as a Career, 1880–1930* (Cambridge: Harvard University Press, 1965), identifies the 1920s as the decade in which casework methodology shifted from an environmental to a psychoanalytic orientation. Most historians accept this dating, citing the rise of the mental hygiene movement. See, for example, the basic textbook in the field, Walter I. Trattner, *From Poor Law to Welfare State: A History of Social Welfare in America,* 5th ed. (New York: Free Press, 1994), pp. 260–263. However, research by scholars in social work has cast doubt on the 1920s as the pivotal decade of methodological change in social casework. These studies demonstrate that except for elite East Coast child placement agencies and psychiatric child guidance centers, the shift to a psychoanalytic casework methodology spread slowly and unevenly beginning in the late 1920s and was not fully accomplished until the early 1950s. Martha Heineman Field, "Social Casework Practice during the 'Psychiatric Deluge,'" *SSR* 54 (December 1980): 482–507; Leslie B. Alexander, "Social Work's Freudian Deluge: Myth or Reality?" *SSR* 46 (December 1972): 517–538. A study of the popularization of Freudian concepts in American mass market periodicals between 1919 and 1939 similarly concludes that Freudian concepts were conspicuous by their absence. See A. Michael Sulman, "The Freudianization of the American Child: The Impact of Psychoanalysis in Popular Periodical Literature in the United States, 1919–1939" (Ph.D. diss., University of Pittsburgh, 1972). For Freud's influence in the child guidance movement see Margo Horn, *Before It's Too Late: The Child Guidance Movement in the United States, 1922–1945* (Philadelphia: Temple University Press, 1989). By the 1930s, Freud was a strong influence in the policy and practice of treating child sexual abuse. See Elizabeth Pleck, *Domestic Tyranny: The Making of American Social Policy against Family Violence from Colonial Times to the Present* (New York: Oxford University Press, 1987), ch. 8.

44. Elizabeth M. R. Lomax, Jerome Kagan, and Barbara G. Rosenkrantz, *Patterns of Child Care* (San Francisco: W. H. Freeman, 1978), p. 112.
45. Lucille C. Birnbaum, "Behaviorism in the 1920's," *American Quarterly* 7 (Spring 1955): 15–30.
46. Herbert E. Rie, "Historical Perspectives of Concepts of Child Psychopathology," in Rie, ed., *Perspectives in Child Psychopathy* (Chicago: Aldine-Atherton, 1971), pp. 28–39; Bernard Rosenblatt, "Historical Perspective of Treatment Modes," ibid., pp. 51–67; William Healy, *Mental Conflicts and Misconduct* (Boston: Little, Brown, 1917), pp. 73–74.
47. Sidney Tarachow, "The Disclosures of Foster-Parentage to a Boy," *American Journal of Psychiatry* 94 (September 1937): 401, 410–411.
48. Robert P. Knight, "Some Problems Involved in Selecting and Rearing Adopted Children," *Bulletin of the Menninger Clinic* 5 (May 1941): 70–71.
49. Carolyn Conant Van Blarcom, "Shall We Tell the Truth to Adopted Children?" *Delineator* 84 (February 1920): 29; Lillian Gatlin, "Adopting a Baby," *Sunset* 46 (February 1921): 85; Francis Lockridge, "How to Adopt a Child," *Children: The Magazine for Parents* 3 (October 1928): 60; Mary E. Milburn to Mrs. M. Mueller, June 9, 1930, CBR, Central File 1929–1932, File 7-3-3-4, Box 406.
50. Mrs. G. H. Unwon to Grace Abbott, Sept. 3, 1929, CBR, Central File 1929–1932, File 7-3-3-4, Box 406; "The Adopted Child Asks Questions: Doctor Crumbine and Cheerio Broadcast Answers," *Child Health Bulletin* 9 (July 1933): 117–118; "Chosen Children," *Time* 33 (May 15, 1939): 39.
51. Valentina P. Wasson, *The Chosen Baby* (Philadelphia: J. B. Lippincott Company, 1939), n.p.; Mary Ruth Colby to Mrs. E. A. Brady, Sept. 8, 1942, CBR, Central File 1941–1944, File 7-3-3-4, Box 170.
52. Lee Brooks and Evelyn C. Brooks, *Adventuring in Adoption* (Chapel Hill: University of North Carolina Press, 1939), pp. ix, 66–67; quotations on pp. 66, 185, 67. *Adventuring in Adoption* sold out its first edition of 1,454 copies. Eventually, it sold a total of 2,366 copies. (UNC Press Assistant Advertising Manager Sue H. Cate, letter to author, Sept. 4, 1991).
53. The following summary is based on Carol S. Prentice, "Manual for Adopting Children," *Good Housekeeping* 111 (August 1940): 168; "Story about Me," *PM* 19 (October 1944): 166; An Adopted Father, "How to Tell Them," *PM* 20 (October 1945): 134; Mackenzie, "Boom in Adoptions," p. 29; "How-What to Tell an Adopted Child," [New York] State Charities Aid Association *News* 36 (November 1946): 2; Douglas E. Lawson, "Choosing Your Child," *Hygeia* (October 1942): 770–771.
54. Benjamin Spock, *The Common Sense Book of Baby and Child Care* (New

York: Duell, Sloan and Pearce, 1946), pp. 480–481; Nancy Pottishman Weiss, "Mother, The Invention of Necessity: Dr. Benjamin Spock's *Baby and Child Care,*" *American Quarterly* 29 (Winter 1977): 534–535; Michael Zuckerman, "Dr. Spock: The Confidence Man," in Zuckerman, ed., *Almost Chosen People: Oblique Biographies in the American Grain* (Berkeley: University of California Press, 1993); Joseph Reid to League Member Agencies, Aug. 29, 1960, CWLA Recs., Suppl.

55. Jean M. Paton, *The Adopted Break Silence* (Philadelphia: Life History Study Center, 1954).
56. "How It Feels to Have Been an Adopted Child," *American Magazine* 90 (August 1920): 72.
57. Martha Vansant, "The Life of the Adopted Child," *American Mercury* 28 (February 1933): 214–222; quotations on pp. 216, 220.

4. The Ephemeral Age of Secrecy

1. "Second Annual Report" (1855), *CAS*, p. 5.
2. Quoted in Miriam Z. Langsam, *Children West: A History of the Placing-Out System of the New York Children's Aid Society, 1853–1890* (Madison: State Historical Society of Wisconsin, 1964), p. 53.
3. Wilfred S. Reynolds, "Standards of Placing Out in Free Family Homes," *PNCCC* (Fort Wayne, Ind.: Fort Wayne Printing Co., 1914), p. 184; Marilyn Irvin Holt, *The Orphan Trains: Placing Out in America* (Lincoln: University of Nebraska Press, 1992), p. 130.
4. CHSW CRs 6, 2502; Cleveland Protestant Orphan Asylum, Fiftieth *Annual Report* (Cleveland, 1902), p. 39.
5. "Whereabouts of Placed-Out Children," *Charities Review* 10 (1900): 8; Julie Berebitsky, " 'To Raise as Your Own': The Growth of Legal Adoption in Washington," *Washington History* 6 (Spring–Summer 1994): 20–21; S. J. Hathway, "Children's Homes in Ohio," *PNCCC* (Boston, 1890), p. 210; Henry W. Thurston, Discussion of "Child Placing by Volunteers," *PNCCC* (Indianapolis: William P. Burford, 1910), p. 137.
6. "Whereabouts of Placed-Out Children," p. 8; Case Record 2472, Children's Home Society of Minnesota, St. Paul, Minn.; Homer Folks, "Some Developments of the Boarding Out System," *Charities Review* 2 (March 1893): 256; George Harrison Durand, "The Study of the Child from the Standpoint of the Home-Finding Agency," *PNCCC* (Indianapolis: William P. Burford, 1907), p. 260; Amos G. Warner, *American Charities: A Study in Philanthrophy and Economics* (New York: Thomas Y. Crowell Co., 1894), p. 228.

7. "Sues Spence Society for Return of Son," *NYT,* August 29, 1925, sec 1, pp. 1, 14.

8. "Wins Plea in Spence Suit," *NYT,* September 27, 1925, sec. 1, p. 34; H. H. R., "Adopted Children," *NYT,* October 7, 1925, sec. 1, p. 26; "Upholds Spence Alumnae," *NYT,* October 24, 1925, sec. 1, p. 16; quotation from ICH&AS, *Home Life for Children* 14 (June 1926): 14.

9. Mary Ruth Colby, *Problems and Procedures in Adoption,* U.S. Children's Bureau pub. 262 (Washington, D.C.: Government Printing Office, 1941), p. 120.

10. "Minimum Safeguards in Adoption," Nov. 5, 1938, CWLA Recs., Box 15, Folder 5.

11. CHSW CRs 11202, 16062, 19582.

12. CHSW CRs 11202, 15072, 15212, 12792, 14573.

13. CHSW CR 12792; CHSW, "Manual of Adoption Family Services," (n.p., 1969), p. 11, CHSW Recs., hereafter cited as "Adoption Manual."

14. CHSW CRs 7942, 7072, 16433. See also CHSW CR 5693, in which caseworker "A" writes, "I did not reveal to AE that he had another sister who had been in the care of our agency, too."

15. See, for example, Arthur D. Sorosky, Annette Baran, and Reuben Pannor, *The Adoption Triangle: The Effects of the Sealed Record on Adoptees, Birth Parents, and Adoptive Parents* (New York: Anchor Press/Doubleday, 1978), pp. 22–23; Hal Aigner, *Adoption in America: Coming of Age* (Greenbrae, Calif.: Paradigm Press, 1986), pp. 7–8.

16. E. Wayne Carp, "The Sealed Adoption Records Controversy in Historical Perspective: The Case of the Children's Home Society of Washington, 1895–1988," *Journal of Sociology and Social Welfare* 19 (June 1992): 38–39, 42.

17. Joseph T. Alves, *Confidentiality in Social Work* (Westport, Conn.: Greenwood Press, 1984), pp. 108–112, 117, 181–182; Mary E. Richmond, *Social Diagnosis* (New York: Russell Sage Foundation, 1917), pp. 160–165, quotation on p. 160; Agnes K. Hanna to Elsa Castandyck, Nov. 27, 1936, CBR, File 7-3-3-4, Central File 1933–1936, Box 549.

18. "Regarding Adoptions," CWLA *Special Bulletin* (March 1937): 5, CWLA Recs., Suppl., Box 41, "Special Bulletins" folder. Contributing to the League's change in policy was the feminist outlook of Children's Bureau officials during World War II who championed the privacy rights of married women who gave birth to illegitimate children while their husbands were overseas. They strenuously objected to court decisions that insisted that husbands must be notified of the birth and encouraged adoption agencies to accommodate the wives' desire for secrecy. Mary

Labaree to Maud Morlock, Oct. 8, 1945, CBR, File 7-3-3-4, Central File 1945–1948, Box 157.

19. California Department of Social Welfare, *Adaptation of Adoption Law and Procedure* (Sacramento: California State Printing Office, 1944), p. 10; Maud Morlock, "Babies on the Market," *Survey* 81 (March 1945): 69; Frank Howard Richardson, "Protecting Child and Parents in Adoption," *Today's Health* 28 (May 1950): 52.

20. Shirley C. Hellenbrand, "Main Currents in Social Casework, 1918–1936" (D.S.W. diss., Columbia University School of Social Work, 1965), chs. 2–4.

21. Nathan G. Hale, Jr., *The Rise and Crisis of Psychoanalysis in the Untied States: Freud and the Americans, 1917–1985* (New York: Oxford University Press, 1995), ch. 11; J. Kasanin and Sieglinde Handschin, "Psychodynamic Factors in Illegitimacy," *American Journal of Orthopsychiatry* 11 (1941): 83; James P. Cattell, "Psychodynamic and Clinical Observations in a Group of Unmarried Mothers," *American Journal of Psychiatry* 3 (November 1954): 337; Florence Clothier, "Psychological Implications of Unmarried Parenthood," *American Journal of Orthopsychiatry* 13 (1943): 548; Florence Clothier, "Problems in the Placement of Illegitimate Children," CWLA, *Bull.* 20 (March 1941): 1–3, 8.

22. Jesse Taft, "A Changing Psychology in Child Welfare," *Annals* 151 (September 1930): 121; Hale, Jr., *Rise and Crisis of Psychoanalysis,* ch. 16.

23. Charlotte Henry, "Objectives in Work With Unmarried Mothers," *The Family* 14 (May 1933): 76; Mary S. Brisley, "The Unmarried Parent-Child Relationship," in *The Unmarried Parent-Child Relationship* (New York: CWLA, 1939), pp. 11–12; Leontine R. Young, "The Unmarried Mother's Decision about Her Baby," *Journal of Social Casework* 28 (January 1947): 27; CWLA, *Standards for Adoption Service* (New York: CWLA, 1958), p. 14.

24. Clothier, "Placement of Illegitimate Children," p. 2; Ruth F. Brenner, "Discussion," in *The Unmarried Parent-Child Relationship,* p. 23; Florence Clothier, "The Unmarried Mother of School Age as Seen by a Psychiatrist," *MH* 39 (October 1955): 645; Frances H. Schertz, "Taking Sides in the Unmarried Mother's Conflict," *Journal of Social Casework* 28 (January 1947): 59–60; Helene Deutsch, *The Psychology of Women* (New York: Grune & Stratton, 1944–1945), vol. 2, p. 376.

25. John Bowlby, *Maternal Care and Mental Health,* World Health Organization Monograph Series, no. 2 (Geneva: World Health Organization, 1951), pp. 15–51, 101–108, quotations on pp. 101, 103. See also Bowlby, *A Secure Base: Parent Child Attachment and Healthy Human De-*

velopment (New York: Basic Books, 1988), ch. 2. For Bowlby's "deep influence on agencies," see the statement by CWLA president Joseph H. Reid, "Principles, Values, and Assumptions Underlying Adoption Practice," in I. Evelyn Smith, ed., *Readings in Adoption* (New York: Philosophical Library, 1963), p. 33.

26. Sarah Evan, "The Unwed Mother's Indecision about Her Baby as a Defense Mechanism," CWLA, *Services to Unmarried Mothers* (New York: CWLA, 1958), pp. 18–30, quotations on p. 18.

27. CHSW CR 18993.

28. CWLA, *Standards for Adoption Service* (New York: CWLA, 1958), p. 47. The CWLA used identical language in its 1968 revision of the *Standards*. CHSW, "Adoption Manual," part 4: "Recording," pp. 1–2.

29. Sigmund Freud, "Family Romances," in James Strachey, ed., *The Standard Edition of the Complete Psychological Works of Sigmund Freud* (London: Hogarth Press and Institute of Psycho-Analysis, 1953–1966), vol. 9, pp. 237–241, quotations on pp. 238, 239, 240–241.

30. Florence Clothier, "Some Aspects of the Problem of Adoption," *American Journal of Orthopsychiatry* 9 (1939): 612–614; Florence Clothier, "The Psychology of the Adopted Child," *MH* 27 (April 1943): 228–230.

31. Viola W. Bernard, "Application of Psychoanalytic Concepts to Adoption Agency Practice," in Marcel Heiman and M. Ralph Kaufman, eds., *Psychoanalysis and Social Work* (New York: International Universities Press, 1953), p. 207, and reprinted in the widely read I. Evelyn Smith, ed., *Readings in Adoption* (New York: Philosophical Library, 1963); "Minutes of General Staff Meeting," Nov. 12, 1958, CHSW Recs.

32. Alves, *Confidentiality in Social Work,* chap. 4, pp. 87–90, 160–163, 182–183.

33. "Adoption Manual," p. 11b; CHSW CR 7082.

34. CHSW CRs 11834, 12812. In September 1971, caseworker Marian Elliott noted that in the last few months "we have had some very strict interpretation of what Washington State Law is and this to the point that it is illegal to give identifying information in these cases and that it can only be done by a court order to open the adoptive file" (CHSW CR 16433).

35. Barbara Kohlsaat and Adelaide M. Johnson, "Some Suggestions for Practice in Infant Adoptions," *SC* 35 (March 1954): 92–94, quotations on pp. 94, 93.

36. Lela Costin, "Readers' Comments," *SC* 35 (June 1954): 259; Constance Rathbun, ibid., p. 261.

37. Michael Schapiro, *A Study of Adoption Practice* (New York: CWLA, 1956), vol. 1, pp. 86–87.

38. "Agency Adoption Practices: Abstracts from the Preliminary Report of the Survey of the Child Welfare League of America" (June 1955), pp. 41–43, 42, CWLA Recs., Box 16, Folder 7; Lela B. Costin, "The History-Giving Interview in Adoption Procedures," *Journal of Social Casework* 35 (November 1954): 398, reprinted in Smith, ed., *Readings in Adoption*, pp. 343–355.

39. CWLA, "Agency Adoption Practices," pp. 43, 42; *Standards for Adoption Service,* rev. ed. (New York: CWLA, 1959), p. 27.

40. Louise Raymond, *Adoption and After* (New York: Harper and Row, 1955), p. 80; Carl Doss and Helen Doss, *If You Adopt a Child* (New York: Henry Holt, 1957), p. 191 (emphasis in the original); Ernest Cady and Francis Cady, *How to Adopt a Child* (New York: Whiteside and William Morrow, 1956), pp. 120–121; Dorothy Barclay, "Chosen Children: A Fresh Look," *NYTM,* Nov. 9, 1958, p. 60.

41. C. V. Williams, "Safeguarding Adoptions," ICH&AS, *Homelife for Children* 14 (December 1927), p. 11; CHSW CR 4342. For similar examples, see CHSW CRs 2232, 2842, 3362, 3682, 4442; Raymond, *Adoption and After,* p. 64.

42. Alexina Mary McWhinnie, *Adopted Children: How They Grow Up* (London: Routledge & Kegan Paul, 1967), p. 241; Benson Jaffee and David Fanshel, *How They Fared in Adoption: A Follow-Up Study* (New York: Columbia University Press, 1970), p. 312. See also Lois Raynor, *The Adopted Child Comes of Age* (London: G. Allen & Unwin, 1980), p. 95.

43. Margo Horn, "The Moral Message of Child Guidance," *Journal of Social History* 18 (Fall 1984): 27–29; Dorothy H. Hutchinson, *In Quest of Foster Parents: A Point of View on Homefinding* (New York: Columbia University Press, 1943), p. 74.

44. Francis Lockridge, *Adopting a Child* (New York: Greenberg, 1947), pp. 152–153; Margaret Kornitzer, *Child Adoption in the Modern World* (London: Putnam, 1952), p. 115.

45. Kathleen Norris, "Drama in Everyday Life," *Reader's Digest* 44 (June 1944): 23–24. *Reader's Digest* circulation figures from Theodore Peterson, *Magazines in the Twentieth Century,* 2d ed. (Urbana: University of Illinois Press, 1964), p. 232.

46. Susan Brubaker to Herbert R. Mayes, Sept. 15, 1959, CWLA Recs., Suppl., Box 7, Folder: Adoption 1925–1966; H. David Kirk, "Guarding the Ramparts: Reader Reactions to a Magazine Article Questioning a Social Work Prescription," *The Social Worker/Le Travailleur Social* (June–July 1962): 31–43; Henrietta Sloane Whitmore, "To My Adopted Daughter: I Wish I Hadn't Told You," *McCall's Magazine* 79 (September 1959): 66–67, 151–153, quotations on pp. 67, 153.

47. Benjamin Spock, *The Common Sense Book of Baby and Child Care* (New York: Duell, Sloan, and Pearce, 1946), p. 480.

48. Marshall D. Schechter, "Observations on Adopted Children," *Archives of General Psychiatry* 3 (July 1960): 21–31, quotations on pp. 21, 31.

49. Lili E. Peller, "About 'Telling the Child' of His Adoption," *Bulletin of the Philadelphia Association for Psychoanalysis* 11 (1961): 145–153, quotations on pp. 153, 146; Lili E. Peller, "Further Comments on Adoption," ibid. 13 (1963): 1–13.

50. Irene M. Josselyn, "A Psychiatrist Looks at Adoption," in Michael Schapiro, ed., *A Study of Adoption Practice* (New York: CWLA, 1956), vol. 2, pp. 16–17, quotation on p. 17; Peller, "About 'Telling the Child' of His Adoption," p. 146.

51. Herbert Wieder, "On When to Disclose about Adoption," *Journal of the American Psychoanalytic Association* 26 (October 1978): 802; Wieder, "On Being Told of Adoption," *Psychoanalytic Quarterly* 46 (1977): 1–22, quotations on p. 16.

52. James Lawton, Jr., and Seymour Z. Gross, "Review of Psychiatric Literature on Adopted Children," *Archives of General Psychiatry* 11 (December 1964): 636–640, quotations on 636, 640. Two years later, similar criticism of the unscientific nature of Schechter and Peller's work came from H. David Kirk, Kurt Jonassohn, and Ann D. Fish, "Are Adopted Children Especially Vulnerable to Stress? A Critique of Some Recent Assertions," ibid. 14 (March 1966): 291–298.

53. Povl W. Toussieng, "Thoughts Regarding the Etiology of Psychological Difficulties in Adopted Children," *CW* 41 (February 1962): 65; "Editor's Note," ibid., p. 65; Toussieng, "Discussion of 'Thoughts Regarding the Etiology of Psychological Difficulties in Adopted Children,'" ibid., 67; Dorothy C. Krugman, "Reality in Adoption," *CW* 43 (July 1964): 350.

54. Viola W. Bernard, *Adoption* (New York: CWLA, 1964), pp. 102–105, quotations on pp. 102, 104; U.S. Department of Health, Education, and Welfare, *When You Adopt a Child*, U.S. Children's Bureau Folder, no. 13–1965 (Washington, D.C.: Government Printing Office, 1965), pp. 23–24.

55. Jaffee and Fanshel, *How They Fared in Adoption*, pp. 274–275. A 1980 British study also discounted the psychoanalytic interpretation of the harmfulness of telling early. See Raynor, *Adopted Child*, p. 94.

56. Catherine Mathews, "Case Work With Unmarried Mothers," *The Family* 13 (October 1932): 185; Raymond, *Adoption and After*, p. 87. For similar advice, see Doss and Doss, *If You Adopt a Child*, p. 187.

57. Bernard, *Adoption*, p. 103.

58. Compare Florence Rondell and Ruth Michaels, *The Adopted Family, Book 2, The Family That Grew: A Picture Story Book for the Child* (New York: Crown, 1951), p. 4, with ibid., rev. ed. (1965), p. 4.

59. Compare Rondell and Michaels, *The Adopted Family,* Book 1, *You and Your Child: A Guide for Adoptive Parents* (New York: Crown, 1951), p. 27, with ibid., rev. ed. (1965), pp. 27–28.

60. John Troseliotis, *In Search of Origins: The Experiences of Adopted People* (London: Routledge and Kegan Paul, 1973), p. 33; Valentina P. Wasson, *The Chosen Baby,* rev. ed. (Philadelphia: J. B. Lippincott, 1977).

61. For a review of the debate of whether or not adopted children are more vulnerable to psychological problems than their nonadopted peers, see David M. Brodzinsky, "Looking at Adoption Through Rose Colored Glasses: A Critique of Marquis and Detweiler's 'Does Adoption Mean Different? An Attributional Analysis,'" *Journal of Personality and Social Psychology* 52 (February 1987): 394–398.

62. Joan Lawrence, "The Truth Hurt Our Adopted Daughter," *PM* 38 (January 1963): 45, 105–106, quotations on 105.

63. This and the next paragraph are based on Joseph G. Ansfield, *The Adopted Child* (Springfield, Ill.: Charles C. Thomas, 1971), pp. 20–21, 35–49, quotations on pp. 37, viii, 40, 47, 49.

64. "White Parents, Black Children: Transracial Adoption," *Time* 98 (Aug. 16, 1971): 42; Elizabeth L. Post, "Adopted Child Asks: 'Who Am I?'— What Can Parents Answer?" *National Adoptalk* 3 (December 1967): 1; Joan McNamara, *The Adoption Adviser* (New York: Hawthorn Books, 1975), pp. 150–151. Cf. H. David Kirk, *Shared Fate: A Theory and Method of Adoptive Relationships* (New York: Free Press, 1964).

5. *The Emergence of the Adoption Rights Movement*

1. Ruthena Hill Kittson [Jean Paton], *Orphan Voyage* (New York: Vantage Press, 1968), pp. 30–31. The phrase "Mutual Registration" can be found in the Life History Study Center's pamphlet "Reunion" (1958), p. 6, in possession of the author.

2. This and the next paragraph are based on Paton, *Orphan Voyage,* pp. 31, 23, 39, both quotations on p. 33.

3. Jean M. Paton to author, May 6, 1996. Paton, *Orphan Voyage,* pp. 39–41, quotation on p. 41.

4. Elaine Tyler May, *Homeward Bound: American Families in the Cold War Era* (New York: Basic Books, 1988); Paton quoted in Jean White, "Adoptee Lib Vs. Sealed Records," *Los Angeles Times,* October 12, 1975, sec. 5, p. 16.

5. Michael J. Crozier, Samuel P. Huntington, and Joji Watanuki, *The Crisis of Democracy: Report on the Governability of Democracies to the Trilateral Commission* (New York: New York University Press, 1975), pp. 74–76; Edward P. Morgan, *The Sixties Experience: Hard Lessons about Modern America* (Philadelphia: Temple University Press, 1991); Stewart Burns, *Social Movements of the 1960s: Searching for Democracy* (Boston: Twayne, 1990).

6. Douglas T. Miller, *On Our Own: America in the Sixties* (Lexington, Mass.: D. C. Heath, 1996), p. 206; Morgan, *The Sixties Experience*; Burns, *Social Movements of the 1960s*; James T. Patterson, *Grand Expectations: The United States, 1945–1974* (New York: Oxford University Press, 1996), pp. 565–568, quotation on p. 568.

7. Florence Fisher, *The Search for Anna Fisher* (New York: Fawcett Crest, 1973), pp. 154, 203; Enid Nemy, "Adopted Children Who Wonder, 'What Was Mother Like?'" *NYT*, July 25, 1972, sec. 1, p. 22.

8. Fisher quoted in Lynn Lilliston, "Who Am I? Adoptees Seek Right to Know," *Los Angeles Times*, July 22, 1973, sec. 10, p. 15, and in Nemy, "Adopted Children Who Wonder," p. 22.

9. Jean M. Paton to author, May 20, 1996; Jean Paton-Kittson, "The American Orphan and the Temptations of Adoption: A Manifesto," World Conference on Adoption and Foster Care, Milan, Italy, Sept. 16, 1971, in possession of the author.

10. *Time*, June 24, 1974, p. 81; Hal Aigner, *Faint Trails: A Guide to Adult Adoptee–Birth Parent Reunification Searches* (Greenbrae, Calif.: Paradigm, 1987), pp. 67, 2–3; Paul Sachdev, "Unlocking the Adoption Files: A Social and Legal Dilemma," in Sachdev, ed., *Adoption: Current Issues and Trends* (Toronto: Butterworths, 1984), pp. 146–147. In 1974, the ARM radicalized adoptive parents, a number of whom founded the North American Council on Adoptable Children (NACAC). NACAC joined adoptees' search organizations in demanding that all adoptive parents recognize that their children's identities involve having two sets of parents, thus implicitly advocating open records. See Ruth G. McRoy, Harold D. Grotevant, and Kerry L. White, *Openness in Adoption: New Practices, New Issues* (New York: Praeger, 1988), p. 9; Mary Ann Jones, *The Sealed Adoption Record Controversy: Report of a Survey of Agency Policy, Practice and Opinions* (New York: CWLA, 1977), pp. 29–30; *EA*, s.v. "American Adoption Congress."

11. Nemy, "Adopted Children Who Wonder," p. 22; R. D. Maxfield to Joseph Reid, Oct. 1, 1975, CWLA Recs., Suppl., Box 10, "Sealed Adoption Records Controversy" folder. Keith Bromery, "He's Battling to Keep Adoption Records Closed," *Chicago Daily News*, Dec. 27, 1994, ibid.; *EA*, s.v.

"National Committee for Adoption"; NCFA, *Adoption Factbook* (Washington, D.C.: NCFA, 1989), p. 108.

12. Nemy, "Adopted Children Who Wonder," p. 22; *Bell & Howell's Newspaper Index to the Washington Post, 1972–1975* (Wooster, Ohio: Bell & Howell, 1979) vol. 3, p. 6; Vanderbilt Television News Archive *Television News Index and Abstracts* (Nashville, Tenn.: Vanderbilt Television News Archive, 1972–1975). Although the evening news ignored the ARM, Barbara Walters's NBC program *Not for Women Only* ran a five-day series on adoption, in which Florence Fisher appeared on a panel discussion and an ALMA member was interviewed about a successful reunion. *ALMA Searchlight*, June 1975, p. 2; *Time*, June 24, 1974, p. 81.

13. For East Coast media bias against the western United States, personified in its coverage of California, see Edward Jay Epstein, *News from Nowhere* (New York: Random House, 1973), pp. 37, 197, 244–246; Herbert Gans, *Deciding What's News: A Study of CBS Evening News, NBC Nightly News, Newsweek and Time* (New York: Random House, 1979), p. 27.

14. For the information about Watergate in this paragraph and the next, I have relied on John Morton Blum, *Years of Discord: American Politics and Society, 1961–1974* (New York: W. W. Norton, 1991), chs. 15, 16; Stanley I. Kutler, *The War of Watergate: The Crisis of Richard Nixon* (New York: W. W. Norton, 1990).

15. Annette Baran, Reuben Pannor, and Arthur D. Sorosky, "Adoptive Parents," *SC* 55 (November 1974): 531–536; Arthur D. Sorosky, Annette Baran, and Reuben Pannor, "The Reunion of Adoptees and Birth Relatives," *Journal of Youth and Adolescence* 3 (1974): 195–206; Reuben Pannor, Arthur D. Sorosky, and Annette Baran, "Opening the Sealed Record in Adoption—The Human Need for Continuity," *Journal of Jewish Communal Service* 51 (Winter 1974): 188–196; Baran, Sorosky, and Pannor, "The Dilemma of Our Adoptees," *Psychology Today* 9 (December 1975): 38; Sorosky, Baran, and Pannor, "Identity Conflicts in Adoptees," *American Journal of Orthopsychiatry* 45 (January 1975): 18–27; Sorosky, Pannor, and Baran, "The Psychological Effects of the Sealed Record on Adoptive Parents," *World Journal of Psychosynthesis* 7 (November–December 1975): 13–18; Pannor, Baran, and Sorosky, "Attitudes of Birth Parents, Adoptive Parents, and Adoptees toward the Sealed Adoption Record," *Journal of the Ontario Association of Children's Aid Societies* 4 (April 1976): 1–7; Sorosky, Baran, and Pannor, "Effects of the Sealed Record in Adoption," *American Journal of Psychiatry* 133 (August 1976): 900–904; Sorosky, Baran, and Pannor, "Adoption and the Adolescent: An Overview," in Sherman C. Feinstein and Peter L. Giovacchini, eds., *Adolescent Psychiatry*, vol. 5: *Annals of the American Society for Adoles-*

cent Psychiatry (New York: Jason Aronson, 1977): 54–71; Baran, Pannor, and Sorosky, "The Lingering Pain of Surrendering a Child," *Psychology Today* 58 (June 1977): 58–60; Pannor, Baran, and Sorosky, "Birth Parents Who Relinquished Babies for Adoption Revisited," *Family Process* 17 (September 1978): 329–337; Sorosky, Baran, and Pannor, *The Adoption Triangle: The Effects of the Sealed Record on Adoptees, Birth Parents, and Adoptive Parents* (New York: Anchor Press/Doubleday, 1978).

16. Interestingly, Sorosky, Baran, and Pannor never used either term previous to the publication of *The Adoption Triangle*. The earliest use of "adoption triangle," or at least a phrase very similar, was in 1974 by Ralph D. Maxfield, founder of an anti-ARM organization, the Association for the Protection of the Adoptive Triangle. See R. D. Maxfield to Joseph Reid, Oct. 1, 1975, CWLA Recs., Suppl., Box 10, "Sealed Adoption Records Controversy" folder. Three years later, in March 1977 the Children's Home Society of California (CHSC) used the term "adoption triangle" in its report on attitudes toward sealed adoption records. Children's Home Society of California, *The Changing Face of Adoption* (Los Angeles: Children's Home Society of California, 1977), p. 34. The earliest use of the term "adoption triad" dates to 1977. See C. Wilson Anderson, "The Sealed Record in Adoption Controversy," *SSR* 51 (1977): 146.

17. Sorosky, Baran, and Pannor, *Adoption Triangle,* pp. 35, 228.

18. Baran, Pannor, and Sorosky, "Adoptive Parents," p. 532; Pannor, Sorosky, and Baran, "Opening the Sealed Record," p. 193; Sorosky, Baran, and Pannor, "Reunion," p. 204; Baran, Sorosky, and Pannor, "Dilemma," p. 42.

19. Baran, Sorosky, and Pannor, "Dilemma," p. 38; Pannor, Sorosky, and Baran, "Opening the Sealed Record," p. 194; Sorosky, Baran, and Pannor, "Reunion," p. 203.

20. Sorosky, Baran, and Pannor, "Identity Conflicts," pp. 19, 24; Sorosky, Baran, and Pannor, "Adoption and the Adolescent," pp. 59–62. But adoption rights activists were selective about what was psychologically unhealthy. They never entertained for a moment the idea that searching for one's biological family was part of the "adoption syndrome." But some leaders accepted the other psychological symptoms, turned them into the causes of adoptees' "illness," and went to court with the rationale that searching and finding their biological family provided the "cure." See Chapter 6 below.

21. Baran, Pannor, and Sorosky, "Adoptive Parents," p. 535; Baran, Sorosky, and Pannor, "Dilemma," p. 42.

22. Baran, Pannor, and Sorosky, "Lingering Pain," p. 59; Baran, Sorosky, and Pannor, "Dilemma," p. 42; Pannor, Baran, and Sorosky, "Attitudes," p. 7.

23. Pannor, Sorosky, and Baran, "Opening the Sealed Record," p. 192; Baran, Pannor, and Sorosky, "Adoptive Parents," pp. 535, 536; Sorosky, Baran, and Pannor, "Identity Conflicts," pp. 23–25.

24. Sorosky, Baran, and Pannor, "Identity Conflicts," p. 25; Sorosky, Baran, and Pannor, "Adoption and the Adolescent," p. 64; Sorosky, Pannor, and Baran, "Psychological Effects," p. 15.

25. H. J. Sants, "Genealogical Bewilderment in Children with Substitute Parents," *British Journal of Medical Psychology* 37 (1964): 133–141, quotation on p. 133. Sants was identified in the article as affiliated with the University College of North Wales, Bangor. Previously, he had worked at Child Guidance Center, Bexleyheath, Kent. E. Wellisch, "Children without Genealogy—A Problem of Adoption," *Mental Health* 12 (Autumn 1952): 41–42.

26. Sants, "Genealogical Bewilderment," p. 139.

27. Sorosky, Baran, and Pannor, "Reunion," p. 199; Pannor, Sorosky, and Baran, "Opening the Sealed Record," pp. 191, 192. No reliable statistics were used in the *Social Casework* article. Sorosky, Baran, and Pannor made a vague reference to "the large number" of letters they received and generalized that "two-thirds" believed this or "the majority of adoptees" responded thusly. There were also statistically worthless references such as "twelve letters were received." Baran, Pannor, and Sorosky, "Adoptive Parents," pp. 534–535. By December 1975, when the *Psychology Today* article appeared, the number of reunions in the sample had risen to fifty. Baran, Sorosky, and Pannor, "Dilemma," p. 38.

28. Baran, Sorosky, and Pannor, "Dilemma," p. 38; Sorosky, Baran, and Pannor, "Effects of the Sealed Record," p. 901; Pannor, Sorosky, and Baran, "Opening the Sealed Record," p. 192.

29. Edmund V. Mech, "Adoption: A Policy Perspective," in Bettye M. Caldwell and Henry N. Ricciuti, eds., *Review of Child Development Research* (Chicago: University of Chicago Press, 1973), vol. 3, pp. 480–489, esp. pp. 484, 486. Four additional studies conducted in the 1980s support these positive evaluations of adoption. See the fine discussion in *CWS*, pp. 613–622.

30. From 1976 through 1980, Sorosky and associates were cited approximately sixty-eight times. See *Social Sciences Citation Index, 1976–1980,* Five Year Cumulation (Philadelphia: Institute for Scientific Information, 1983), s.v. "Sorosky"; Alfred Kadushin, "Children in Adoptive Homes," in Henry Maas, ed., *Social Service Research: Reviews of Studies* (Washington, D.C.: National Association of Social Workers, 1978), p. 71; Patrick A. Curtis, "The Dialectics of Open versus Closed Adoptions of Infants," *CW* 65 (September–October 1986): 439. See also the criticism in Paul Sachdev, *Unlocking the Adoption Files* (Lexington, Mass.: D. C.

Heath, 1989), pp. 17–19; John P. Triseliotis, "Obtaining Birth Certificates," in Philip Bean, ed., *Adoption: Essays in Social Policy, Law, and Sociology* (New York: Tavistock, 1984), p. 48; *CWS,* pp. 583, 584; NCFA, *Adoption Factbook,* pp. 108–109.

31. Lilliston, "Who Am I?" p. 14; Baran, Pannor, and Sorosky, "Adoptive Parents," p. 535.

32. *Los Angeles Times,* October 23, 1973, sec. 4, pp. 1, 5, quotations on p. 5.

33. Ibid., March 6, 1974, sec. 4, pp. 1, 15, quotation on p. 15; ibid., April 15, 1974, sec. 4, p. 1.

34. Ibid., May 12, 1974, sec. 4, p. 3; ibid., August 11, 1974, sec. 1, p. 1; ibid., September 15, 1974, sec. 2, p. 9; Judith Modell, "In Search: The Purported Biological Basis of Parenthood," *American Ethnologist* 13 (November 1986): 651.

35. "Searching for Myself," *Seventeen* 30 (November 1971): 118–119, 148; Jeanie Kasindorf, "Who Are My Real Parents?" *McCall's* 101 (May 1974): 53; "The Adopted Child Has a Right to Know Everything," *PM* 50 (October 1975): 40–43; Elizabeth Pope Frank, "We're a Family Again," *Good Housekeeping* 185 (October 1977): 111, 224–227; Gordon S. Livingston, "Search for a Stranger," *Reader's Digest* 110 (June 1970): 85–89, quotation on 89.

36. "Adopted Child Has a Right to Know Everything," p. 41; Baran quoted in Kasindorf, "Who Are My Real Parents?" p. 53.

37. Carol Schaefer, *The Other Mother: A Woman's Love for the Child She Gave Up for Adoption* (New York: Soho, 1991), p. 181; Katrina Maxtone-Graham, *An Adopted Woman* (New York: Rémi Books, 1983), p. 267; Fisher, *Search for Anna Fisher,* p. 178.

38. Maxtone-Graham, *Adopted Woman,* p. 267.

39. "Adoptees Pleased Meeting Parents," *NYT,* May 11, 1975, sec. 1, p. 33.

40. Lorraine Dusky, "Yearning," ibid., March 1, 1975, sec. 1, p. 25; "Court Challenge by Adoptees," ibid., May 29, 1977, sec. 4, p. 16; Betty Jean Lifton, "The Search," *NYTM,* Jan. 25, 1976, pp. 15–19.

41. Betty Jean Lifton, *Twice Born: Memoirs of an Adopted Daughter* (New York: McGraw Hill, 1975).

42. Lifton quoted in Richard Flaste, "Adoptees and the Truth—Adoptive Family's Role," *NYT,* Nov. 28, 1975, sec. 1, p. 32; Lifton, "The Search," pp. 15, 18; Lifton, "So That Adoptees Do Not Have to Vent Their Rage," *NYT,* September 19, 1977, sec. 1, p. 34.

43. Leslie Fishbein, "*Roots:* Docudrama and the Interpretation of History," in John E. O'Connor, ed., *American History, American Television: Interpreting the Video Past* (New York: Ungar, 1983) p. 282; Les Brown, *Encyclopedia of Television,* 3d ed. (Detroit: Gale Research, 1992), p. 467.

44. Fishbein, *"Roots,"* pp. 289, 291, 287, quotation on p. 289; Stuart H. Surlin, *"Roots* Research: A Summary of Findings," *Journal of Broadcasting* 22 (Summer 1978): 319.

45. "Everybody's Search for Roots," *Newsweek* (July 4, 1977): 25–38, quotations on pp. 38, 30; David A. Gerber, "Haley's *Roots* and Our Own: An Inquiry into the Nature of a Popular Phenomenon," *Journal of Ethnic Studies* 5 (Fall 1977): 87; Cynthia Ortega, "Adoption Records: Buried Roots," *NYT*, February 25, 1977, sec. 1, p. 22.

46. *New York Times Book Review,* April 2, 1978, p. 20.

6. The Adoption Records Wars

1. CWLA, *Adoption Resource Exchange of North America* (New York: CWLA, 1968); U.S. Department of Health, Education, and Welfare, National Center for Social Statistics, "Adoptions in 1969," Supplement to *Child Welfare Statistics—1969* (Washington, D.C.: Government Printing Office, 1969). The phrase "special needs," referring to minority and mixed racial groups, older children, children with siblings, and the physically and mentally disabled, was first used in 1958. See Helen Fradkin, "Adoptive Parents for Children with Special Needs," *CW* 37 (January 1958): 1–6; Harriet Fricke, "Interracial Adoption: The Little Revolution," *SW* 10 (July 1965): 92–97; CWLA, *Standards for Adoption Service,* rev. ed. (New York: CWLA, 1968), p. 34; Opportunity: A Division of the Boys and Girls Aid Society of Oregon, "1971 Survey of Adoption of Black Children," (Portland, Ore., 1972, typescript). In 1968, there were 733 transracial adoptions nationwide (ibid.).

2. Harvard Sitkoff, *The Struggle for Black Equality, 1954–1992,* rev. ed. (New York: Hill and Wang), ch. 7.

3. Wayne Vasey, "The San Francisco Story," *Social Welfare Forum* (New York: National Conference on Social Welfare, 1968), pp. 156–163. Russell quoted in C. Gerald Fraser, "Disease Programs Scored by Blacks," *NYT*, April 9, 1972, sec. 1, p. 29; Judy Klemesrud, "Furor over Whites Adopting Blacks," *NYT*, April 10, 1972, sec. 1, p. 38. The harshest critics argued that transracial adoption was a white conspiracy to commit cultural genocide and destroy the black race. See Joyce A. Ladner, *Mixed Families: Adopting across Racial Boundaries* (New York: Anchor, 1977), pp. 98–99. Surprisingly, neither side raised the issue of secrecy and disclosure in the context of transracial adoption.

4. Ladner, *Mixed Families,* pp. 103–114; Howard Altstein and Rita James Simon, "Transracial Adoption: An Examination of an American Phenomenon," *Journal of Social Welfare* 4 (Winter 1977): 65.

5. Rita Dukette, "Perspectives for Agency Response to the Adoption Record Controversy," *CW* 54 (September–October 1975): 545–555. During the same period, *CW* published fifty-two articles on other aspects of adoption; see CWLA, *Adoption Service: A Ten Year Bibliography of CWLA Publications, 1968–1978* (New York: CWLA, 1979), pp. 1–4. *Social Work* did not publish an article on the ARM until 1977; see Joel Freedman, "An Adoptee in Search of Identity," *SW* 22 (May 1977): 227, 229. Erica Haimes and Noel Timms, *Adoption, Identity, and Social Policy: The Search for Distant Relatives* (Hants, England: Gower, 1985), ch. 2. Arlene Nash, review of *The Search for Anna Fisher* by Florence Fisher, *CW* 53 (May 1974): 331.

6. Joseph H. Reid to Sproesser Wynn, Sept. 4, 1975, CWLA Recs., Suppl., Box 10, "Sealed Adoption Records Controversy" folder; Editorial, " 'Adoptee Liberation'—A Fight for Legal Rights," *Today's Health* 52 (August 1974): 59; Reid quoted in Richard Flaste, "Adoptees and the Truth—Adoptive Family's Role," *NYT,* November 28, 1975, sec. 1, p. 32.

7. CWLA, *Standards for Adoption Service,* 1968 rev. ed. (New York: CWLA, 1973), sects. 2.3, 5.2, 5.16, 6.30, 7.23, 7.36.

8. Deborah Shapiro, "The Right to Know—Adoption," March 31, 1975, pp. 1–4, CWLA Recs., Suppl., Box 10, "Sealed Adoption Records Controversy" folder; all quotations on p. 2.

9. Rebecca Smith, "The Sealed Adoption Record Controversy and Social Agency Response," *CW* 55 (February 1976): 74, 73.

10. CWLA, "Proposal for Analysis of the Sealed Adoption Record Issue," April 22, 1976, CWLA Recs., Suppl., Box 10, "Sealed Adoption Records Controversy" folder; quotations on pp. 4, 6.

11. Mary Ann Jones to Betsy Cole, Emily Gardiner, Becky Smith, Clara Swan, memorandum, February 24, 1976, CWLA Recs., Suppl., Box 10, "Sealed Adoption Records Controversy" folder; Ann Shyne to "Mr. Reid," memorandum, March 25, 1976, ibid.

12. Mary Ann Jones, *The Sealed Adoption Record Controversy: Report of a Survey of Agency Policy, Practice and Opinion* (New York: CWLA, 1976), pp. 6, 29–30, quotation on p. 30.

13. CWLA Advisory Committee on Adoption Records, "Synopsis of Meeting, September 17, 18, 1976," p. 1, CWLA Recs., Suppl., Box 10, "Sealed Adoption Records Controversy" folder; CWLA Advisory Committee on Adoption Records, "Issues Statement," September 17, 18, 1976, p. 2, ibid., Box X.

14. Mary Ann Jones to Members of the CWLA Advisory Committee on Adoption Records, memorandum, Oct. 20, 1976, CWLA Recs., Suppl., Box 10, "Sealed Adoption Records Controversy" folder.

15. CWLA, *Standards for Adoption Service,* rev. ed. (New York: CWLA, 1978), sects. 4.26, 4.27, quotation from sect. 2.4. In addition to the demand for open records, other factors, such as differences in the population of children coming into the adoption system and changes in adoptive parents' attitudes toward special-needs children, influenced the CWLA's advice on disclosing nonidentifying information. See E. Wayne Carp, "Adoption and Disclosure of Family Information: A Historical Perspective," in Eve P. Smith and Lisa A. Merkel-Holguín, eds., *A History of Child Welfare* (New Brunswick, N.J.: Transaction, 1995): 227–228.

16. For an overview, see James R. Carter, "Confidentiality of Adoption Records: An Examination," *Tulane Law Review* 52 (June 1978): 817–855. Space does not permit listing them all, but there are more than twenty law review articles on the sealed adoption records controversy.

17. Milessa Arndt, "Severed Roots: The Sealed Adoption Records Controversy," *Northern Illinois University Law Review* 6 (Winter 1986): 118, 103; Laura M. Purdy, *Reproducing Persons: Issues in Feminist Bioethics* (Ithaca: Cornell University Press, 1996), p. 95.

18. Marshall A. Levin, "The Adoption Trilemma: The Adult Adoptee's Emerging Search for His Ancestral Identity," *University of Baltimore Law Review* 8 (Spring 1979): 514, 515. See, for example, the discussion of two cases where judges denied that adoptees had a constitutional right to the information in their files, in Andrea Saltzman and Kathleen Proch, *Law in Social Work Practice* (Chicago: Nelson-Hall, 1990), pp. 214–216.

19. *ALMA Searchlight* (Summer 1976), pp. 2–3, emphasis in the original.

20. Ibid., quotations on pp. 3, 4, emphasis in the original; 601 F.2d 1225 (2d Cir.) *cert denied,* 100 S. Ct. 531 (1979).

21. Debra D. Poulin, "The Open Adoption Records Movement: Constitutional Cases and Legislative Compromise," *Journal of Family Law* 26 (1987–1988): 405–407.

22. Ibid., p. 398; Leslie Allan, "Confirming the Constitutionality of Sealing Adoption Records," *Brooklyn Law Review* 46 (Summer 1980): 731.

23. Allan, "Constitutionality," p. 729; quotation from *ALMA Society, Inc., v. Mellon,* 601 F.2d 1232 (2d Cir.) *cert denied,* 100 S. Ct. 531 (1979).

24. *ALMA Society, Inc., v. Mellon,* 601 F.2d 1238–1239 (2d Cir.) *cert denied,* 100 S. Ct. 531 (1979); Allan, "Constitutionality," pp. 732–735.

25. Florence Kreech to Mary Ann Jones, Dec. 6, 1976, CWLA Recs., Suppl., Box 10, "Sealed Adoption Records Controversy" folder. In the same year, the Children's Home Society of Virginia initiated a similar intermediary system for adult adoptees wishing to be reunited with their birth parents. See Carole Hopp Depp, "After Reunion: Perceptions of Adult

Adoptees, Adoptive Parents, and Birth Parents," *CW* 61 (February 1982): 115–116.

26. Mary Ann Jones to Clara J. Swan, Dec. 14, 1976, CWLA Recs., Suppl., Box 10, "Sealed Adoption Records Controversy" folder.

27. Clearly in the minority were articles defending the system of sealed adoption records. See Donald L. Newborg, "Legal Developments in New York State Regarding the Sealed Adoption Record Controversy," *CW* 58 (April 1979): 276–283; Austin Foster, "Who Has the Right to Know," *Public Welfare* 37 (Summer 1979): 34–37; Richard Aeilenger, "The Need vs. the Right to Know," ibid., pp. 44–47.

28. C. Wilson Anderson, "The Sealed Adoption Record Controversy," *SSR* 51 (1977): 141–154; Elizabeth Cole, review of *The Adoption Triangle* by Arthur Sorosky, Annette Baran, and Reuben Pannor, *CW* 57 (July–August 1978): 457; Joan Ferry DiGiulio, "The 'Search': Providing Continued Service for Adoptive Parents," *CW* 58 (July–August 1979): 460–465. The entire issue of *Public Welfare* 37 (Summer 1979) is devoted to the sealed adoption records controversy.

29. Joseph D. Harrington, "Legislative Update on Sealed Adoption Records," *Public Welfare* 39 (Spring 1981): 29–31; *Public Hearing Before [New Jersey] Assembly, Institutions, Health and Welfare Committee, [Bill] No. 2051 (Adoption)*, Dec. 9, 1981 (Trenton: 1981), quotations from pp. 53–54, 160X, 48.

30. Ibid., pp. 33, 60X; Harrington, "Legislative Update," pp. 29–31. And some states, like Montana, went in the opposite direction by restricting access to adoptees' original birth certificates; ibid., p. 30.

31. Ruth C. Weidell, "Unsealing Sealed Birth Certificates in Minnesota," *CW* 59 (February 1980): 113–119; Jeannine J. Fay, "The Mutual Consent Voluntary Adoption Registry," *Rutgers Law Journal* 18 (Spring 1987): 672–673.

32. Weidell, "Unsealing Sealed Birth Certificates"; *ALP,* 1995 Suppl., vol. 2, p. 51, Appendix 13-A, pp. 74–75.

33. "Model State Adoption Act and Model State Adoption Procedures," *Federal Register* 45, no. 33 (February 15, 1980): 10622–10691.

34. Title II, sec. 201, of the law stated that its purpose was "to facilitate the elimination of barriers to adoption and to provide permanent and loving home environments for children who would benefit by adoption, particularly children with special needs." *Child Abuse Prevention and Treatment and Adoption Reform Act of 1978*, *U.S. Code*, vol. 1, secs. 201–205 (1978). Most scholars have overlooked this piece of federal adoption legislation, which was the precursor to the better known Adoption Assistance and Child Welfare Act of 1980, the so-called federal "perma-

nency planning" law. For the convoluted legislative background to Public Law 95-266, see Barbara A. Pine, "Child Welfare Reform and the Political Process," *SSR* 60 (September 1986): 352–353.

35. Diane D. Broadhurst and Elaine J. Schwartz, "The Right to Know," *Public Welfare* 37 (Summer 1979): 6; "Model State Adoption Act and Model State Adoption Procedures," *Federal Register* 45, no. 33 (Feb. 15, 1980): 10686–10690, microfilm; quotations on pp. 10691, 10686, 10688, 10689, 10690.

36. Mary Jo Rillera, *Adoption Encounter: Hurt, Transition, Healing* (Westminster, Calif.: Triadoption Publications, 1987), p. 28; "Sealed Records Committee," CWLA Recs., 1993 Suppl., Box 5A; Edwin Watson to Member Agencies and League Board, memorandum, April 10, 1980, pp. 10–11, CWLA Recs., Suppl., Box 9, "Model States Adoption Act" folder, quotation on p. 10; Edwin F. Watson to League Board and Member Agencies, memorandum, Sept. 2, 1980, ibid., p. 7; Department of Health and Human Services, "Model Act for Adoption of Children with Special Needs," *Federal Register* 46, no. 195 (Oct. 8, 1981): 50022, microfilm.

37. Francine Klagsbrun, "Debunking the 'Adopted Child Syndrome,' " *Ms.* 15 (October 1986): 102.

38. Betty Jean Lifton, "How the Adoption System Ignites a Fire," *NYT*, March 1, 1986, sec. 1, p. 27.

39. Jeffrey Rosenberg, "1988 Survey of State Laws on Access to Adoption Records," *Family Law Reporter* 14 (Aug. 16, 1988): 3017–3019, quotation on 3018.

40. *EA*, s.v. "International Soundex Reunion Registry"; Joseph D. Harrington, "Legislative Reform Moves Slowly," *Public Welfare* 37 (Summer 1979): 55–56; Fay, "Mutual Consent Voluntary Adoption Registry," pp. 674–676; Joseph D. Harrington, "Adoption and the State Legislatures, 1984–1985," *Public Welfare* 44 (Spring 1986): 25; Rosenberg, "1988 Survey of State Laws," p. 3019.

41. U.S. Senate, Committee on Labor and Human Services, *Adoption in America, 1981: Hearing before the Subcommittee on Aging, Family, and Human Services,* 97th Cong., 1st sess., 1981 (Washington, D.C.: Government Printing Office, 1981), pp. 83–85, 117–128, quotations on pp. 84, 118; hereafter cited as *Adoption in America, 1981.*

42. Ibid., pp. 19–20, 92–93, 109–110, quotation on 92. For the senators' objections see ibid., pp. 108–109; Harrington, "Legislative Update," p. 31. Levin reintroduced a similar bill in January 1988, when it again met with defeat. See Rosenberg, "1988 Survey of State Laws," p. 3019.

43. Rosenberg, "1988 Survey of State Laws," p. 3018; Madelyn DeWoody,

"Adoption and Disclosure of Medical and Social History: A Review of the Law," *CW* 72 (May–June 1993): 195–218.

44. *Burr v. Board of County Commissioners,* 23 Ohio St. 3d 69, 491 N.E. 2d 1101 (1986). There are a number of accounts of the Burr case. See, for example, Janet Hopkins Dickson, "The Emerging Rights of Adoptive Parents: Substance or Specter," *UCLA Law Review* 38 (April 1991): 955–958.

45. Kenneth Watson, *Report of the Child Welfare League of America National Task Force* (Washington, D.C.: CWLA, 1987), p. 9; *Standards for Adoption Service,* rev. ed. (Washington, D.C.: CWLA, 1988), sec. 4.27, p. 44.

46. *Adoption in America, 1981,* p. 126; CWLA officials quoted in Rosenberg, "1988 Survey of State Laws," p. 3019; H. David Kirk, *Adoptive Kinship: A Modern Institution in Need of Reform,* rev ed. (Port Angeles, Wash.: Ben-Simon, 1985), p. 139. Moreover, searching was expensive. One Connecticut agency charged more than $300 for a search. For a breakdown of agency expenses, see ibid., p. 144, n. 20.

7. From Open Records to Open Adoption

1. Priscilla Ferguson Clement, "Families and Foster Care: Philadelphia in the Late Nineteenth Century," *SSR* 53 (September 1979): 410; "Minutes of the Board of Managers, 1878–1903," June 1901, Records of the Hillcrest Children's Center [Washington, D.C.], Cont. 44, Manuscript Division, Library of Congress, Washington, D.C.; "Copy of Agreement between Mrs. —— and Mrs. ——," Jan. 7, 1902, ibid., Cont. 43; CHSW CR 2132; Lawrence W. Cook, "Open Adoption: Can Visitation with Natural Family Members Be in the Child's Best Interests?" *Journal of Family Law* 30 (1991–92): 481.

2. Arthur D. Sorosky, Annette Baran, and Reuben Pannor, *The Adoption Triangle: The Effects of the Sealed Record on Adoptees, Birth Parents, and Adoptive Parents* (New York: Anchor Press/Doubleday, 1978), p. 217. The authors present no evidence for this statement, and I have found no reference to any such practice.

3. For an example of the self-imposed secrecy, shame, and fear surrounding unwed pregnancy, see Carol Schaefer, *The Other Mother: A Woman's Love for the Child She Gave Up for Adoption* (New York: Soho Press, 1991).

4. H. David Kirk, *Shared Fate: A Theory and Method of Adoptive Relationships,* 2d rev. ed. (Port Angeles, Wash.: Ben-Simon, 1984; orig. pub. 1964), p. 154 and n. 3. Four years later, in 1968, Jean Paton was the

first person to use the term "open adoption," though she meant only that adoptive parents should talk openly to the child about his or her original parents. See Ruthena Hill Kittson [Jean Paton], *Orphan Voyage* (New York: Vantage Press, 1968), p. 96 and n. 20.

5. Annette Baran, Reuben Pannor, and Arthur D. Sorosky, "Open Adoption," *SW* 21 (March 1976): 97–100, quotations on p. 97. I will quote from the published version of the talk. Detailed notes of Baran's talk suggest that there was little change between the two. Cf. Deborah Shapiro, "The Right to Know—Adoption," March 31, 1975, pp. 2–3, CWLA Recs., Suppl., Box 10, "Sealed Adoption Records Controversy" folder.

6. Shapiro, "The Right to Know—Adoption," pp. 2–3, 5, 12. Baran, Pannor, and Sorosky, "Open Adoption," pp. 97–100.

7. John D'Emilio and Estelle B. Freedman, *Intimate Matters: A History of Sexuality in America* (New York: Harper and Row, 1988), pp. 250–252, 315; NCFA, *Adoption Factbook* (Washington, D.C.: NCFA, 1988), p. 18; Christopher Tietze, Jacqueline Darroch Forrest, and Stanley K. Henshaw, "United States of America," in Paul Sachdev, ed., *International Handbook of Abortion* (New York: Greenwood Press, 1988), p. 484; *CWS,* p. 471.

8. Christine Bachrach, "Adoption Plans, Adopted Children, and Adopted Mothers," *Journal of Marriage and the Family* 48 (May 1986): 250; Alan Guttmacher Institute, *Teenage Pregnancy: The Problem That Hasn't Gone Away* (New York: Alan Guttmacher Institute, 1981), p. 27; Michael Bracken, Lorraine Klerman, and Maryann Bracken, "Coping with Pregnancy Resolution among Never Married Women," *American Journal of Orthopsychiatry* 48 (April 1978): 320–332; *CWS,* p. 495.

9. A seminal study rejecting a psychoanalytic interpretation of illegitimacy was Clark E. Vincent, *Unmarried Mothers* (New York: Free Press, 1961); *CWS,* pp. 473–474; NCFA, *Adoption Factbook,* p. 19; Susan Phipps-Yonas, "Teenage Pregnancy and Motherhood," *American Journal of Orthopsychiatry* 50 (July 1980): 409–410, 413; quotation from Madeleine Simms and Christopher Smith, "Teenage Mothers and Adoption," *Adoption and Fostering* 6 (1982): 45.

10. NCFA, *Adoption Factbook,* p. 14; Alfred Kadushin, *Child Welfare Services,* 3d ed. (New York: Macmillan, 1980), p. 470.

11. Lynn J. Witkin, "Bridging the Gap: Natural Parents and Adoptive Families," *SW* 16 (October 1971): 96; Ruth G. McRoy, Harold D. Groevant, and Kerry L. White, *Openness in Adoption: New Practices, New Issues* (New York: Praeger, 1988), pp. 15–16.

12. Carol J. Storich and Roberta Siebert, "Toward Humanizing Adoption," *CW* 61 (April 1982): 211, 213, 214–215.

13. McRoy, Groevant, and White, *Openness in Adoption,* pp. 17–18; ch. 4.

14. Betty Jean Lifton, *Lost and Found: The Adoption Experience* (New York: Dial Press, 1979), p. 209; Judith S. Modell, *Kinship with Strangers: Adoption and Interpretations of Kinship in American Culture* (Berkeley: University of California Press, 1994), pp. 172–173; CUB activist quotation from Kathleen Silber and Phyllis Speedlin, *Dear Birthmother: Thank You for Our Baby* (San Antonio: Corona, 1983), p. 46; U.S. Senate, Committee on Labor and Human Services, *Adoption in America, 1981: Hearing Before the Subcommittee on Aging, Family, and Human Services*, 97th Cong., 1st sess., 1981 (Washington, D.C.: Government Printing Office, 1981), p. 125. The CUB membership figure of 2,500 given by Campbell at the 1981 Senate hearing is problematic. Three years later, in an article coauthored by Campbell, the figure given was 1,500 (Eva Y. Deykin, Lee Campbell, and Patricia Patti, "The Postadoption Experience of Surrendering Parents," *American Journal of Orthopsychiatry* 54 (April 1984): 272). Moreover, the most knowledgeable scholar of CUB notes that "records of membership were not kept" (Modell, *Kinship with Strangers*, p. 255, n. 3).

15. Ann Murphy, "A Familiar Stranger," *NYT*, July 31, 1978, sec. 1, p. A15.

16. Lorraine Dusky, *Birthmark* (New York: M. Evans, 1979), pp. 50, 75, 100.

17. Betty Jean Lifton, *Twice Born: Memoirs of an Adopted Daughter* (New York: McGraw Hill, 1977), p. 209; Sorosky, Baran, and Pannor, *Adoption Triangle*, p. 220; Lee H. Campbell, "The Birthparent's Right to Know," *Public Welfare* 37 (Summer 1979): 24–27, quotations on pp. 25, 27; CUB material quoted in Mary Ann Kuharski, "Open Adoption Means 'Adopted for Now,' " *A.L.L. about Issues* (August 1984): 17.

18. Pam Lamperelli and Jane M. Smith, "The Grieving Process of Adoption: An Application of Principles and Techniques," *Journal of Psychiatric Nursing and Mental Health Services* 17 (October 1979): 24–29, quotation on p. 24.

19. "Model State Adoption Act and Model State Adoption Procedures," *Federal Register*, vol. 45, no. 33 (Washington, D.C.: Government Printing Office, 1980), p. 10654; Edwin Watson to Member Agencies and League Board memorandum, April 10, 1980, p. 10, CWLA Recs., Suppl., Box 9, "Model States Adoption Act" folder; Department of Health and Human Services, "Model Act for the Adoption of Children with Special Needs," *Federal Register* 46, no. 195 (Oct. 8, 1981): 50022.

20. Lifton quoted in Children's Home Society of California, *The Changing Picture of Adoption* (San Francisco: Children's Home Society of California, 1985), p. 39; Austin Foster, "Who Has the 'Right' to Know?" *Public Welfare* 37 (Summer 1979): 37.

21. Letter from D. Bower, Corona Publishing Company, to author, July 13, 1996.

22. Silber and Speedlin, *Dear Birthmother,* chs. 1–4, quotations on pp. 4, 43, 64, 189.

23. Sorosky, Baran, and Pannor, *Adoption Triangle,* p. 208; Reuben Pannor and Annette Baran, "Open Adoption as Standard Practice," *CW* 63 (May–June 1984): 245.

24. Ibid., pp. 247, 248. Kirk felt that Pannor and Baran had misused his work. See H. David Kirk, *Adoptive Kinship: A Modern Institution in Need of Reform,* rev. ed. (Port Angeles, Wash.: Ben-Simon, 1985; orig. pub. 1981), pp. 166–169.

25. Pannor and Baran, "Open Adoption as Standard Practice," pp. 248–249. These arguments were later elaborated on with references. See Annette Baran and Reuben Pannor, "Open Adoption," in David M. Brodzinsky and Marshall D. Schechter, eds., *The Psychology of Adoption* (New York: Oxford University Press, 1990), pp. 317–318.

26. Pannor and Baran, "Open Adoption," pp. 246–247, quotation on p. 246.

27. Pierce quotation from a 1984 Dallas newspaper article quoted in McRoy, Groevant, and White, *Openness in Adoption,* p. 23. The next two paragraphs are based on the Dallas newspaper document reproduced in ibid.

28. Kuharski, "Open Adoption," p. 17.

29. Adrienne D. Kraft et al., "Some Theoretical Considerations on Confidential Adoptions, Part 1: The Birth Mother," *Child and Adolescent Social Work* 2 (Spring 1985): 19–21, quotation on 21.

30. Ibid., p. 21; quotation from Adrienne D. Kraft et al., "Some Theoretical Considerations on Confidential Adoptions, Part III: The Adoptive Child," ibid. (Fall 1985): 151.

31. Adrienne D. Kraft et al., "Some Theoretical Considerations on Confidential Adoptions, Part II: The Adoptive Parent," ibid. (Summer 1985): 77–81, quotations on 79, 81.

32. Kraft et al., "Some Theoretical Considerations, Part III," p. 151. In the following year *Child and Adolescent Social Work* gave equal time to the proponents of open adoption by publishing three articles rebutting Kraft et al. The articles, written by Cathy Chapman, Patricia Dorner, Kathleen Silber, and Terry Winterberg, appeared in the Winter 1986, Spring 1987, and Summer 1987 issues. None of them sheds any new light on the subject.

33. Nathan G. Hale, Jr., *The Rise and Crisis of Psychoanalysis in the United States: Freud and the Americans, 1917–1985* (New York: Oxford University Press, 1995), chs. 17–18, esp. pp. 331–335. For penetrating criticism of the entire psychoanalytic enterprise, see Frederick Crews, *Skeptical Engagements* (New York: Oxford University Press, 1986), chs. 1–5; Crews, *The Memory Wars: Freud's Legacy in Dispute* (New York: New York Review of Books, 1995), pp. 3–73; Richard Webster, *Where*

Freud Was Wrong: Sin, Science, and Psychoanalysis (New York: Basic Books, 1995). For criticism of Kohut, see Crews, *Skeptical Engagements,* pp. 28–34. For penetrating criticism of Bowlby's attachment theory and the concept of mother-infant bonding, see Diane E. Eyer, *Mother-Infant Bonding: A Scientific Fiction* (New Haven: Yale University Press, 1992), chs. 1–3.

34. Kraft et al., "Some Theoretical Considerations, Part I," pp. 17, 20; Kraft et al., "Some Theoretical Considerations, Part III," p. 145.

35. Patrick A. Curtis, "The Dialectics of Open versus Closed Adoption of Infants," *CW* 65 (September–October 1986): 437–445; Deborah Churchman, "The Debate over Open Adoption," *Public Welfare* 44 (Spring 1986): 11–14; National Association of Social Workers, "Open Adoptions: What Effect on Families," *News* (May 1986): 3, 8; Barbara Kantrowitz and Elisa Williams, "Life with Two Mothers," *Newsweek,* May 12, 1986, p. 86.

36. Curtis, "Dialectics of Open versus Closed Adoption," pp. 437, 443; Kantrowitz and Williams, "Life with Two Mothers," p. 86.

37. Baran and Pannor, "Open Adoption," p. 318; CWLA, *Standards for Adoption Service,* rev. ed. (New York: CWLA, 1988), sect. 0.10.

38. Kathleen Silber and Patricia Martinez Dorner, *Children of Open Adoption and Their Families* (San Antonio: Corona, 1990); Mary Jo Rillera, *Adoption Encounter: Hurt, Transition, Healing* (Westminster, Calif.: Triadoption, 1987); Judith S. Gediman and Linda P. Brown, *BirthBond: Reunions Between Birthparents and Adoptees—What Happens After* (Far Hills, N.J.: New Horizon, 1989); John Y. Powell, *Whose Child Am I? Adults' Recollections of Being Adopted* (New York: Tiresias, 1985); Mary Jo Rillera and Sharon Kaplan, *Cooperative Adoption: A Handbook* (Westminster, Calif.: Triadoption, 1987); Jeanne Warren Lindsay, *Open Adoption: A Caring Option* (Buena Park, Calif.: Morning Glory, 1987). Lindsay's book is still in print and has sold over 13,000 copies (letter from Jeanne Lindsay to author, Sept. 12, 1996).

39. Miriam Komar, *Communicating with the Adopted Child* (New York: Walker Publishing Co., 1991); Mary Watkins and Susan Fisher, *Talking with Young Children about Adoption* (New Haven: Yale University Press, 1993).

40. David M. Brodzinsky, Leslie M. Singer, and Anne M. Braff, "Children's Understanding of Adoption," *Child Development* 55 (1984): 869–878; David Brodzinsky, Dianne Schechter, and Anne Braff Brodzinsky, "Children's Knowledge of Adoption: Developmental Changes and Implications for Adjustment," in Richard D. Ashmore and David M. Brodzinsky, eds., *Thinking about the Family: Views of Parents and Children* (Hillsdale,

N.J.: Lawrence Erlbaum Associates, 1986), pp. 205–232; quotation from David M. Brodzinsky, "New Perspectives on Adoption Revelation," *Adoption and Fostering* 8 (1984): 28.

41. For their attitude toward the adoption establishment, see Baran and Pannor, "Open Adoption," p. 316; Annette Baran and Reuben Pannor, "It's Time for Sweeping Change," *Decree* (Summer 1990): 5.

Epilogue

1. See, for example, "Unusual Family Reunions," *The Maury Povich Show,* Sept. 8, 1992, Show 260; Sara Rimer, "Across a Barrier, a Family Waited," *NYT,* July 17, 1996, sec. 1, p. A7; Linda Hodges, "Blood Ties," ibid., July 19, 1996, sec. 1, p. A15; *Mighty Aphrodite* (1995); *Flirting with Disaster* (1995).

2. Jayne Askin, *Search: A Handbook for Adoptees and Birthparents,* 2d ed. (Phoenix, Ariz.: Oryz Press, 1992), pp. 217–232. The Adoptee Mailing List can be found on the Internet World Wide Web at htpp://webreflec-tion.com/aiml. See also Focus: An Adoption Reunion Support Group at http://www.openadoption.org/focus/ and Adopt: Talking to Your Child about Adoption at http://www.adopting.org/talk.html. These are only a few examples of the hundreds of Web pages dealing with search-ing, open records, and open adoption.

3. Susan Wadia-Ells, ed., *The Adoption Reader: Birth Mothers, Adoptive Mothers, and Adopted Daughters Tell Their Stories* (Seattle, Wash.: Seal Press, 1995); LaVonne Harper Stiffler, *Synchronicity and Reunion: The Genetic Connection of Adoptees and Birthparents* (Hobe Sound, Fla.: FEA Publishing, 1992), p. 175.

4. Paul Sachdev, "Adoption Reunion and After: A Study of the Search Pro-cess and Experience of Adoptees," *CW* 71 (January–February 1992): 53–68, quotations on 64, 67. For similar conclusions, see also Paul Sachdev, *Unlocking the Adoption Files* (Lexington, Mass.: D. C. Heath & Co., 1989); Karen March, *The Stranger Who Bore Me: Adoptee–Birth Mother Relationships* (Toronto: University of Toronto Press, 1995).

5. *ALP,* 1995 Suppl., vol. 2, p. 51, and Appendix 13-A, pp. 73–75; Tamar Lewin, "Tennessee Is Focus of Debate on Adoptees' Birth Data," *NYT,* March 18, 1996, sec. 1, p. A1.

6. Madelyn DeWoody, "Adoption and Disclosure of Medical and Social History: A Review of the Law," *CW* 72 (May–June 1993): 198–201, 203; Wade Lambert and Jonathan M. Moses, "Couple Gets $3.8 Million in Adoption Suit," *Wall Street Journal,* October 30, 1991, sec. 2, p. B6.

7. DeWoody, "Adoption and Disclosure," pp. 213–216.
8. Lincoln Caplan, "A Reporter at Large: An Open Adoption—I," *New Yorker*, May 21, 1990; Lincoln Caplan, "A Reporter at Large: An Open Adoption—II," ibid., May 28, 1990; Lincoln Caplan, *An Open Adoption* (New York: Farrar, Straus & Giroux, 1990); Phyllis Theroux, "'Tell Them I'm Carrying Their Baby,' " *New York Times Book Review*, July 8, 1990, p. 7.
9. Harriet E. Gross, "Open Adoption: A Research-Based Literature Review and New Data," *CW* 72 (May–June 1993): 273, 274; Bruce M. Rappaport, *The Open Adoption Book* (New York: Macmillan, 1992); Lois Ruskai Melina and Sharon Kaplan Roszia, *The Open Adoption Experience* (New York: HarperCollins, 1993).
10. Mary Beth Whitehead with Loretta Schwartz-Nobel, *A Mother's Story: The Truth about the Baby M Case* (New York: St. Martin's Press, 1989); "The Steinberg Trail: A Case of Child Abuse," *Newsweek*, Nov. 7, 1988, p. 64; "A Tale of Abuse," ibid., Dec. 12, 1988, pp. 56–61. The Steinbergs never legally adopted Lisa.
11. For Allen, see *NYT*, September 25, 1993, sec. 1, p. 25; "Adoption Rules Criticized," *NYT*, February 26, 1987, sec. 1, p. A7; the defense called child psychologist David Kirschner to testify. See *NYT*, July 26, 1993, sec. 2, p. 1. Publications sympathetic to the ARM continue to give Kirschner a forum to discuss the adopted child syndrome as if it exists. See *Adopted Child* 11 (February 1992): 3. For criticism of transracial adoption, see LeRoy Ashby, *Endangered Children: Dependency, Neglect, and Abuse in American History* (New York: Twayne, 1997), p. 169; for criticism of intercountry adoption, see Diana Jean Schemo, "Adoption in Paraguay: Mothers Cry Theft," *NYT*, March 19, 1996, sec. 1, p. A1; Michael S. Serrill, "Going Abroad to Find a Baby," *Time*, Oct. 21, 1991, pp. 86–88; "Toward a Policy That's No Longer Foreign," *NYT*, February 4, 1996, sec. 1, p. 14; for rumors of adopted children used for organ transplants, see Todd Leventhal, "Traffic in Baby Parts Has No Factual Basis," ibid., February 26, 1996, sec. 1, p. A16.
12. Nancy Newton Verrier, *The Primal Wound: Understanding the Adopted Child* (Baltimore: Gateway, 1993), ch. 6, quotations on pp. 16, 69, 182. The book's continuing popularity is suggested by its third printing in 1996. Marcie A. Griffin, "The Adult Adoptee: The Biological Alien," *Adoption Therapist* 2 (Fall 1991): 8–9; Robert Childs, "The Orphaned Element of the Adoptive Experience," ibid. 4 (Spring 1993): 1–4.
13. "Natural Mother Is Exempted from Federal Kidnap Statute," *NYT*, April 3, 1993, sec. 1, p. A11.
14. Nancy Gibbs, "In Whose Best Interest?" *Time*, July 19, 1993, pp. 45–50;

Lucinda Franks, "The War for Baby Clausen," *New Yorker,* March 22, 1993, pp. 56–73. For the adoptive parents' perspective, see Robby DeBoer, *Losing Jessica* (New York: Doubleday, 1994); Ashby, *Endangered Children,* p. 172.

15. For Hasegawa's current campaign, see Ron Marsico, "Senate Panel Rejects Bill Opening Files to Adoptees," [New Jersey] *Star-Ledger,* January 13, 1995, sec. 1, p. 1.

16. Susan Chira, "Law Proposed to End Adoption Horror Stories," *NYT,* August 24, 1994, sec. 1, p. A12; "Model Adoption Law Promotes Baby Market," ibid., September 1, 1994, sec. 1, p. A26. NASW quoted in William Pierce, "What Do CWLA, NASW, and CCUSA Have against UAA?" *National Adoption Reports* (February 1995): 1–2, quotation on p. 2.

17. Antoinette Martin, "Adoptees Debate Intermediary's Role," *NYT,* October 10, 1995, sec. 3, pp. C1, C4.

18. Tamar Lewin, "Woman Convicted of Fraud in Efforts to Find Adoptees," *NYT,* July 30, 1993, sec. 1, p. 8; Jason Kuhns, "The Sealed Adoption Records Controversy: Breaking Down the Walls of Secrecy," *Golden Gate University Law Review* 24 (Spring 1994): 297, n. 222.

19. National Council for Adoption, "After Baby Jessica," *National Adoption Reports* 14, no. 3 (Summer 1993): 1; Elizabeth Bartholet, *Family Bonds: Adoption and the Politics of Parenting* (Boston: Houghton Mifflin, 1993); Alison Mitchell, "President Tells Government to Promote More Adoption," *NYT,* December 15, 1996, sect. 1, p. 24; Brenda W. Donnelly and Patricia Voydanoff, "Parenting versus Placing for Adoption: Consequences for Adolescent Mothers," *Family Relations* 45 (October 1996): 432–434; Tamar Lewin, "Study of Adopted Finds Nothing Unusual," *NYT,* June 23, 1994, sec. 1, p. A8. Ironically, Betty Jean Lifton criticized the study for its faulty methodology and unrepresentative samples. See the letter to the editor, "What the Teen-Age Adoption Study Left Out," ibid., July 9, 1994, sec. 1., p. A14.

20. Richard P. Barth and Marianne Berry, *Adoption and Disruption: Rates, Risks, and Responses* (New York: Aldine De Gruyter, 1988), pp. 3–8; *EA,* s.v. "Independent Adoption."

21. Peggy Orenstein, "Looking for a Donor to Call Dad," *NYTM,* June 18, 1995, sec. 6, pp. 28–35.

. . . .

Acknowledgments

This book has been a long time coming, and it is a great pleasure for me to acknowledge my many debts. I would like to thank Charlie Langdon and D. Sharon Osborne, past and present Executive Directors of the Children's Home Society of Washington (CHSW), for permission to use the CHSW's case records, and Randy Perin, former Supervisor of the CHSW's Adoption Resource Center, whose enthusiasm for this project has been inspirational. I am also grateful to Roger W. Toogood, Executive Director of the Children's Home Society of Minnesota (CHSM), for permitting me access to the Society's case records, and Marietta E. Spencer, Program Director of the Post-Legal Adoption Services at the CHSM, for being my sponsor during my stay at the CHSM and guiding me through the case records.

Librarians and staff at archives and research centers across the United States have provided me with expert advice and guidance. I wish to single out for special thanks several people who assisted me in the search for adoption materials. Archivist extraordinaire David Klaassen, at the Social Welfare History Archives of the University of Minnesota, made my two visits to the Archives particularly enjoyable and productive. Over the years, he has kept me apprised of new acquisitions, which have contributed greatly to my research. Jeffrey M. Flannery made my trip to the Library of Congress productive. At the University of Washington's Social Work library, Mary Jo Johnson facilitated my acquiring a number of uncommon works. At Pacific Lutheran University the library staff, especially Patty Koessler and

Sharon Chase, have been immensely helpful and encouraging. I also want to thank Laura Lewis, head of the inter-library loan department, for cheerfully tracking down my innumerable requests for rare materials. Other institutions whose staff provided assistance include the U.S. National Archives at College Park, Maryland, the City University of New York's Cohen Library, and the Bancroft Library at the University of California, Berkeley.

I am also grateful to the following publications for permission to draw on my previously published articles: to *Journal of Sociology and Social Welfare* for "The Sealed Adoption Records Controversy in Historical Perspective" (19:2, June 1992); to *Journal of Policy History* for "Professional Social Workers, Adoption, and the Problem of Illegitimacy, 1915–1945" (6:3, 1994); and to *Child Welfare* for "Adoption and Disclosure of Family Information" (74:1, January–February 1995).

Several Pacific Lutheran University colleagues—Philip A. Nordquist, Christopher R. Browning, Paul T. Menzel, and Earl Smith—deserve thanks. Their encouragement and commitment to the support of my research were instrumental in the completion of this project. For financial assistance I am grateful to Pacific Lutheran University for a sabbatical leave in 1992–93 and for a Research Assistance Grant and Regency Advancement Award; the Evangelical Lutheran Church in America for a study grant; the National Endowment for the Humanities for a Summer Stipend and a Fellowship for College Teachers and Independent Scholars; the Institute for Humane Studies for an F. Leroy Hill Summer Faculty Fellowship; and Robert Middlekauff, former director of the Huntington Library, for inviting me to be a Visiting Fellow. Special thanks also to the John M. Olin Foundation for a year-long Faculty Fellowship (1986–87), which gave me a jump start to make the transition from an early Americanist to a twentieth-century social historian.

While writing this book I accumulated many intellectual debts, which I happily acknowledge. I have profited immensely from corresponding with adoption rights activists Jean M. Paton and Pam Hasegawa. I owe special thanks to George Behlmer, Ruth Bloch, Susan B. Carlton, Paula S. Fass, Ray Jonas, Patricia O. Killen, Beth M. Kraig, William J. Rorabaugh, the late Eugene Sheridan, Paula Shields, and Barbara Temple-Thurston, all of whom read and commented on my work as it progressed. LeRoy Ashby, Clarke A. Chambers, and Barbara Melosh read a first draft of the entire manuscript. Their criticism forced me to rethink, modify, or recast my ideas and saved me from numerous errors of fact. Over the years, my friend Mark Jensen, of PLU's Foreign Languages and Literature Department, cheerfully read every word, sometimes twice, and improved virtually every sentence. Finally, at Harvard University Press I am especially grateful to Joyce Seltzer and Cherie Weitzner Acierno for their encouragement and perceptive advice and to Donna Bouvier for her expert copyediting. If I have not followed every suggestion or agreed with every criticism, this book is certainly the better for the many I received.

Index